T0340310

Air Cargo Management

This is the third edition of a popular introductory guide to the function and future of the air cargo supply chain, an industry which responded with remarkable efficiency when faced with the challenges and impact of the COVID-19 pandemic. The book reviews the role and strategy of air cargo and its contribution to world trade and international economies. This industry, which accounts for more than 35% of the world's trade in value, will be even more vital in the coming years.

Building on the success of previous editions, *Air Cargo Management* now puts the emphasis on basic functionality, economics and historical precedents, but most of all it focuses on how traditional legacy methods are being replaced by the adoption of technologies and cloud-based applications – new methods which are changing and streamlining the entire industry. The book reviews the supply chain process and the technology applications as well as the effects of the pandemic and the fundamental lack of cargo capacity hitherto supplied by passenger aircraft. It also explores the increased use of freighter aircraft and the need for faster and more efficient processing, particularly on the ground and in road transport.

The third edition features new content on:

- Security and crime, including pharmaceutical counterfeiting and fraud
- The role of airports and road feeder services
- Typical air cargo products, including the heavy-lift sector
- Regulations and treaties
- Aircraft in use, historically and currently
- New technologies

The book is illustrated with statistical evidence, examples and photographs and is enriched with comments from industry leaders and experienced professionals. The style and breadth of content are designed to be easily readable and should be of practical interest to anyone either currently working in the logistics, supply chain or transport industries, or contemplating a career in this sector.

Michael Sales has worked in international business magazine publishing since 1977 but joined *Air Cargo News* in 1990 to develop the newspaper's global impact and influence. Michael has published three books about the air logistics industry, this volume being the fourth. He is also consulting with the Rotterdam Business School to create a new Air Logistics course.

Sebastiaan Scholte has been the CEO of Kales Group since 2020 and a senior advisor for Boston Consulting Group since October 2020. In April 2010 he was appointed CEO of Jan de Rijk Logistics, based in Roosendaal, the Netherlands, and in May 2012 was appointed Chairman of the Cool Chain Association. In 2013 he joined the board of TIACA, where he was elected Vice Chairman in April 2015 and Chairman in 2017 until 2019.

Air Cargo Management

Air Freight and the Global Supply Chain

Third Edition

Michael Sales and Sebastiaan Scholte

LONDON AND NEW YORK

Designed cover image: Getty Images

First published 2023
by Routledge
4 Park Square, Milton Park, Abingdon, Oxon OX14 4RN

and by Routledge
605 Third Avenue, New York, NY 10158

Routledge is an imprint of the Taylor & Francis Group, an informa business

© 2023 Michael Sales and Sebastiaan Scholte

British Library Cataloguing-in-Publication Data
A catalogue record for this book is available from the British Library

Library of Congress Cataloging-in-Publication Data
Names: Sales, Michael, author. | Scholte, Sebastiaan, author.
Title: Air cargo management : air freight and the global supply chain / Michael Sales and Sebastiaan Scholte.
Description: Third Edition. | New York, NY : Routledge, 2023. | Revised edition of Air Cargo management, 2017. | Includes bibliographical references and index.
Subjects: LCSH: Aeronautics, Commercial—Freight. | Business logistics.
Classification: LCC HE9788 .S25 2023 | DDC 387.7/44—dc23/rnh/20220926
LC record available at https://lccn.loc.gov/2022046536

ISBN: 978-0-367-76489-0 (hbk)
ISBN: 978-0-367-76487-6 (pbk)
ISBN: 978-1-003-16716-7 (ebk)

DOI: 10.4324/9781003167167

Typeset in Bembo
by codeMantra

Contents

Contributors

Alessandro Bombelli, PhD is Lecturer and Researcher in the Air Transport and Operations section, Faculty of Aerospace Engineering, Delft University of Technology (NL).

Gerton Hulsman is Ex Managing Director at Dusseldorf Airport Cargo, Air Logistics Consultant.

Kevin Smith is Founder of Cargo Hub.

Stan Wraight, Editor International Railway Journal.

Vladimir Vyshehirsky is Head of engineering and logistics at Volga–Dnepr UK Ltd.

Raoul Paul is President and CEO of Strategic Aviation Solutions Int'l.

Mike Yarwood is Managing Director in Loss Prevention Department at Through Transport Mutual Services (UK) Limited for the TT Club.

Foreword

GLYN HUGHES DIRECTOR
GENERAL TIACA

The COVID-19 pandemic of 2020/2021 impacted the world in ways never thought imaginable. The planet was faced with a global crisis that taught us how to live differently, work differently, think of our health differently and think of the health of others differently. It also taught the world the value of logistics, and in particular, the value of air cargo.

Air cargo has a proud history extending back for over 110 years to that first consignment of silk transported a mere 65 miles. From those small beginnings, air cargo grew to support society through international air mail and things progressed further to support the expanding global economy and to enable first responders during times of humanitarian and civilian disasters.

Prior the COVID-19, air cargo was the global economy's silent partner. Transporting over 35% of international trade by value but was rarely acknowledged by those outside of the industry except during times of disruption, such as erupting volcanoes which closed air supply chains and disrupted commercial activity or during times of security or safety breaches, such as unfortunate accidents involving lithium batteries.

But COVID-19 changed all that. As 70% of passenger networks were grounded due to travel restrictions, air cargo continued to fly. Initially bringing much needed Personal Protective Equipment (PPE) to countries struggling to control the spread of the virus, then to support communities in their fight to treat its citizens with therapeutics and medical devices, while at the same time supporting consumers who were forced to shop online as traditional retail channels shuttered their doors and finally by mobilizing the entire air cargo ecosystem to move vaccines in a temperature controlled environment to over 200 countries and territories.

Air cargo served as a lifeline to the planet and its citizens. Nightly news broadcasts proudly showed freighters and passenger aircraft bringing much needed supplies and as national economies reopened air cargo was there to support the restarted production.

But how was this possible? What made the industry work? What lessons were learnt and how will it continue to support global society and industry as they continue to evolve?

This book, *Air Cargo Management*, third edition, is the latest in a series written by the author Michael Sales, and in his edition, he co-authors with Sebastiaan Scholte. Two globally recognized experts in the field of logistics and leaders in operational and analytical assessments and strategic thinking.

They perform a detailed analysis of how the industry was able to achieve the success during the COVID-19 crisis and how new solutions, new working processes and technical applications were adopted to ensure operations could continue despite unprecedented challenges resulting from the crisis.

They explore how supply chains shifted to enhanced utilization and optimization of freighter networks as passenger belly capacity disappeared over night. They look at how the industry innovated by operating passenger flights for cargo only operations.

They analyse technological applications and how the industry responded to the need for faster and more efficient processing as the cargo being moved was in some cases a matter of life or death for patients waiting for much-needed medicines and vaccines.

This edition provides a basic guide to the function and future of the air cargo supply chain and how the air cargo industry must evolve its strategic priorities to further enhance its contribution to world trade and international economies.

Building on the success of the previous editions, the authors focus on basic functionality and economics, and its historical precedents, but most of all how traditional legacy methods are being replaced by the adoption of technologies and cloud-based applications to achieve the greater efficiency, transparency and predictability demanded by todays and tomorrow's air cargo customers.

Air cargo is no longer about moving a box, it's now about the impact on the consumer of what's inside the box. E-commerce, special cargo, perishables, pharmaceuticals, electronics, fashion and almost anything one can think of could move by air cargo.

Therefore, the industry must evolve to provide enhanced solutions.

This edition explores these new methods and solutions which are changing and streamlining the entire industry.

In addition, there are dedicated chapters on:

- Security and crime including pharmaceutical counterfeiting and fraud
- Special focus on the role of airports and road feeder services
- Typical air cargo products including the heavy-lift sector
- Synopsis of regulations and treaties
- Review of aircraft in use historically and currently

The book is illustrated with statistical evidence, case studies and photographs and is enriched with comments from industry leaders and experienced professionals.

The style and breadth of content are designed to be easily readable and should be of practical interest to anyone either currently working in the logistics industry or contemplating a career in this business. Everyone should read at least one book on logistics, and I have no reservations in recommending this book as that one.

Preface

Welcome To Air Logistics Management Third Edition

The sudden arrival of the COVID-19 pandemic in January 2020 completely overturned living patterns of nearly all world societies, causing global and catastrophic damage to health, education, trade and daily life. It has generated a new way of living and surviving, but its long-term effects are yet to be defined. The aviation industry, which hitherto had been rapidly expanding, was especially devastated, and probably changed forever, while the air logistics industry, so heavily dependent on the belly hold capacity of passenger aircraft, was catapulted into emergency mode, with the need to move vast quantities of medical equipment and medicines with very limited resources.

When planning this book, we were unaware of what was about to hit the world and again, when going to press, with many months of adaptation behind us, there is much yet to happen and change which we cannot predict. Despite this, we have taken an objective view of the industry including its evolution, structure, practices, achievements and future prospects. We assess what its role will be in the future and how the aviation and transportation sectors will adapt to new challenges.

We are honoured that several leading figures from the Aviation Logistics industry have given valuable time and effort to share their knowledge and experience. Our aim is to underline the massive contribution that Air

Logistics contributes to the global economy and health. Aviation has always had many enemies and has suffered badly at the hands of bad weather, earthquakes, tidal waves, wars, fuel price hikes, terrorism, politicians and repressive regulation and most recently the impact of the COVID pandemic which hit the aviation and travel industries so badly. Air cargo feeds the world with produce, medicines, clothing and industrial goods.

Unfortunately, there is not an "air cargo university." Even in the most prestigious logistics schools, the function of air cargo, which accounts for more than 1/3 of the value transported in the world, is not being discussed in sufficient depth and students do not see the opportunities which exist for great careers.

The aim of this book is to give better insight into the drivers, economics and complexity of air cargo at all levels. Whether you are a student, a shipper, an airline, freight forwarder, a logistics or IT company, airport or a ground handler, you will definitely find valuable information in this book that eventually will make you stand out in your day-to-day activities at work. Our ultimate goal is to share the extensive knowledge of many industry experts so eventually the air cargo supply chain will be improved and that there is more common understanding for each other's role.

We, therefore, highlight the interaction between the different players in the air cargo supply chain and as well its shortcomings. There is as well practical information on what the right decision-making metrics are per sector. We hope that by sharing these business management practices in a practical way, we can help the current and future managers make their job do better.

Transport accounts for a high proportion of the final cost of the product, in some cases up to 40%. Due to the varied factors involved, international consignments clearly demand careful and detailed costings. The choice of transport mode will depend on the type of goods, the urgency of delivery and the destination. Frequently, there will be a combination of some, or all, of these to form eventually a major component of the total supply chain. Intermediate warehousing, re-packaging and partial assembly may also be part of the process. The decision to employ air cargo is based on a number of factors, including urgency, value of shipment, protective environment, access and product shelf life. Price is not the only consideration, as some products are needed urgently as in the case of a broken machine needing a new part or a consignment of fresh seafood as well as the market demand of a new fashion.

Many people are not aware that much of what we need to sustain our lifestyle, including energy, communications, pharmaceuticals, food, flowers, entertainment, clothes and transport, depends substantially on the air cargo logistics supply chain which works alongside all other transport modes. Air Logistics Management provides the practical knowledge and explanations about the processes involved and an explanation of the vital role played by the air cargo industry in maintaining the global logistics supply chain. The choice of air cargo is not only reserved for high value commodities or perishable items but includes just about everything that touches our lives. If you like F1 motor racing, symphony concerts, strawberries at Christmas, the latest fashions or you need diabetic drugs and medication, air freight will be acting on your behalf behind the scenes. At the same time, protecting the environment is one of the industry's top priorities. Aviation and air transport account for 3% of global carbon emissions, which we review in the chapter on Environment. Aviation is a source of goods that connects people around the world; for example, it delivers agricultural produce from Africa, the Far East to South America, and it facilitates trade and is the only industry that has globally committed to specific actions to neutralize carbon emission growth and reduce emissions by 50% by 2050. The fast-evolving global economy is connected by events that impact us within hours, not days. We have seen over the last few years the economic growth of the developing countries such as Brazil, Russia, India, China and South Africa (BRICS). As these countries and other developing nations begin to compete and attract foreign direct investment, we witness their increasing prosperity and new emerging middle classes. That is manifesting itself into the desire for branded consumer goods, travel and leisure activities.

Security has become a major part of air cargo and has evolved further since terrorist's attack on New York's twin towers on 9/11. There have been countless other criminal assaults on cargo shipments of cash and valuables over the years and today, considering the high value of goods moving by air, such as computers, mobile phones, fashion, pharmaceuticals and diamonds, nearly every shipment can be considered as a potential target. The temptation and opportunities are even greater than ever, and the problem is exacerbated in many cases by reluctance on the part of the victims to report the crime or even acknowledge its occurrence.

Cargo theft affects everyone as it damages economies and companies, forces up prices and feeds the world's black markets that are often sources of funding for terrorists and large criminal gangs. In the United States alone, it is estimated that some $30 billion worth of cargo is stolen annually by highly sophisticated and well-organized gangs. Cargo is at its most vulnerable when it is on the ground, especially in transit by road. Trucking companies may respond by raising prices or employing expensive security guards, the costs of which will be passed onto customers.

The main challenge of this industry now is the implementation of electronic cargo processing (E-Freight) which would speed up the entire air freight chain as well as increasing security and cutting a great deal of cost. It has been and will continue to take a long time to gain acceptance by the whole industry, but currently a major proportion of international shipments are being processed electronically led by airlines, handling companies, forwarders and leading logistics companies. We sincerely hope you enjoy this book and I urge you to visit the various websites which we have listed where you will find more details, facts and figures.

The COVID pandemic which continues to bite into economic and social recovery has multiplied and accelerated a number of significant changes which are occurring in the way business is done and people live their lives.

One of the most significant is in the workplace, underlining the need to pay proper wages to drivers, warehouse staff and final mile delivery personnel and at the same time balance the pressure to do the same for hard pressed medical staff. Shortages of skilled labour have in turn forced the industry to find alternative ways of operating deliveries warehouses and just about every aspect of the industry, automation can only go so far. The rapid rise of e-commerce, while creating a new industry, has also increased the amount of pollution, packaging and waste. Integrators such as DHL and FedEx are turning to electric vehicles and other forms of technology, while large distribution companies begin to look at nearer manufacturing sites in order to avoid not only some of the long-distance shipping, but some of the political conflict that is developing throughout the world. With millennials, who have grown up in the digital and technical environment, now holding positions with decision-making powers, there will be even more reliance on technical processes.

Even as we write this, the world is still embroiled in the conflicts in Iraq, Syria, Libya and Ukraine. The possibility of trade barriers between Russia, the United States and Europe could result in the return to cold war routes which are longer and more expensive to operate than the trans Russia route. Aviation is never without challenge and threat, but it goes on and continues to deliver people and cargo throughout the world. We sincerely trust that this small book will lead to a greater understanding of this vital industry, the challenges it faces and the solutions it delivers.

A Message to Our Student Readers

Shortly before this book went to the press, a vicious and cruel war broke out in Europe. Not just any war, but a confrontation of a world power, Russia, with a small neighbour Ukraine, a brutal attempt to subjugate a smaller weaker nation, who fought back with unbelievable bravery and with great suffering, not only for its population but also with enormous consequences for the world.

The supply of gas and oil has never been made so critical to the free world as it is now, resulting in rising energy prices, inflation and complete dislocation and relocation by fleeing people. It is not yet possible to estimate the impact on international transport via all modalities after weeks of war, but it is certain that this will be enormous.

I hope that during your studies it will become clear what a massive influence air transport has on our daily lives. Not only the provision of humanitarian resources for the victims, but also the great importance in our world of flows of goods and the associated communication. Take a good look at this industry and decide if there is a bright future for you in Air Logistics.

By Michael Sales and Sebastiaan Scholte

Acknowledgements

The AIR LOGISTICS INDUSTRY has been experiencing a long hard battle to survive the Pandemic, the effects of the war in Ukraine, fuel price rises and rapid changes in the international trading landscape. We have set out in this book to reflect the background and events which are the fundamentals of this business. We would not have been able to achieve this without the input and help of those industry leaders and publication editors who have generously contributed and helped. We thank you all.

1 Basics of Air Logistics

Air Cargo Supply Chain

We sometimes take many products for granted without thinking how they end up in our hands or in our stores, for example, papayas from Brazil or smart phones sent from China. The air cargo supply chain is quite complex with different companies playing different roles (Figure 1.1).

Air cargo spends most of its time on the ground rather than in the air since it must be transported and stored. Therefore, the efficiency and quality on the ground are very important.

It starts with a shipper in a certain country wanting to export or import a certain product from another country. Given the value density and the need for speed, the shipper decides himself to opt for airfreight instead of other modalities. Most of the larger multinational companies have logistics experts, but in some cases a smaller company with no previous experience gets advised by the freight forwarder on what modality to choose.

In any case, in almost all the cases, nowadays air cargo is booked through freight forwarders, who consolidate large quantities with the airlines in order to get a better negotiated price. Some forwarders are local and others multinational. The shipper can select a forwarder or already has a contract with a certain forwarder. The forwarder will negotiate the price and books the space with the airlines. The airline can outsource its sales to a general sales agent (GSA), who represents more airlines in a certain territory.

Many forwarders also will pick up and pack the goods and even customs clear it on behalf of the shipper. Either the forwarder arranges the road transport to and from the airport or the airline does. This is called the road feeder

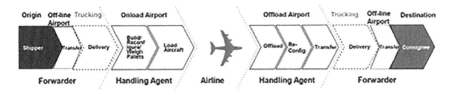

Figure 1.1 "Air cargo supply chain."

DOI: 10.4324/9781003167167-1

service (RFS) and is done mostly bonded, meaning the trailer is customs sealed at its origin or destination and no longer needs to clear customs at the airport of departure or arrival.

Once the shipment arrives at the airport it will be delivered to the handling facilities, either operated by the airline or by dedicated worldwide or local general handling agents (GHA). Either the same or another GHA will also take care of the handling on the tarmac from the terminal to the plane, loading or unloading the aircraft. Some airlines, mainly at their hubs, opt for self-handling at the ramp.

The airline will fly the shipment to the destination and the reverse process will start there.

Hereunder follows a description of the different stakeholders in the air cargo supply chain, their roles, benefits and interaction:

The Shipper

Consumers buy products that are manufactured all over the world. Certain products, for example, cars have supply chain sourcing over multiple countries for cost and quality reasons. In a globalized world with still a relatively lot of free trade goods are being moved between different countries. Large multinationals may have different production sites globally. Obviously supply chain plays a vital role in the success of these small and larger multinational shippers and also air freight is a crucial enabler for global trade.

There are three reasons why a shipper decides to send a shipment by air:

1 Due to an urgency: Imagine a production standstill where spare parts must be flown in urgently. Another example is the urgent air shipments of personal protective equipment and medicines during the outbreak of COVID-19 in 2020. Or relief aid goods to a territory affected by war. There are also occasions in which other modes of transport fail and the product needs to be flown in due to contractual obligations. As the term urgency implies, it is mostly not planned and therefore this is also unplanned air cargo. Some companies in certain industries never forecast air cargo in their budgets but nevertheless must airlift products due to unforeseen disruptions

2 Because a product otherwise would perish: Flowers and food are for example perishables that if not transported in time will lose their quality and value. The proportion of air freight cost of total cost is quite high and at the end is calculated in the end consumer price. Air cargo is definitely planned and budgeted in the supply chain processes. Thanks to air cargo we are able to eat exotic fruits and other food from all over the world.

3 Because of cost: Even though air cargo is more expensive on a per kilogram basis or in absolute terms than other modalities, in some situations air cargo is more economical than for example sea freight. In the box below there are two clear examples of the economics of sea versus air freight. Also, this type of air freight is planned in advance.

Air freight can be cheaper than sea freight for a shipper: Economics of sea vs air freight

Example a: A company needs to ship automotive parts from Milan to Los Angeles.
The door-to-door transit time is:

- 5 days via air
- 30 days via sea

It concerns expensive goods with a high value. The spare parts weigh 200 kg and have a value of USD 1000,000. Moreover, the cost of borrowing for the company is 4% per year. Therefore, the cost of capital tied up in inventory is worth USD 0.05 per kg/day (0.04×100,000/(200×365)).
The inventory cost will be

- By sea: USD 1.50/kg (30 days × 0.05)
- By air: USD 0.25/kg (5 days × 0.05)

The cost of sea freight is USD 0.20/kg and that of air freight is USD 1.00/kg. Thus, air freight is actually USD 0.45/kg cheaper than sea freight (1.50 + 0.20−0.25−1.00)

Example b: A company wants to ship 6,000 kg fashion clothes with a retail value of USD 100,000 from Barcelona to Shanghai
The door-to-door transit time is:

- 5 days via air
- 30 days via sea

These fashion clothes have an economic life cycle of 90 days, after which they are either not sellable anymore or will have to be sold at such a discount the company will incur losses.
The shipment is ready for transport on March 15, and the new sales campaign in the Shanghai shop starts on March 21. Hence:

- Every day the shipment arrives later than March 21 is a cost of USD 0.18/kg/day (100,000/6000/90)
- Cost of non-sales for 25 days is USD 4.5/kg
- If the rate of air freight is USD 2.20/kg and sea freight USD 0.20/kg, you still have an advantage of USD 2.50/kg by using air instead of sea freight

At the end cost, speed, quality and reliability are very important factors for the shipper who uses a freight forwarder for the air freight booking, since a forwarder has many advantages and specializations.
Forwarders are mostly selected on a tender basis, where the shipper will first select on the basis of RFI (request for information) and then finally decide on RFP (request for proposal) or RFQ (request for quotation). The

shipper normally only has a contract with a freight forwarder and not with any of the other players on the air cargo supply chain.

The Freight Forwarder

There is a general misconception in the market that the freight forwarder cuts the air waybill (AWB) and only is the middleman between the airline and the shipper. Another misconception is that digital platforms will replace the traditional forwarders. Digitization will and has to revolutionize this industry and perhaps the rates of airlines will become more transparent and there will be bookings made via online platforms. However, the freight forwarder does so much more than just buying and selling air freight.

The freight forwarder basically unburdens the shipper's logistics needs. Many shippers outsource their external logistics completely to one or several forwarders. Many large forwarders have a division for air freight, sea freight, contract logistics (like warehousing and other added value logistics) and road transport. A forwarder will choose the best modality for the shipper given the cost and time constraints and arrange the whole logistics globally.

There are thousands of different forwarders across the world (Figure 1.2).

Total metric tonnes transported were 63,300,00 (*www.statista.com) in 2018. The share of the top 25 forwarders was only 26% of total which implies a fragmented market.

Most of the freight forwarders are "asset-light" or "asset-less." They out-source to airline and trucking companies who are rather asset-heavy. The main cost factor for a forwarder is therefore labour and the intangible asset most invested in is IT and software.

With air freight shipments the forwarder makes a margin, driven by price and volume and occasionally offers the air cargo or other services at a cost in order to be able to make a margin on other complementary services, like sea freight or contract logistics.

In a downturn a forwarder should be able to get better rates from the airlines, even though volumes are less. In an upturn the rates are obviously lower but somehow offset by higher volumes. It could well be that in both situations the absolute margins are similar.

The risk the forwarder could take is to engage in longer term contracts with fixed prices when there could be fluctuations due to changes in demand.

Since the industry of forwarding is very fragmented, the shippers have ample choice and therefore through tender processes can select the best prices. A forwarder can differentiate itself through added services and digitization and automation. Size does matter as well do a forwarder can get a better network and economies of scale. This explains the consolidation taking place in the last years.

Some examples of consolidations:

- CMA, CGM investing in AIR FRANCE-KLM 2022
- CSV AND AGILITY in 2021

Top 25 airfreight forwarders 2021						
Rank	+/-	Company	Air metric tons	YoY change (%)	Gross logistics revenues ($m)	Headquarters
1	+1	Kuehne + Nagel	2,220,000	54.9	40,838	Switzerland
2	-1	DHL Supply Chain and Global Forwarding	2,096,000	25.7	37,707	Germany
3	0	DSV	1,510,833	18.7	28,901	Denmark
4	0	DB Schenker	1,438,000	31.4	27,648	Germany
5	+1	Expeditors	1,047,200	26.0	16,523	United States
6	-1	UPS Supply Chain Solutions	988,880	*N/A	14,639	United States
7	+1	Nippon Express	971,763	34.9	18,612	Japan
8	+4	Sinotrans	804,000	32.2	19,097	China
9	+1	Kintetsu World Express	728,534	40.5	9,010	Japan
10	-1	Bolloré Logistics	656,000	14.3	5,701	France
11	0	Hellmann Worldwide Logistics	652,100	18.0	4,718	Germany
12	+1	Kerry Logistics	520,415	5.4	10,516	Hong Kong
13	+9	AWOT Global Logistics Group	486,216	*N/A	4,058	China
14	+1	CEVA Logistics	474,000	30.6	12,000	France
15	-1	CTS International Logistics	416,190	4.5	3,822	China
16	+2	Yusen Logistics	410,000	28.9	7,788	Japan
17	+2	DACHSER	365,000	17.4	8,333	Germany
18	+2	GEODIS	346,667	19.3	11,900	France
19	-2	Crane Worldwide Logistics	337,300	*N/A	1,600	United States
20	+5	C.H. Robinson	300,000	45.5	22,356	United States
21	+2	NNR Global Logistics	288,837	18.1	1,828	Japan
22	+2	Pilot Freight Services	280,000	16.6	1,350	United States
23	-2	FedEx Logistics	265,600	*N/A	1,920	United States
24	N/A	Dimerco Express Group	251,967	N/A	1,395	Taiwan
25	N/A	cargo-partner	239,400	33.0	2,123	Austria
		Total	18,094,902	19.2		

Revenues and metric tons are company reported or Armstrong & Associates, Inc (A&A) estimates
Revenues have been converted to US$ using the average annual exchange rate
Year-on-year volume growth rates calculated by Air Cargo News
* = due to restated figures
Copyright © 2022 Armstrong & Associates, Inc.

Figure 1.2 Top global forwarders.

- CMA CGM and CEVA in 2019
- DSV and UTI in 2015, followed by the acquisition of Panalpina by DSV in 2019
- XPO acquiring Norbert Dentressangle and Con-way in 2015
- Deutsche Bahn and Schenker in 2007
- Deutsche Post and DHL in 2002, followed by the acquisition of Excel in 2005

A forwarder makes money on air cargo by consolidation, basically combining different shipments to the same destination and optimize chargeable weight and rates. The airline charges shipments with a higher volume with a volume: weight ratio of 6 m^3: 1,000 kg. This is logical since volume takes up space that otherwise could have been used by cargo with a higher weight. If for example an aircraft pallet with feathers would be charged with its actual weight the airline would lose this space for other shipments and therefore lose money. The example of 12 m^3 with feathers weighing only 100 kg would get charged a chargeable weight of 2,000 kg.

Hereunder are two clear examples of how the forwarder makes money with consolidations.

Example 1: Volume/weight consolidations

Let us assume that there are two different shipments with different weight and volume dimensions going to the same destination (Figure 1.3).

The forwarder charges the customer 3,000kg for shipment/HWB # 1 and 1,333kg (8,000/6) for shipment/HWB # 2, which brings the total chargeable weight to the shipper to 4,333kg. The rate by the airline is USD 1/kg.

If these two shipments are tendered in consolidation to the airline under one AWB, the airline would charge based on 3,800kg only (because that is the higher amount between [3,800kg actual weight] and [18 m^3 × 166.67 = 3,000 kg chargeable weight].

Hence the forwarder would make USD 533 on the consolidation of these shipments.

Example 2: Consolidations of various smaller shipments to one destination

Let us assume that there three customers with different shipments to the same destination (Figure 1.4).

In this case the forwarder will charge customer A and B: 45 × 2.25 = USD 101.25 each and customer C: USD 75, resulting in a total revenue of USD 277.50 from the three customers.

The forwarder will consolidate these three shipments into one shipment and booking with the airline. The forwarder will then make one master air waybill (MAWB) (for the three customers) of 110 kg (45+45+20).

If the general rate of the airline for +100kg is USD 1.50 p/kg, the airline will bill the forwarder USD 165 and the forwarder will then have USD 112.50 profit (277.5-/-165).

Example 3: No transparency on rates

Not all forwarders tell their customers transparently what their buying rates are with the airline.

Let us assume a forwarder has a shipment of 5,000 kg and charges the shipper USD 1.20 per kg when the actual buying rate with the airline is USD 1.00 per kg. The forwarder would make USD 1,000 profit.

Any combination of the above-mentioned examples is also possible.

The forwarder has a contractual relationship with the shipper and airline, and in some occasions also with the trucking company.

Most of the airlines and forwarders are IATA members and therefore settle their invoices through the Cargo Account Settlement Systems (CASS), a neutral settlement platform.

PRODUCT/Density	Weight in KG	Volume in m³
1. shipment/HWB, disc drives 300k/m3	3000	10
2. shipment/HWB, slot machines 100k/m3	800	8

Figure 1.3 Weight and density.

Shipment per customer	Weight in KG	General rate in USD
shipment/HWB, customer A	45	2.25
shipment/HWB, customer B	45	2.25
shipment/HWB, customer C	20	Min. 75

Figure 1.4 Shipment comparison.

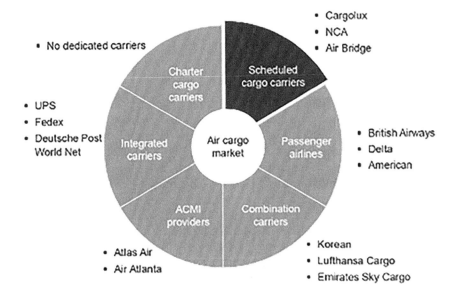

Figure 1.5 Carrier market share.

The Airline

Air cargo is being transported on different types of aircraft operated by different kinds of aircraft operators.

Around half of the global air cargo is flown on passenger aircraft, while the other half is flown on freighters. As the following image shows, there are different types of carriers:

Type of carriers for air cargo (Figure 1.5)

Passenger Airlines

Cargo is transported in the bellies of these passenger aircraft of airlines who do not operate any freighters. Not on all routes there is an equal demand for air cargo. Especially on beach holiday destinations there tends to be less cargo than between industrial hubs. For example, there is more cargo between

Shanghai and Frankfurt than between the Maldives and Frankfurt, even though the same aircraft with the same belly hold capacity is being operated on both routes. On routes with less demand obviously the load factor (percentage of transported cargo divided by the available capacity) is lower and therefore also most likely the rate/yield is lower.

Cargo can make the difference between a profitable or loss-making passenger route. Any cargo carried with a positive contribution margin (revenue minus variable cost) contributes to the fixed cost and therefore the route's profitability. The passenger airline has the following variable costs:

- GSA commission: % of gross sales, excluding surcharges and interline
- Handling cost: p/kg import/export
- Trucking cost: p/kg import/export
- Variable IT cost per kg
- Additional fuel cost, depending on different aircraft types

Example of bottom line contribution of cargo to a passenger route:

A passenger airline flies between Chicago and Mexico City. The handling cost in Chicago is USD 0.08 per kg and in Mexico City USD 0.06 per kg. A forwarder has a shipment of 5,000 kg from Detroit to Mexico City and the trucking cost between Detroit and Chicago is USD 0.10 per kg. The additional fuel and IT cost on this route is USD 0.02 per kg. If the selling rate to the forwarder is USD 0.80 per kg, then the GSA's commission of 5% will be USD 0.04 per kg. The total variable cost is USD 0.30 per kg, and therefore the contribution to the overhead and other fixed costs is USD 0.50 per kg. If given the total revenues the overhead per kg would have been USD 0.10 on all routes, then in this case the passenger airline would have a net contribution to the bottom line of this route of USD 2,000 (5,000 × 0.40).

Now let us assume that the payload is 10,000 kg both ways and that the same net revenue can be generated from Mexico City to Chicago. If the airline has an average of 70% load factor, it will result in a net contribution of USD 5,600 (70% of 10,000 kg × 2 (both ways) × 0.40) on this route.

Hence cargo can make a difference on profitability or not for a passenger airline.

Given the relative low variable cost per kg and the extensivity of the network of passenger airlines, it would be difficult to replicate and disrupt this industry. The high barriers of entry and the high frequencies combined with low cost will result that cargo always will be transported on passenger airlines.

However, some low–cost carriers/budget airlines have decided not to carry any cargo in their bellies because it could affect their turnaround time on the ground and moreover since the routes are short the competitive rates of trucking are similar or even lower than the variable cost of the airlines.

Cargo departments and transfer pricing at passenger airlines:

Most of the larger passenger airlines have their own cargo department and depending on its importance the head of cargo could (and should) report to the CEO. Airlines may outsource some of their sales to GSAs, especially in non-core markets. Even smaller airlines may outsource their whole cargo departments to a GSA. Most of the passenger's airlines cargo departments have their own P&L with an organizational structure with an MD/CEO at the head and finance, operations (mainly handling and trucking) and sales and marketing VP or director. In some occasions the HR function can be combined with the head office.

Like in the example of the bottom line contribution before, it is important to allocate the right cost and revenues in order to optimize the total bottom line for the whole airline.

The cargo department has normally its own overhead cost (building, personnel, etc.) and its own variable cost (trucking, handling, GSA, incremental fuel and IT).

Now how are the cost and revenues of the cargo department allocated/transferred in the passenger airlines?

Basically, there are three different ways of transfer pricing:

- Fixed charge per kg
- Variable % of revenues
- Lump sum

Transfer pricing: fixed charge per kg P 19
Advantage:

- Simple, no administrative burden

Disadvantage:

- Potential loss of contributing revenues for the airline

Example: An airline charges its cargo division a fixed charge of USD 0.75 per kg for every shipment moved on its bellies

- The cargo division will now no longer accept any shipments below USD 0.75/kg
- If the variable cost per kg on a certain route is USD 0.35, it should actually accept shipments above USD 0.35
- Assuming there is a route with the potential of 200 tonnes per month, which would fit in the bellies, and the market rate is USD 0.65, the airline would lose (200,000 × (0.65−0.35)) USD 60,000 of profits per month, of course provided that rest of revenues cover all fixed costs

Advantage:

- Simple, no administrative burden
- Contributing revenues will be accepted

Disadvantage:

- Potential loss due to acceptance of non–contributing cargo

Example: An airline charges its cargo division a variable charge of 30% of the revenues for every shipment moved on its bellies

- The cargo division might now accept loss–making shipments
- If the variable cost per kg is average $ 0.35, it should actually accept shipments above $ 0.35, but not below
- Assuming there are about 100 tonnes per month at an average of $0.30 p/kg, the cargo division will still record net revenues of $21,000 for these shipments, while the airline overall has actually lost $5,000
- One way of avoiding this problem is to give the cargo division P&L responsibility so it allocates its own variable cost in the right way

Transfer pricing: Lump sum
Advantage: Passenger airlines

- Simple, no administrative burden
- Contributing revenues will be accepted
- Flexibility

Disadvantage:
  Potentially "overcharging" the cargo division
  Example: An airline charges its cargo division a lump sum of $ 20 million per year for the utilization of its bellies

- The cargo division has generated $ 30 million in revenues.
- The variable costs were $ 8 million and overhead $ 5 million.
- The cargo division made a loss of $ 3 million, while the airline group made a profit of $ 17 million.

So, what is the conclusion?
  Fixed cost per kg transfer price is definitely not a desirable option since it will lead most likely to missed overall contribution.
  All the other transfer price methods are valid, depending on whether the cargo division is a stand–alone organization or not.
  At the end the option should be chosen where the overall airline benefits most, as long as everyone understands the right costs. The cargo division of a passenger airline should be lean and mean, but at the same time agile to be able to take swift actions on its own without putting a heavy bureaucratic burden. The cargo industry is more dynamic than the passenger industry so the structure should be organized accordingly.

Scheduled All Cargo Carriers

These are airlines that only operate freighters on a scheduled service. They do not have any passenger aircraft and have their own maintenance and flight crew departments. In essence they operate like a passenger airline, only instead of passengers they only transport cargo.

There are global and regional all cargo carriers. The global airlines tend to operate wide body freighters whereas the regional carriers operate smaller narrow body aircraft.

Hereunder an overview of the different freighter aircraft (Figure 1.6):

The economics of the various freighters are quite different. For example, the bigger aircraft in general have a lower operating cost per unit at full pay-load utilization, but at the same there is a bigger commercial and financial risk to fill the aircraft. It takes an equivalent of 6 B727F to fill a B747–8F.

Older aircraft can be cheaper to acquire, but also have higher maintenance cost and can be utilized less hours during a month than newer aircraft. At the end total cost of ownership (TOC) is what counts. TOC includes operating and ownership (depreciation) cost.

Every flight that leaves with a low load factor is basically economically unrecoverable since margins are quite low.

A (cargo) airline has the following fixed costs:

- Aircraft depreciation or lease: An aircraft is purchased, either new or older and then is subsequently being depreciated every year with a certain residual value. The aircraft can also be leased. There are 2 forms of leasing:
  - Dry lease, which is like a financial lease, where there is a long-term financial commitment and the airline has to take care of its own crew, maintenance and interest payments. Usually dry lease deals are made with aircraft owners/investors/lessors like AirCap, GECAS, Air Lease Corporation and Avalon and are always for a period of at least 5 to 8 years. It is actually very similar to ownership.

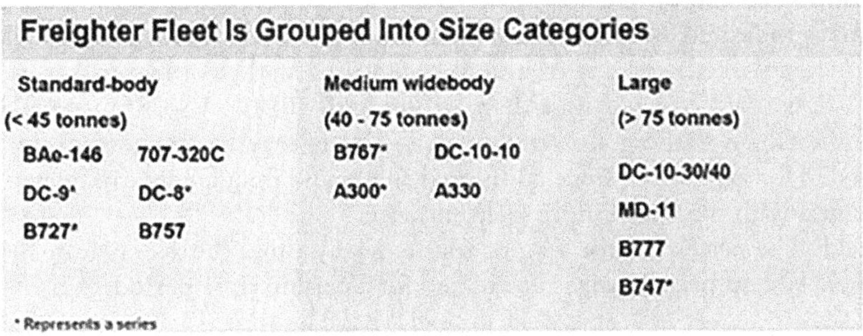

Freighter Fleet Is Grouped Into Size Categories

Standard-body (< 45 tonnes)		Medium widebody (40 - 75 tonnes)		Large (> 75 tonnes)
BAe-146	707-320C	B767*	DC-10-10	
DC-9*	DC-8*	A300*	A330	DC-10-30/40
B727*	B757			MD-11
				B777
				B747*

* Represents a series

Figure 1.6 Freighter sizes.

- Wet lease, also called Aircraft Crew Maintenance and Insurance (ACMI). There are different ACMI Carriers, like Atlas or Air Atlanta. They lease an aircraft on an hour rate including crew, maintenance and insurance with a minimum guaranteed hours per months for a certain period to an airline.
- Crew salaries: These are the monthly fixed salaries of the crew, mainly pilots
- Maintenance: This is the fixed and scheduled maintenance cost for an airline.
- Insurance: Cost to insure the aircraft
- Overhead: Fixed salaries and rental cost
- Finance cost: The cost/interest of a loan, mainly to finance the aircraft and working capital

The variable costs are:

- Fuel: One of the highest cost elements for an airline
- Handling (warehouse and ramp): on a per kg basis; see next chapter on handling agents (GHA)
- Landing: Airports charge a landing fee in every airport. If the aircraft stay longer there will be a parking fee as well
- Overflying: A country charges a fee to overfly its country.
- Variable maintenance and crew: Non-planned maintenance and hotel accommodation for crew

There are three basic drivers to operational profitability for a (freighter) airline:

1 Load factor: The utilization rate of the space of an aircraft based on the chargeable weight. Mostly expressed in flown ton km (FTK) as a percentage of available ton km (ATK)
2 Asset utilization: The more the airline flies the aircraft (obviously with commercial cargo), the lower the fixed cost per unit (kg/flight/hour). This is indicated as block hours (BH: block off when leaving and block on when parked) per day of month. An airline with 15 BH per day has 50% less fixed cost per unit than airline with 10BH. Also, if more BH can be flown with an aircraft, at the end there may be less new aircraft needed for expansion, since additional routes and frequencies can be performed with the same (more efficient) fleet.
3 Yield: The price paid for a kg or tonne. Many times the average for the whole system or city pair is calculated for a certain time period.

These Key Performance Indicators (KPIs) should be positively combined and not stand-alone. When in a given period the load factor and yield are high and the aircraft have flown many hours, the airline for sure will make a good result, provided that fixed costs remain low.

How are new routes developed with an all-cargo airline? With passenger aircraft the routes are already defined, but a freighter airline has to determine where to deploy its aircraft and with what frequencies.

Below are some criteria for the evaluation of new routes:

• Market demand: What has the past growth been and what is the size of the market? What are the factors that could determine future growth? Is it politically stable?
• Seasonality: Is the demand steady throughout the year or are there seasonal influences, either due to demand or supply (like some perishables only grow a certain period of the year?
• Directional imbalances: Air trade is almost never in balance between two city/country pairs. There always tends to be more going from A to B than vice versa. In that case will the yield offset the lower demand from one direction or is it possible to combine the route with another economically viable destination nearby?
• Traffic rights: Is it possible to operate the route and does the airline have to request traffic rights according to the two nations bilateral air services agreement. (See flight freedoms.)
• Competition: Is there a lot of competition already, how strong, what frequencies and most importantly is there room for another airline and based on what?
• Rates: What are the market rates?
• Support from local forwarder community: Talk to the forwarders at origin and destinations.
• Costs: fixed and variable: What are the rates for parking, landing, handling and trucking?
• Profitability: Is the route profitable or not
• Operational feasibility: Is the airport safe, does it have enough slots, etc.?
• Aircraft availability and opportunity cost: Is there availability within the system and if not, can an aircraft be leased? There may be other more attractive routes in the system, which could imply that there may be an opportunity cost

When new aircraft are being developed it is always somehow a gamble if the promised benefits will offset the higher purchase price. Of course, things can be negotiated with the aircraft manufacturer.

Ideally an airline orders a new freighter a one of the first, in order to have fist mover advantage of the lower operating cost. Hopefully, this purchase moment is anticyclical.

Image: To ensure long-term viability, airlines need to bridge the gap between older aircraft exit and new aircraft entry (Figure 1.7).

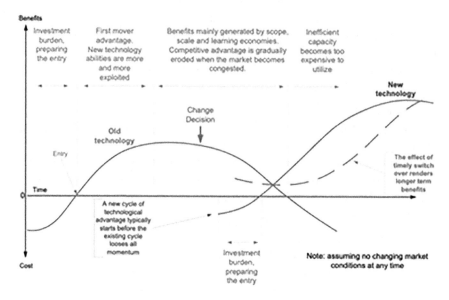

Figure 1.7 Old and new aircraft benefits.

Unfortunately, the order cycle of aircraft is still far from perfect. Traditionally aircraft are ordered after some time of economic growth where first of all management and then after some time shareholder boards are convinced that the markets are growing. They subsequently order large quantities of aircraft based on the present facts which will then be delivered some years after, in many occasions when there is an economic downturn. Ideally these planes should be ordered in a recession when prices are low and they will be delivered when there is sufficient growth to make economic use of these expensive assets. However, this countercyclical investment behaviour will require different cash flow management where savings in good times only will be used to acquire assets in an economic slowdown.

Combination Carriers

Like the term already implicates, combination carriers are airlines who operate passenger bellies and freighters. The same dynamics apply as earlier described with passenger and freighter airlines. Freighters and bellies should be complementary, feeding each other and creating the maximum overall result. Since the profit or a loss of a freighter operation is seen and felt immediately there could be a risk that the attention goes more towards filling the freighter instead of the bellies. Also here applies that any additional business through a freighter that is transported with a positive contribution margin on a belly afterwards, adds to the overall bottom line of the airline.

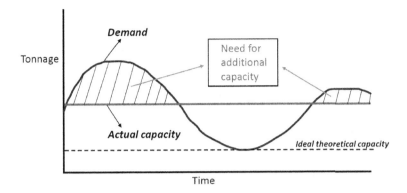

Figure 1.8 Capacity and demand.

The combination of freighters and the high frequency of bellies gives the airline a competitive edge in terms of network coverage.

ACMI providers or also called wet lessors own a fleet of aircraft who they lease out on a short or medium term to airlines, integrators but also to forwarders. The wet lessor charges the customer the cost of the aircraft, crew, maintenance and insurance. All the other costs, like handling, fuel, etcetera, are the responsibility of the customer.

The other form of leasing is a dry lease, which is a longer term financial lease of the aircraft. There are several financial institutions, like AirCap, Gecas and Air Lease Corporation, who are the three biggest with a combined fleet of over 2,000 aircraft.

Whether during the course of a year or during various years, there are fluctuations in demand and sometimes in supply as well. The difference is that the supply side could be controlled by an individual airline, whereas the demand cannot be influenced that easily.

The underlying graph shows the fixed capacity of an airline during a certain period and the fluctuations in demand, either cyclical or structural.

Ideally any asset operator maintains fixed capacity at the bottom of the demand curve and copes with the extra demand through variable capacity. Here is where ACMI carriers play an important role (Figure 1.8).

Integrators

Ahead of the game, control the whole supply chain, IT driven (see chapter 2).

Traffic Rights

Airlines are heavily regulated and in order to have the rights to carry cargo and passenger on a route, the airline needs to apply for traffic rights. The market has become more open with some countries offering open skies, which means two nations basically agree to have unlimited air travel between them. Air travel is much more regulated than sea travel.

Freedoms of the Air IndustryEven though aviation is more liberated through more global access to traffic rights than in the past, complete open skies will also allow airlines worldwide to make use of all traffic rights and as a result create a level playing field where cost and prices will come down and thus will contribute to more economic growth. Since 1992 the inter-European liberalization caused a rise of 33% in European air travel, which again resulted in 1.4 million extra full-time jobs and a GDP growth of $85 billion (Figure 1.9).

However, there are still some countries in the world that prefer to protect their flag carriers, rather than improving the overall welfare of the broader public interest. This places European carriers in a relative competitive disadvantage since Europe is more deregulated than certain other areas in the world.

Ownership rules in the aviation industry in many countries limit necessary integration and therefore further growth. For example, the United States, China and Brazil are some of the large markets that restrict foreign ownership. Eliminating these ownership rules would result in a unified global and fully liberalized market for the aviation industry. It would also result in further necessary integration where inefficient national airlines will no longer distort the mechanisms of an open market economy in which consumers benefit from better service and lower prices.

Airline subcontracts GSA. GHA and RFS all have a relationship with the forwarder.

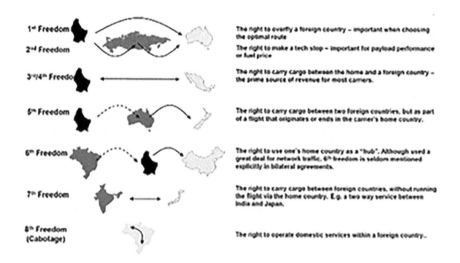

Figure 1.9 Flight freedoms.

General Sales Agent

Back in the 1980s and 1990s most GSAs were small independent units providing service for smaller airlines or in markets where there was an insufficient business for an airline to justify establishing its own cargo office. Alternatively, they were acting as an off-line agent in places such as Europe, fed by off-line trucking or even co-loading with other carriers. Certain regions for example in Latin America or Africa where markets were either small or difficult to manage, were the main areas for GSA operations.

In the early 1990s an organization was formed entitled FAGSA (Federation of Airline GSAS) in an attempt to consolidate the financial backing of GSA operations which depended on personal bank loans, a substantial disadvantage for entrepreneurs. During the 1990s, some GSAs evolved into groups, offering wider service to their airline customers, such as warehousing, dangerous good clearance and road feeder servicer, but in most cases the trend was to keep within a country boundary but having offices in key cities. Companies such as Aerotrans, Globe Air began to develop significant revenue on the part of their diverse clients. GSAs offered several advantages. They were willing to work longer hours and to access a useful personal client network thus seeking and bringing new business to the airline. They paid their own operating expense, relying on commission from the airline, the cheaper win-win option for the airline. They were on short term contracts which meant that the carrier could switch to another GSA at very short notice. Whereas this was advantageous to the carrier, it meant in reality, that the GSA was extremely vulnerable which is one of the reasons why the bank guarantee was insisted upon.

In that era, it was also considered that to represent airlines that might be in competition, to be inappropriate and to overcome this, often other trading names were used in order to disguise any possible conflict. In fact, it was almost impossible to disguise this and today, with so much transparency, it is no longer necessary.

One of the big traditional challenges of any GSA has always been to be too successful! If the GSA takes over a territory with low production and turns it into a success story, there is a very good chance that the airline will decide that they do not wish to pay out large commissions by outsourcing, but would rather take the territory back in-house and save money. GSAs have always been on very short contracts, thus making it easy for carriers to fire them and replace them with their own cargo department or to engage another GSA, possibly at a lower rate. In a worst-case scenario the airline may appoint an alternative rival GSA in the same territory. Recent events however have brought about some substantial changes in the relationship between airline and outsourced agent.

The keyword in the modern era is transparency and the introduction of cloud-based digital processing and booking platforms, is making information more easily available, including in some cases, even rates and conditions.

Thus, the old practice of keeping information hidden has mostly disappeared to be replaced with efficient real time data, making the cargo process more efficient and cost-effective. The ability to utilize block space agreements, for example, has become a major part of the GSA's armoury. Today the leading GSAs are acting as entire outsourced cargo management departments, responsible for handling, road feeder service (RFS), dangerous goods and security checking and every other aspect of the cargo process. This is why the title has changed into GSSA (General Sales and Service Agent) with the accent on service. In some cases, these services are offered at cost price or even lower in order to attract clients in much the same way as a supermarket offers loss leader products in order to entice customers into the store.

Because of his wide experience with different airlines and systems, a GSSA is able to consider, evaluate or include the best practices from different sources thus giving a balanced and competitive performance profile. This incorporates all the best available technology, systems and platforms, in order to provide a total air cargo management service and not having to pay homage to old legacy systems operated by some airlines. The GSA above all else is an entrepreneur, able and willing to use all possible skills, leverage contacts and technology to achieve success.

The GSA market operates at several different levels and varies considerably in different parts of the world. More GSAs are based in Europe but other areas such as Latin America, Africa and parts of the Far East are well served by GSAs where conditions may be difficult and cargo loads not viable for full scale airline operations.

The market is dominated by a handful of large multinational GSAs such as the ECS group with offices in 47 countries serving 180 carriers, the air logistics group with a worldwide network and the Kales group with offices in around 40 locations in EuropeThen there are a number of smaller more regional GSAs who specialize in a particular sector or country. In the Far East it has been the practice for one company to operate as a GSA and freight for that and the handler simultaneously, a practice that is not so likely in Europe. However with the advent of the service element, the GSA is much more likely to offer a wider range of service which will include a pricing strategy and capacity management as well as ground services. It is estimated that prior to the COVID-19 pandemic, that on average around 20% to 25% of all air cargo capacity volume sold was in the hands of GSSAs.

Airlines now struggling to cut costs and stay in business, consider that outsourcing of cargo can be an excellent solution but the selected GSA must come with a good reputation in the industry, sound financial backing and a good trading record, and of course the ability to produce high level sales at the right price.

The maximum use of appropriate technology is now a vital element in success and allows the GSA to operate more efficiently and effectively. This is likely to expand in the future as more proven operating platforms become available.

ECS Group continues to introduce its own special style of the GSA concept with the addition of several new options for its customers, allowing them and allows customers to pick and choose which services and products they would like to utilize rather than a "one-size-fits all" solution. The concept is based on four pillars: Commercial, New Abilities, Technology and Sustainability, including sales, marketing, revenue optimization, operations, interline management, claims handling, all the way through to chartering operations.

Adrien Thominet, ECS Group executive chairman, said that the air cargo industry has been undergoing massive disruption, already visible prior to the pandemic.

"Digitalisation as well as emerging digital platforms, ever-developing safety and security regulations, the e-commerce boom, greater cargo community collaboration, multimodal... All these factors and more are leading to changes in age-old air cargo processes. The traditional GSA model is no longer enough."

All successful GSSAs are now following much the same direction and becoming an even more influential part of the developing industry.

The General Sales and Services Agent

The GSSA as its name already suggests offers sales services to the airlines. It is not always limited to sales only. Therefore, the second "s" implies services, like supervision of cargo, or bookings, accounting, trucking, etc. Basically, all services that a cargo department of an airline should perform.

There are different types of GSSAs. There are the local companies, specialized in a certain market but there are also a couple of larger group GSSAs that have office all over the world and achieve synergies in the back office and offer one stop shop services to airlines.

The GSSA functions like the cargo division of an airline in a certain territory, selling to the local forwarding community

Why would an airline outsource its sales to a GSSA?

There are various reasons for outsourcing:

- If the cargo volumes and revenues of an airline are not sufficient to justify an own organization. In this way the variable commission cost of a GSSA will be less than the overhead costs of an own office. As an example, if an airline cannot generate more than USD 2 million sales per year in a certain country they fly from and putting their own organization will cost them USD 400,000 per year (between personnel, rent and travel costs), it makes sense to outsource. Let's assume the GSSA charges around 5% commission. This will imply that the cost of the GSSA will be USD 100,000 versus the USD 400,000 of their own organization. So, it makes perfect sense from a cost point of view.
- To remain flexible in case volumes and flights will increase or decrease. It could make sense from a cost point of view to have their own staff in a

country, but in case due to market circumstances volumes could decline which ultimately could lead to the decision of the airline to cease operations, it would be better to have a flexible GSSA organization. Otherwise ultimately the airline may end up with a large overhead and maybe even no sales.

- For market knowledge and experience: In some cases, the GSSA has superior market knowledge and expertise which could take some time for the airline to build it up themselves.
- In case the airline has limited network destinations: The forwarder would like to deal with airlines/GSSAs that cover a wide range of network destinations and products. In case the airline only serves a limited market, outsourcing to a GSSA that represents more (non-conflicting) airlines would give the forwarders a more comprehensive service.

How does the relationship between the airline, the GSSA and forwarders work?

The revenue model and value proposition of the GSSA can be in different forms or even combinations:

- On a commission basis: The GSSA sells on behalf of the airline either in or outside IATA CASS, where applicable and gets a commission on the rates. The commission can be either applicable on all in rates, including fuel and other surcharges or on net rates, excluding surcharges. The GSSA will optimize its workforce by presenting various airlines and in this way get a profit.
- On a net rate basis: The airline will ask the GSSA a certain net rate per route and the GSSA will sell on top of that rate in the market.
- Total Cargo Management (TCM): This model applies mostly for smaller passenger airlines who do not want to bother with the investment and fixed operational expenses of having an own cargo department. The GSSA will take over the whole cargo department, including, sales, bookings, operations and finances. There are different forms of TCM:
  - On a lump sum basis: The GSSA offers to take over the bellies for a certain amount and will try to generate more revenues than the cost. The disadvantage of this system is that it does not consider the growth or even decline of flights and volumes. If for some reasons the airline decides to half its fleet, it would become very difficult to regain the lump sum.
  - On a fixed/variable basis: The GSSA will give a minimum fixed revenue guarantee to the airline but will have either a commission or an add on top of the net rates.
  - Completely variable: The GSSA pays a net rate to the airline on a per kg basis per different sectors, thus taking into account seasonality and market dynamics in volumes.

- Large airlines tend to have their own staff instead of a GSSA but could consider a GSSA in smaller non-core markets.

Like in so many other industries, there are more digital booking platforms that will make the whole booking process more efficient. The goal of these platforms is to make the bookings more efficient and in even in some cases make it a transparent rate system. The advantage of such a booking system will and should be that the bookings will get done electronically system to system, cutting personnel time and eventually also errors. This is not necessarily a threat to the GSSA model, since this will only help improving the booking system with existing rates.

Air Charters

In the early days the broker was very much the "post office," literally taking the enquiry from the would-be charterer and asking the airline for a quote and passing the quote back to the client and retaining a commission. In those days the centre of the broking world was the Baltic Exchange; beyond that in cities like Hamburg and Rotterdam there were other brokers. There was a reason – a large part of the work of a broker was the movement of urgent ships spares for a vessel that had broken down.

In the days of the Baltic Exchange's pre-eminence, the airlines had their broker representatives on the exchange – known as the "carrier's broker" and a charterer would use another broker, the "charterer's broker," who was obliged to negotiate the charter price through the carrier's broker. Today, the Baltic Exchange for the world of aircraft charter has become the Baltic Air Charter Association and has become a meeting place for the aircraft charter industry.

The brokers of the age on the Baltic Exchange were part of the Airbrokers Association, which was actually formed in 1949 and were in many cases byproducts of the ship brokers and part of the shipping world – companies like Clarksons, Furness Withy, Lambert Brothers, E.A. Gibson and many others. With JIT inventory we first started to see the auto manufacturers cut their factory stocks and rely on their suppliers to get their goods to the factory line just as they became needed – saving along the way a vast amount on both storage and premature capital outlays. Of course, suppliers could get "stymied" by weather, strikes and their own internal problems. These events were a bonanza to the charter broker, who became the point of focus as usually speed was of the essence, the broker usually knew which aircraft was where and from the moment of enquiry to the moment of fixture was often less than 1 hour. Sometimes an aircraft would be chartered one way for one factory and in exactly the reverse direction for another – in the words of a well-known TV comic, "a nice little earner."

This charter airline in the 1970s was heavily involved, as were others in transport of heavy materials to the Far East, with aircraft frequently returning empty. How curious when we look at today's market, where the trade works in the reverse direction with aircraft frequently light loaded into the Orient and fully laden coming back.

The other massively influential cargo aircraft in the charter market is the Antonov AN-124 Ruslan, which was first commercially certified in 1992. This is in effect the largest freighter aircraft after the destruction of the AN 225 in 2022.

The brokers were the first to realize the potential for these machines and started putting them to work on an almost global basis – although to start with some authorities resisted their lure, many others were quick to embrace them. To this day some of these older aircraft can be found in distant corners of the globe, but now many of the major authorities have introduced a list of banned operators and sometimes countries.

The brokers began to sell the services of these freighters – especially the large Antonov AN-124 – to governments who could see that using chartered aircraft like these would cut the cost of their military support operations. This is happening even today, although the age of the Ilyushin aircraft in many cases makes them less suitable and acceptable. So it is that brokers, and this is key to their usefulness in the market, are forever searching for ways of operating at ever lower costs. Much changes in the economics of operation with the cost of fuel; as this rises, more fuel-efficient aircraft have a greater value – aircraft such as the Boeing 747-400; but when fuel prices drop heavily then the older classic Boeing 747s can come into their own.

The broker of today has to be aware of market conditions – as demand drops and recession bites, available capacity increases, especially in the belly-hold space of passenger aircraft, which today are far larger than 30 years ago. But at the same time the traditional scheduled airline, which has been trying to build its own cargo fleet, starts to suffer a massive downturn in demand and starts to axe these scheduled freighters. This creates holes in the market that the broker is called upon to fill.

Today, the major brokers are global companies and are constantly being fed information from their worldwide offices and using the network to piece together an operation that keeps the costs down as well as having someone on hand to ensure the smooth transfer of freight from one service to another or ensure the speedy approval of traffic rights. More than ever the business is a 24/7 one and no broker worth his weight would not carry a mobile phone at all times.

In line with all air transport, the use of aircraft is heavily weighted towards passengers, and so it is in the broking world – there are far more specialist passenger charter brokers than air freight brokers. In turn, many of these passenger brokers specialize in particular niches in the market – be it sport (and even this breaks down), entertainment, executive and so on. In the air freight world this is less the case, although there are areas of specialization, such as livestock and automotive, but these are few and far between. There are freight brokers now around the globe, but the larger international ones tend to be Europe-based, particularly in the UK, which is fitting as that is pretty much where it all started. However, the same cannot be said for the airlines being used, as they are far more widely spread.

As we face the future, looking forward from 2013 the broker is looking at the IL-76s, where we have gone from a market of 30 operators with 100 machines to barely 10–12 air operator's certificates with 30-odd aircraft. Only four or five can now operate in EU airspace; two of these have Stage 4 noise-compliant aircraft only – a total of seven airframes – the rest have Stage 2 versions and it is much tougher for them to operate in the commercial market. If it carries on like this, and with no Afghan traffic, there are likely to be only four or five carriers by 2015 or 2016, with a total of 20–25 aircraft in service.

As for the Boeing 747s, the last big downturn in 2009 caused virtually all the classics to leave the major league, with almost no exceptions. There is now perhaps a crisis with the mortgaged, financed or lessor-owned Boeing 747-400Fs and converted BCFs.

It is just starting, but there could be terrible troubles ahead for airlines, especially charter ones, in the near future. The reasons are varied, but the crisis is both economic conditions on the one hand and the steep decline since the spring of U.S. military flying on the other (affecting the U.S. 74F majors that rely on AMC/MAC and ACMI/charter operations).

On top of that are two other factors. First, freighters ordered 2 or 3 years ago, such as the Boeing 777F and the delayed B747–8F – which came to the market nearly 2 years late – are coming online now in 2012. Fortunately, there are very few, if any, conversions left to be done to Boeing 747 passenger aircraft. Second, the huge number of large-capacity passenger widebody equipment coming online now, especially the "freight-friendly" Boeing 777, with some of the Middle East airlines alone having around 80 of these aircraft to come still from the manufacturer. This will create a great volume of belly-hold space on global routes that will eat away at charter demand.

Airbus and Boeing had orders on their books for 2,240 widebody aircraft – A330s, A350s, A380s and Boeing's 777, 787 and 787–88 models – all of which can carry more than 15 tonnes of cargo in their bellyhold space. The B777 can lift as much as 40 tonnes, even with a full passenger load, which is as much as a DC-8 freighter, the very aircraft that was at the heart of some charter broker programmes less than 10 years ago. Compared to the Boeing 767s and A330s, and at the top end of the range, the A350 and (above all) the Boeing 777, can load more freight than a B747-400. These aircraft will be flying frequent scheduled passenger services between many of the cities that did have such big birds in their skies a few years ago and will mop up cargo that would have been the basis for a charter operation even 5 years ago.

What does this mean for the broker? Probably retrenchment, but as always, in 50 years it means looking for innovative answers in niche markets to meet sudden and unexpected demands. Many experts believe the day of the pure freighter aircraft is over and certainly some major airlines are pulling back from full-freighter service. This will create spot demand – an area where the broker can always be "first to the post" with a ready solution.

The Internet Generation

As with nearly every field of activity in our modern world, the power of the internet has either taken over or changed the way we do business. The charter broker has not been immune to this movement and many have disappeared. However, many have not only survived this revolution but have found ways of enhancing and upgrading their usefulness for their customers. Charter broking can be relatively simple when a single shipment such as a piece of industrial equipment must be flown to an uncomplicated destination. The aircraft and price might well be handled online. But in most cases the transaction may be open to interpretation as to the correct equipment and crew, loading and unloading at the destination airport. The price and delivery timetable may need negotiation and the client may feel the need for expert and reliable advice. For example, providing logistics service for an orchestra or music group on a tour of several locations will require specialist knowledge, understanding of the specific needs and limitations. As the cost of most charters is very high, the customer must ensure that he is getting the best possible solution. This type of expert consultancy is unlikely to be found on the internet. Thus overall, the charter brokers can feel sure that their services will be required for many years to come but that they must work hard at providing extra value added personal service.

The Federation of GSAs

Back in the 1990s GSAs were regarded as peripheral to the main air cargo industry, and indeed were seen with some suspicion by many airlines. A large proportion of GSAs at that time were small or even one-man companies selling airline capacity to carriers which had few resources for this job. The main carriers mostly avoided GSAs except in minor or strategically difficult markets, preferring to sell their own cargo space in major markets. GSAs also suffered the restriction of providing substantial bank guarantees to airlines so that there could be no loss of income.

The formation of FAGSA (Federation of Airline GSAs) was an attempt by pioneer Helge Luhr to create a team spirit and present a unified front to the airlines. Despite valiant attempts to provide financial backing, no serious solution emerged. Also, many of the member GSAs were in competition with each other and thus cooperation was minimal. Over the years, however, the industry and the role of GSAs have changed out of recognition.

The Federation of Airline General Sales Agents (FEDAGSA) is today headquartered in Geneva, Switzerland and is a not for profit trade federation, dedicated to representing the interests of airline GSAs throughout the world.

The Federation continues to attract new members and provide much needed help and benefits.

Applicants who meet the criteria are welcomed into this Federation and quickly learn that despite the Federation itself being not for profit many profitable networking and business opportunities exist within FEDAGSA. Professional services are easily accessible including initial "free" consultations with legal counsel where necessary. Newsletters, news updates, business referrals, statistics and finance plus the lobbying of government and non-government organizations are just some of the benefits. Business Conferences/AGM meetings provide well qualified networking opportunities and set the priorities for each year. Discounts on IATA CASS, accreditation, manuals, conferences and other services including courses are available through your membership. Indeed many members have found discounts to be greater than their membership fees making FEDAGSA essentially free. We also offer prompt and discounted access to IATA accreditation for those qualifying for this excellent joint programme.

With various challenges faced by the airline industry over three decades, the situation has been completely revolutionized. The main driver of this has been cost reduction. The expense of maintaining a fully manned sales office with a staff of essentially, "nine to fivers," could not be justified, with low volume and yield and increasing competition. The GSA, on the other hand, was and is an entrepreneur, willing to work long unsocial hours using local contacts. As the airline had only to pay commission on paid-for sales, all the risk was eliminated. If the GSA did not perform they could be replaced by another at short notice. All the cost of the GSA operation was borne by the GSA. Economic downturns and volatile fuel prices very often meant unpredictable results. It was a tough job, some survived and some did not.

During the noughties the trend amongst airlines to outsource as much activity as possible developed. This allowed them to concentrate on the core business of passengers and GSAs had more opportunities to secure more solid and lucrative contracts. The additional element of service was introduced turning them into GSSAs (General Service and Sales Agents). The additional tasks of documentation, trucking, customs clearance, dangerous goods handling, warehousing and ground handling were some of these new responsibilities. This changed the whole relationship between airline and agent and in many cases created a complete outsourced cargo management function. It was at this point that GSAs formed themselves into strategic groups. By acquiring existing GSAs or opening new ones in different countries, the emerging groups were able to benefit from the local expertise of the individual GSAs while creating an umbrella management structure. Financial guarantees thereafter were in the hands of banks and financial institutions and many airline customers could be represented in several offices in the group. This gave the advantage of across the board collaboration, but at the same time an airline could choose one office only if required.

Companies such as Air Logistics, ECS, Kales and Wexco began to build and strengthen their market share and clout.

One example is ECS (European Cargo Services), a Paris-based GSSA group with offices in 35 countries employing over 800 people. The group was launched in 2012 by the joining of several French GSAs which at the time were fiercely competitive with one another – Globe Air Cargo and Aero Cargo being the two principal companies. Despite their competition they were able to work as a team and from that point expanded into most European hub airports – Brussels, Frankfurt, Madrid and Milan and sub-sequently to other European centres, as well as Miami and Bogota. Today the group is represented by 104 offices, including 59 subsidiaries, together producing an annual turnover of more than $1 billion and representing many airlines.

The global network approach is regarded by the airlines as a real and legitimate business, and as such has surpassed any of the old GSA stigma. According to Bertrand Schmoll, Chairman of ECS, the company is now in partnership with its airline customers and very much part of the airlines' organizations.

Today our group puts around 50% of its resources and efforts into service for the clients, but the sales function is still our primary contribution, after all that is what the GSA does!! Airlines don't want to have to employ people, preferring to outsource wherever possible. Although we are a multinational group explains Schmoll,

> it is in the local manager's hands to really create the business. He has the contact and local market knowledge, but at the same time can collaborate with colleagues in the other group offices when necessary. Competition is of course as tough as ever, which is fine as long as it is fair and on a level playing field. However, in air cargo, as in any modern business, there are always people undercutting price and willing to do loss making deals to secure new business.

As in any modern business successful companies, including GSSAs are obliged to take risks and to back their local managers to the hilt. The ECS Group has been very successful at this and by encouraging its entrepreneurial spirit it has gained a strong traction in markets such as India where it's pharmaceutical business is flourishing.

Kales Airline Services, HQ in Amsterdam, has over 40 offices in around 30 countries and represents 70 airlines handling over 200,000 tonnes pa.

Global GSA group, also headquartered in Amsterdam, operates in over 50 countries and generates around 850,000 tonnes of cargo annually.

A quick glance at the number of GSAs in different countries reveals that this is a largely European business. For example, in Netherlands there are 24, the United Kingdom 30, Germany 20, the United States 15, Canada 10 and China11. Many of these are branches of European groups. The number of GSAS based in other countries is proportionately much smaller than in Europe. EG China has only 12, Brazil 2, South Africa 6 and India 23.

There is no doubt that the GSSA function will expand in the future as more airlines seek to outsource various functions, especially in markets that are either small or which are considered difficult. The entire cargo operation will often be managed by the GSSA including –sales, marketing, handling, Customs, trucking and dangerous goods declarations.

For the airlines it is a win-win business as they have no overheads or staff costs and obligations.

The Ground Handler

See Chapter 3 (ON THE GROUND)

Road Feeder Services

The road feeding service, or also referred to as trucking, plays an important part in the air cargo supply chain. Sometimes the freight spends more time on the road than on a plane or even in a warehouse. For airlines it is essential to be able to count on an efficient road (de) feeding network to deliver the goods in good quality and on time.

The RFS provider typically works for more airlines and distributed the cargo between airports or other bonded facilities. The truck is considered as a flight and is bonded, meaning that the cargo will not be cleared in customs until it has arrived at its destination.

There are airlines, usually the larger network carriers, that have fixed schedules of trucking, mainly in Europe and the United States. They contract the RFS on a fixed bases, paying for Full Truck Load (FTL) and therefore taking the responsibility and risk to optimize the trailer capacity themselves. This obviously only works when these airlines have sufficient constant demand between certain airports.

For other airlines these is also the option to contract RFS companies who provide Less than Truck Load (LTL) services. These services are offered in a network of consolidating different shipments in order to optimize the load factor. The airline in these cases usually pays per kilo or per pallet position. An LTL service is not always as quick as a FTL service since the truck has to pick up and deliver various shipments at airports and/or bonded facilities.

In most cases the RFS service is between handling agents at airports on behalf of the airline. There is a contractual relationship between the airline and the RFS and between the airline and the GHA, but not between the GHA and the RFS. In some cases, it is difficult to interact between the GHA and the RFS because they do not have a contractual obligation between each other, but they do have to cooperate together.

Similar KPI dynamics are applied to RFS suppliers as to airlines:

- Load factor: RFS is trying to achieve the highest load factor of the trailers behind the trucks. The more volume, the better result
- Yield: ideally you have a high load factor with good paying cargo, be it the rate per kg, pallet or full truck
- Asset utilization: the more km you drive with high paying load factor, the lower the fixed unit cost and therefore the better the contribution margin. Considering the driving time restrictions and congestion, it should be possible to achieve an asset utilization of around 15,000 kms per months, mostly using two drivers.

Trucking companies could be either asset-heavy or asset-light. The advantages of being asset-heavy are that the RFS company can ground some fleet in case of a downturn, without having to continue to pay, meaning the deprecation will continue but it is not a cash out. Another big advantage of having your own fleet is that you will be able to offer capacity guarantees to your customers, especially when the demand for capacity is high.

Obviously, the disadvantage is that it requires a lot of investment and therefore a lot of cash out or higher debts.

Ideally a trucking company will have its own capacity at lowest level of demand during the cycles in the year, like the image below symbolizes (Figure 1.10):

A RFS can hire charters, who are companies that subcontract their trucks and drivers to other trucking companies. These charters can operate in two different ways:

1 On a fixed basis per month: The charter company will be included in the trucking network of the RFS, operating with their board computer. The charter will get a fixed per km charge, with often a guaranteed minimum

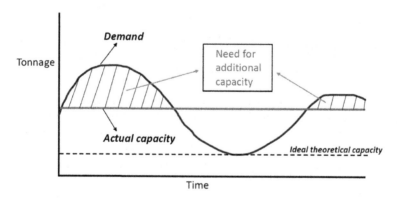

Figure 1.10 Capacity demands.

kilometres per month. The contract duration can vary between a couple of months and a year.

2 On an ad-hoc basis: When there is an ad-hoc need between a certain city pair where the RFS does not have the capacity in an economically timely way, the RFS could outsource that sector to an ad-hoc charter which in most of the times are similar "friendly" competitors. This happens on a per kg of FTL basis.

Nowadays almost all trucks have board computers, where instructions are sent to the driver, fuel consumption is monitored and driving times and salaries are determined.

Like the AWB is the official document for air cargo so is the CMR for trucking. CMR stands for Convention on the contract for the International Carriage of Goods by Road and was signed at a United Nations convention in Geneva in 1956. It covers several legal issues regarding road transport and has been ratified by most of the European countries.

RFS companies face different challenges in network dynamics and planning:

- **Time**: It is essential to deliver on time, while being flexible in changing customer demands.
- **Place**: Having the required availability at the right place trying to balance the network as much as possible.
- **Drivers**: Some companies have fixed drivers per truck, but considering the driving times restrictions, you can achieve more revenue kilometres by changing drivers and even utilizing two drivers per truck. In a dynamic network good crew planning is essential
- **FTL versus LTL**: Depending on customer demands and load factor optimization, the customer may decide to go for an LTL service when the volumes do not justify the FTL. Since an RFS company needs to optimize its network, it must find more LTL loads to optimize the load factor. This will result in more stops and therefore a longer service than with a straight FTL. Obviously the LTL rate will be more expensive on a per kg basis, since the RFS provider will have the risk of filling the space, whereas with a FTL the full truck is paid for.
- **Hubs**: Operating from hubs from where the network is optimized. These hubs function as gathering points where traffic flows are combined to achieve the highest load factor.
- **Import/Export ratio (in vs out)**: Trying to complement imbalances in the network, by combining different routes, since there is almost never a perfect import/export balance between cities and countries.
- **Availability of equipment or third parties:** Having a strong network of external providers to accommodate surges in demand or ad-hoc requests when their own trucks are not available.

- **Congestion:** In many parts of the world roads, but also airport can be congested. The advantage of air cargo is that most of it will be trucked in the night when there is less traffic. However, congestion around certain cities and airports results in longer waiting times and less asset utilization, putting a higher cost burden on the RFS companies.

Control Towers

Digitalization and automation are key. Of course, there will always be a need for asset-heavy operators – businesses with physical trucks and warehouses. But the future leaders will be the ones with the right digital platforms. For example, if you were able to see all the transport flows worldwide with all their available capacity, you could optimize your operations and have 20% fewer trucks on the road. Why? Many trucks on the road today aren't full. Without even knowing it, several trucks could be travelling in the same direction, each with, for example, only 70% capacity.

With better visibility, there could be really useful advice. For example, you could go to a customer and say that we've analysed their flows and that, on a Wednesday, if they could hold out for a 6 pm rather than a 3 pm pickup, we could combine cargo and save them money.

You can only do that with smart platforms.

A Thursday in November is not the same as a Monday in November. And a Thursday without rain is different to a Thursday with rain. So, if you have all this big data and you combine it and you perform predictive analytics, you can plan ahead better, be more efficient and offer better on-time service to your customers.

To optimize large fleet networks you need a smart system. It helps achieve operational excellence and improve customer interaction. System-to-system integration, booking systems, on-time performance, digital feedback and smart reporting are all big differentiators and enable the company to be more open and transparent with customers.

Logistics and world trade are very correlated. Digitalization is very important, as is the growing use of new technologies. Think autonomous driving, robotics in warehouses, pilotless planes; it's all going to happen.

But, while there are a lot of trends and hype, let's not underestimate that, for the time being, we'll continue to have business-to-business flows. So while we must continue to be agile, we also have to acknowledge that the pace of change isn't going to be continuously at the same level or higher.

Airports

The airport is the central mechanism of the entire air supply chain. As Figure 1.11 shows, there are different contractual relationships between the various sectors in the air cargo supply chain. An airline has a separate contract and

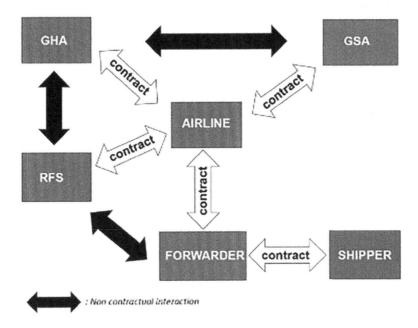

Figure 1.11 Aircargo team.

sometimes even standard operating procedures with an RFS and GHA, but there is no contractual relationship between the RFS and GHA, even though they interact quite frequently. This can lead to suboptimization of the air cargo supply chain where one party will blame the other for not complying with agreed KPIs without having any contractual enforcement. Also, the GSA interacts with the GHA on behalf of its airline, who will have a contract.

The Relevance of Contribution Margin for Airlines

The contribution margin (CM) is defined as revenues minus the variable costs. A positive CM means that additional revenues cover the variable costs and contribute to the fixed cost base.

In order to understand the impact of CM better, it is relevant to understand airline specific dynamics:

- High Fixed Costs per calendar period (aircraft depreciation/lease, salaries)
  - Aircraft is typically depreciated over 18 years with a small residual value
- High Fixed Costs per round-trip (aircraft depreciation/lease, salaries, landing, over-flying)

- Global business
  - It does not matter whether one is China-based or Europe-based if it wants to fly between Europe and China
- Constraints
  - Curfews – In many airports a night curfew is applied with possible penalties
  - Slots – parking positions, arrival and departure times are limited at many large airports (e.g., HKG, TPE, JFK)
  - Traffic rights – aviation is still heavily regulated, in sharp contrast to "freedom of the seas"
  - Heavy and line maintenance – regular downtime on aircraft between day and several weeks depending on the type of check
  - Unforeseen delays – loading delays, strikes, breakdowns on aircraft can compromise utilization plan.

What Are the Relevant Cost Drivers?

Like in many other industries it is important to use the right cost drivers to allocate certain costs. Changing from a cost driver X to cost driver Y can have an impact on the economic viability of projects, divisions, flights, etc.

- It is a given that every flight that leaves with a low load factor is economically unrecoverable
- A cargo airline has the following fixed costs: aircraft, crew salaries, maintenance, insurance, overhead
- The variable costs are: fuel, handling, landing, overflying and variable maintenance and crew
- Marginal costing means that the extra revenue generated in certain actions (like, for example, taking an extra shipment onboard an aircraft) will trigger additional (marginal/variable) costs.

There are different cost drivers for an airline:

- BH (Block Hours): the time from the moment the aircraft door closes at departure of a revenue flight until the moment the aircraft door opens at the arrival gate following its landing. Block hours are the industry-standard measure of aircraft utilization.
- FH (Flight Hours) is defined as "when an aircraft moves under its own power for the purpose of flight and ends when the aircraft comes to rest after landing." Time spent taxiing and performing pre-flight checks on the ground is included in flight hours, provided the engine is running.
- EH (Elapsed Hours): actual time an airplane spends in the air, as opposed to time spent taxiing to and from the gate and during stopovers.
- Ton: 1,000 kgs

- FTE: full-time employee
- Aircraft
- Cycles: the operation of an engine from the time an aircraft leaves the ground until it touches the ground at the end of a flight. This definition is especially relevant for maintenance

Relevance of Contribution Margin (CM): Introduction and Application in the Air Cargo Industry

- Different cost drivers: EH, BH, FH, flight, cycles and tons
- Depending on what kind of cost driver is used, a certain route might be profitable or not
- Take, for example, a route where the aircraft is parked for 12 hours for commercial reasons, and the route loses $20,000:
  - If the aircraft cost and overhead (let's assume $3,000 per EH) are charged per EH, the impact of parking would be -/-$36,0000
  - If there is in fact no better use of this time in the system, the profitability of this flight should be +$16,000, when the cost is viewed per BH
- Most of the cost can be driven by BH, except for some crew cost (FH), M&E (besides BH also cycles), some handling (tons) and aircraft cost and overhead (EH)
- Whatever system is used, it is important to understand the reasons behind it and its impact on the overall profitability
- Like in the example above, it is OK to use EH, but it would be wrong to cancel the flight if there would be no alternatives

There are two ways of viewing CM: on a shipment level and on a per freighter flight level.

- What if the flight is not full and operates anyway and you have to accept a shipment at a lower rate?
  - The minimum rate you can accept this shipment should be at least slightly higher than the variable cost this shipment will trigger
- The CM is also relevant to decide whether you should operate one particular flight or not
  - The minimum revenues needed to operate a flight should cover at least the variable cost of this flight

Bottom line is:

- At the end you have to make money and choose the best alternative:
  - Accept shipment or not (yes if CM positive)
  - Operate flight or not (yes if CM positive)

Example of CM on Flight Basis

Airline X with B747–400F (115T payload) on route from Barcelona (BCN) to Hong Kong (HKG) with 12 hrs BH, has the following cost structure:

- Aircraft, crew, maintenance and insurance of USD 15,000 per BHr
- Overall fuel cost of USD 3,000 per BHr, but USD 0.07 for every kg of extra pay load
- Overhead of USD 1,000 per BHr
- Landing/airport/overflying fees of USD 1,000 per BHr
- Airport handling in BCN of USD 0.05/kg and in HKG of USD 0.10/kg
- Trucking from Alicante (ALC) to BCN of USD 0.05/kg

The flight is 70% full and a customer in ALC has a last-minute shipment of 10,000kg: *What is the minimum rate you can offer without losing money?*

Answer: The additional variable cost that this shipment will trigger is: additional fuel (USD 0.07/kg), handling at airport (USD 0.15 /kg in HKG and BCN) and trucking (USD 0.05/kg). So, the total extra variable cost will be USD 0.27/kg. If the airline would offer a rate of USD 0.40 per kg, it would still contribute USD 0.13/kg or USD 1,300 for the additional 10,000 kgs. All other fixed cost per flight will stay the same regardless of the payload.

Example of CM on Freighter Flight Basis

Airline X with B747–400F routing (Frankfurt) FRA-HKG-FRA (24 BH, 28 EH) has the following cost structure:

- Aircraft depreciation: USD 1,800 per EH
- Fixed crew and maintenance: USD 2,200 per BH
- Variable crew and maintenance: USD 1,000 per BH
- Insurance of USD 300 per BH
- Fuel cost of USD 7,000 per BH
- Overhead of USD 1,000 per EH
- Landing/airport/overflying fees of USD 1,000 per BH
- Airport handling (import and export) in FRA of USD 0.05/kg and in HKG of USD 0.10/kg

HKG can generate 85 ton at a net revenue of USD 175,000 and FRA can generate 55 ton at a net revenue of USD 75,000: *Should you operate the flight or not?*

Answer: The total revenue will be USD 250,000. The variable costs are:

- *Variable crew and maintenance: USD 24,000*
- *Fuel: USD 168,000*
- *Landing/airport/overflying: USD 24,000*
- *Airport handling in HKG and FRA: USD 21,000 (140,000 x USD 0.15)*

The total variable cost is USD 237,000, while the revenue is USD 250,000, meaning a positive CM of USD 13,000 for this particular flight. So yes, it should be operated because it contributes to the fixed cost basis.

CM in Transfer Pricing for Cargo with Passenger Flights

- Wrong transfer pricing can lead to bleed in revenues and profits for pax aircraft
- Cost allocations, keep it basic and simple:
  - Variable costs:
    - GSA commission: % of gross sales, excluding surcharges and interline
    - Handling cost: p/kg import/export
    - Trucking cost: p/kg import/export
    - Variable IT cost per kg
    - Additional fuel cost, depending on different aircraft types
  - Fixed costs:
    - Overhead, IT (fixed part), ULD (could be variable as well)
- CM should cover the variable cost

Network Contribution

Definition: The difference between the revenues and variable cost of a shipment that originates from the network and connects from its hub to another destination.

Many airlines operate through a hub where they feed other flights to other destinations. The objective should be to get the highest total contribution across the network.

There are three basic ways of calculating network contribution:

- On pro mileage:
- On market rates
- On "value", always seeking positive CM

Example: An airline with two old B747-200F with 100-ton capacity and its hub in (Chicago) ORD sells a shipment at USD 1.80 p/kg from CDG (Paris) to MEX (Mexico City)

- Pro Mileage (Figure 1.12):

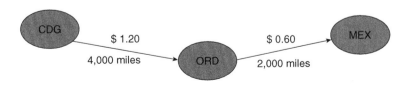

Figure 1.12 Market Pricing.

The flight CDG-ORD gets $1.20 (4000/6000 x 1.80) allocated per kg and the sector ORD-MEX gets $0.60 per kg allocated. Subsequently the route profitability of the flights is calculated based on these sector revenues

Advantage:

• Simple system

Disadvantage:

• Does not take market rates and load factors into account

– Market rates (Figure 1.13):

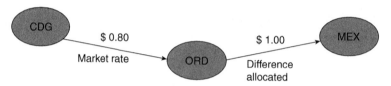

Figure 1.13 Market pricing.

The flight CDG-ORD gets the market selling rate of $0.80 allocated per kg and the second sector ORD-MEX gets the difference of $1.00 per kg allocated.

• If the market rate between ORD and MEX is $0.90 the CM is $0.10 p/kg

Advantage:

• Based on real market rates for the first sector

Disadvantage:

• Does not take load factors into account, and the second sector might get too much or too little allocated depending on the market yields

– Value, positive CM (Figure 1.14):

Figure 1.14 Market pricing.

• The variable cost (extra fuel, handling, trucking) for sector ORD-MEX is $0.40.
• Assuming always minimum $0.10 on top of variable cost of the sector ORD-MEX (to contribute to fixed cost on sector), the CM or "value" of this shipment would be $0.50 (1.80 – 0.80 – 0.40 – 0.10)

- The flight CDG–ORD gets the market selling rate of $1.30 allocated per kg and the second sector ORD–MEX gets the difference of $0.50 per kg allocated
- In case first sector's Load Factor (LF) is also low, than you can also apply the variable cost on the first sector

Advantage:

- Based on real market rates, variable cost and CM principle, where you can make commercial decisions based on value to the network and the areas of full flights get rewarded and low flights get penalized

Disadvantage:

- Complex

Conclusion

- CM very important for shipment level and flight level decision
- Flights are interlinked and, by using network CM, the areas selling full flights at higher yields get rewarded
  - Therefore, the incentive to sell better is on the correct flights in the areas where it is needed
  - In our previous example, those responsible for the Central America flights would be complacent and relaxed when judged based on pro mileage and market rate network contribution
  - When actually the room for improvement is almost only on the Central American flights, which is reflected in the Network CM method
- As standalone wrong decisions can be made about certain routes
- If well managed each method can be used as long as overall picture is not lost and incentives are placed in the right places (Figure 1.15; Table 1.1)

Table 1.1

2007 Market Share (Volume)	
Perishables	12.74%
Live animals, special handling, waste	1.64%
Capital equipment machinery	5.99%
Pharmaceuticals	2.24%
Chemicals and products (excl. pharmaceuticals)	3.90%
Consumer fashion goods	8.30%
Consumer and household goods	6.61%
Telecommunication	4.15%
Semiconductors	2.23%
Computers and related	6.46%
High technology (excl. telecommunication, semiconductors, computers and related)	5.82%
Land vehicles and parts	5.34%
Machinery parts, industrial components	17.87%
Raw materials, industrial consumables, food	16.69%

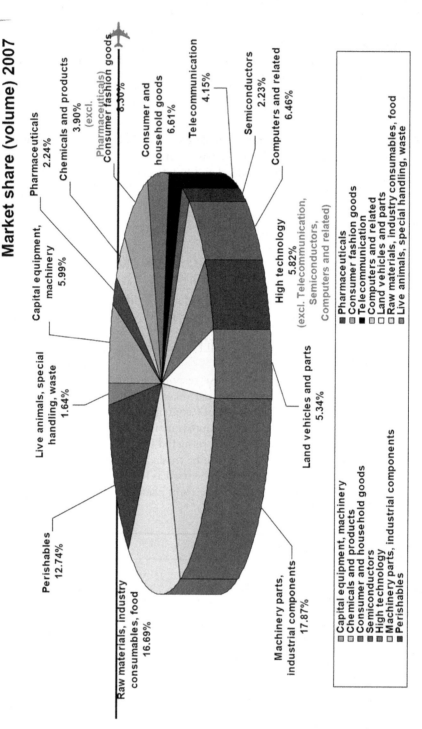

Market share (volume) 2007

Pharmaceuticals
2.24%

Chemicals and products
3.90%
(excl.
Pharmaceuticals)
Consumer fashion goods
8.50%

Consumer and
household goods
6.61%

Telecommunication
4.15%

Semiconductors
2.23%

Computers and related
6.46%

High technology
5.82%
(excl. Telecommunication,
Semiconductors,
Computers and related)

Capital equipment,
machinery
5.99%

Live animals, special
handling, waste
1.64%

Land vehicles and parts
5.34%

Perishables
12.74%

Machinery parts,
industrial components
17.87%

Raw materials, industry
consumables, food
16.69%

- Capital equipment, machinery
- Chemicals and products
- Consumer and household goods
- Semiconductors
- High technology
- Machinery parts, industrial components
- Perishables

- Pharmaceuticals
- Consumer fashion goods
- Telecommunication
- Computers and related
- Land vehicles and parts
- Raw materials, industry consumables, food
- Live animals, special handling, waste

Figure 1.15 Typical product traffic.

2 Integrators

Insights into Current and Future Players and Business Directions

They are full-cargo airlines that integrate, as the name suggests, ground transportation with air transportation, hence providing a door-to-door service to customers. More specifically, integrators combine their own aircraft fleet with a set of warehouses that serve the purpose of freight forwarders and ground handlers, and a truck fleet that carries out first- and last-mile routing and ground transportation across warehouses.

Given the multimodal and complex nature of such a business, only a handful of integrators have emerged in the last decades. In principle, this is a business dominated by the "three-headed monster" composed of the American Federal Express (FedEx) and United Parcel Service (UPS) and the European DHL. While new players are entering the market, our focus will be initially on these three integrators that paved the way for newcomers. Historically speaking, common historical factors can be identified that favoured and facilitated their birth and growth between the 1960s and 1970s.

The push for advanced capitalism during those decades, mostly in the United States and in Europe, resulted in a sudden and somehow unprecedented increase in the speed of the economy. As such, global supply chains had to keep up with the pace to remain competitive in a world that was witnessing the first steps towards a complete globalization. This provided an extremely fertile soil to integrators, which aggressively developed new business products such as overnight delivery. In addition, mass consumer markets were swiftly being replaced by niche markets driven by a change from supply-push to demand-pull supply chains (Hesse & Rodrigue, 2004). Finally, the globalization and de-localization of productions, especially in the context of technology, made it paramount to have fast and reliable door-to-door services that integrators were just ready to offer (Bowen, 2012).

The rest of the section is structured as follows. Initially, we briefly go over the history of FedEx, UPS and DHL. Then, an analysis of the network structure (and business implications) of the three integrators is provided. Finally,

DOI: 10.4324/9781003167167-2

a thorough analysis of the new players entering the market and of the future challenges is carried out.

History

FedEx

Federal Express was founded in Little Rock, Arkansas, in 1971 by Frederick W. Smith, as a follow-up of a paper he wrote while being a graduate student at Yale University. In the paper, he advocated for a new logistic paradigm where one air cargo carrier would own and be responsible for all means of transport and warehouses involved in the door-to-door service. Initially, the primary goal of Federal Express was urgent deliveries. A couple of years later, in 1973, the headquarter of the company was moved to Memphis, making Memphis International airport (MEM) their main (and sole, at that time) hub. The reason for choosing Memphis was two-fold. First, it proved to be a strategic point in the Midwest because of its location close to the mean population centre, not extremely close to any major metropolis, yet reasonably close to all of them. Second, for the general clement weather of the region, which would have positively affected air transportation in and out of MEM. Initially, a fleet of 14 Dassault Falcon 20s was used to perform deliveries in a network comprising 25 cities. In Figure 2.1, we report the Dassault Falcon 20 that carried the very first air package for Federal Express, currently on display at the Udvar Hazy Air and Space Museum, in Virginia. The comparison

Figure 2.1 Dassault Falcon 20 that carried the first air package for FedEx.
Source: Reddit, 2021.

in terms of size and transportable tonnage with respect to the current full freighters, which will be listed later in the section, is quite striking.

After some years with financial struggles, the company became profitable in 1976 and started its ascent. The ascent was also favoured by a 1977 legislative change that removed restrictions on routes operated by full-cargo airlines. This fostered the purchase of the first large full-freighter aircraft by the company, i.e., seven Boeing 727-100s. In 1981, the network of Federal Express almost reached triple digits in terms of cities covered and became international by expanding operations to Canada as well. The need for new hubs became clear, and hence Newark Liberty International airport (EWR), Indianapolis International airport (IND), Oakland International airport (OAK) and Ted Stevens Anchorage International airport (ANC) became all hubs by 1989 (FedExa, 2021). While the first three focused on different domestic regions (respectively, East Coast, Midwest and West Coast), the last one was the perfect transshipment stop to foster international services towards and from Asia.

In 1994, the company was rebranded FedEx, translating a nickname that had been used for years into the official name. In the same year, the logo as we know it, and that was made famous worldwide thanks to advertisement and cinema (e.g., Cast Away with Tom Hanks), was created. Interestingly, the hidden arrow between the capital E and lower case x was not intentional, but perfectly summarized the motto of the company. Due to the advent of the Internet, FedEx launched its own website and was the first integrator to offer online package tracing capabilities. Continuing its expansions, FedEx opened a hub in South-East Asia, Subic Bay International airport (SFS) in the Philippines and one in Europe, Charles de Gaulle airport (CDG). Another big boost to FedEx business operations was given by an agreement, signed in 2001 and currently still in place until 2024, with United States Postal Service (USPS) that makes FedEx the sole carrier for USPS Express mail and Priority mail. While the late-2000s recession took a toll on FedEx operations, for example forcing the closure of the hub in SFS (but simultaneously witnessing the opening of a new Asian hub in Guangzhou Baiyun International Airport (CAN)), business continue to prosper as testified by the opening of another European hub in Cologne Bonn airport (CGN) in 2010 and the acquisition of international courier TNT Express in 2015.

As of now, FedEx has a fleet size of roughly 680 aircraft (considering its own aircraft and contracted fleet) and a network reaching almost 400 airports and is one of the largest airlines in the world when considering the fleet size and freight tonnes transported.

UPS

UPS was founded as American Messenger Company by James Casey and Claude Ryan in Seattle in the early 1900s. Deliveries were carried out mostly on foot and with bicycles, with a Model T Ford as the first purchased vehicle in 1913 (UPSa, 2021). After a few mergers, that resulted in a first name change (Merchants Parcel Delivery), the company expanded outside the state of Washington to Oakland, California, and was rebranded UPSs. UPS relied on limited air service initially and then disconnected the service due to the limited revenues and the effect of the Great Depression.

Between the 1950s and the 1960s a revamped economy made UPS resume air services, serving all of the 48 contiguous states of the United States. Similarly, to FedEx, the first step towards internationalization was to expand the business to Canada. Regarding Europe, while a domestic service had already been established in West Germany since 1976, the fall of the Berlin Wall made it possible to extend operations in the whole Germany. The Airline Deregulation Act of 1978 enabled UPS to significantly expand its business, since flying between cities was not simpler and with fewer bureaucratic issues. As a consequence, in 1980 UPS chose Louisville Muhammad Ali International airport (SDF) as the main hub. Like FedEx, the choice of an airport located in the Midwest was strategic since SDF could be reached from anywhere in the continental United States in maximum 3 hours. At this stage, unlike FedEx, UPS was still operating a contracted fleet using a fleet of passenger aircraft converted to full freighters.

Between the 1980s and the 1990s UPS aggressively pursued acquisitions to expand the business and, in particular, to strengthen the ground transportation network. In addition, UPS started purchasing its own fleet, buying several Boeing 757s and 767s. This fleet expansion resulted in the need to add hubs to the existing airport network, and hence hubs in Rockford (Illinois) (RFD), Philadelphia (PHL), Dallas/Fort Worth (DFW), Columbia (South Carolina) (CAE) and Ontario (California) (ONT) were established. Due to the expansion in North-East Asia, UPS launched "around-the-world" flight rotations stemming from SDF and flying East with intermediate stops in Europe, the Middle-East and North-East Asia before returning to the main hub.

In more recent years, a fleet modernization was carried out by purchasing McDonnell Douglas MD-11 freighters, Boeing 747-400 freighters and, in late 2016, Boeing 747-800 freighters. As a consequence, older models such as the McDonnell Douglas MD-8 freighters were phased out. The introduction of the newer Boeing 747-800 freighter made it possible a direct flight from SDF to the Middle-East hub in Dubai International airport (DXB) as part of the "around-the-world" routes.

As of now, UPS can rely on a fleet of approximately 300 aircraft that can serve roughly 800 destinations, equally divided between domestic and international.

DHL

The idea behind DHL stemmed from Larry Hillblom's job as a courier for an insurance company in Northern California (DHLa, 2021). His job was to run courier duties between OAK and Los Angeles International airport (LAX) every weekday, picking up packages for the last flight of the day and returning with the first flight of the next day. Together with his friends Adrian Dalsey and Robert Lynn, they started a company in the late 1960s whose name combined their three initials (DHL). Initially, their main focus was to fly between LAX and Honolulu International airport (HNL) to carry bills of lading.

DHL became an international courier sooner than its competitors FedEx and UPS, but quickly expanded nationally as well, creating the de-facto integrator triumvirate with FedEx and UPS. Between 1998 and 2002, Deutsche Post began an acquisition process of DHL that led to the creation of the new major European hub on German soil, in Leipzig/Halle airport (LEJ), in 2004. Similarly, to the other integrators, an aggressive acquisition strategy incorporated many logistics companies under the DHL umbrella, considerably increasing its workforce.

Due to being, formally, a German company, DHL stopped operating domestic services in the United States in 2009. This did not stop DHL from opening a new major hub on American soil in 2013, to pair the original one in LEJ and improve worldwide connectivity. Not surprisingly, and consistently with FedEx and UPS, the chosen location was in the Midwest, with Cincinnati/Northern Kentucky International airport (CVG) being the final choice.

Differently from FedEx and UPS, which owns all their fleet and only resort to chartering or leases due to spikes in demand, DHL operates a more hybrid strategy. In fact, on top of its own fleet (divided into different airlines according to the region of interest), DHL has stakes in several other airlines that generally operate under the DHL brand and livery (but that can offer some capacity to competitors FedEx and UPS as well). The five airlines directly owned by DHL are European Air Transport Leipzig (European network), DHL Air UK (Transatlantic flights), DHL Aero Expreso (Central and South America), SNA/DHL (Middle-East network) and Blue Dart Aviation (Indian network). Some of the airlines that are partially owned by DHL are, for example, AeroLogic, Polar Air Cargo and Tasman Cargo Airlines.

As of now, the fleet of DHL is slightly shy of 200 aircraft that can reach roughly 250 destinations.

Network Structure

In this section, a brief complex network theory analysis is carried out that provides insights into the network structure of the three integrators FedEx, UPS and DHL. A complex network is a network whose characteristics are non-trivial and can highlight specific connectivity patterns: most transportation networks are complex networks. We base our description on (Bombelli, 2020), where publicly available data from global flight track services was used to determine and analyse such networks. It is important to highlight that the original source used supply data (i.e., recorded frequencies) to generate the networks, while the demand data (e.g., load factor per flight) was not used at all, being the latter an extremely sensitive piece of information in the cargo industry.

For each integrator, a network was generated where airports were nodes, and connections between airports were edges. An edge was defined between two airports O and D if at least a recorded flight in the dataset from O to D was identified. Given the high directionality of air cargo flows, edges were also directed: the definition of edge O-D does not imply the definition of edge D-O, unless recorded flights in the other direction are also identified.

Networks were initially analyzed in terms of the degree distribution, being the degree the number of incoming and outgoing edges of each node. All three networks displayed a similar trend, as shown in Figure 2.2, where many nodes (airports) are characterized by a few connections, and only a few nodes (airports) are connected to many other airports in the network. For each network, the three highest-ranked airports are labelled in the plot (Figures 2.3 and 2.4).

Not surprisingly, the latter are the hubs in each integrator's network. The airports with the most connections are MEM for FedEx, SDF for UPS and LEJ for DHL. As highlighted in the description of the historical development of each integrator, the two main markets in the initial developmental phase were the United States and Europe. As such, if we focus on the first two airports per integrator, we find the first hub located in the United States and

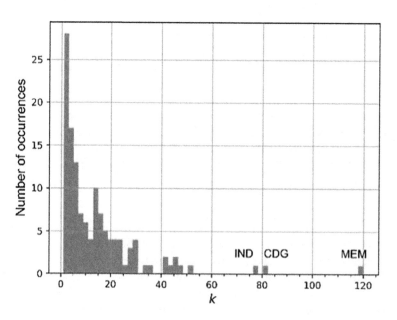

Figure 2.2 Degree distribution for the networks of FedEx, UPS and DHL. From (Bombelli, 2020).

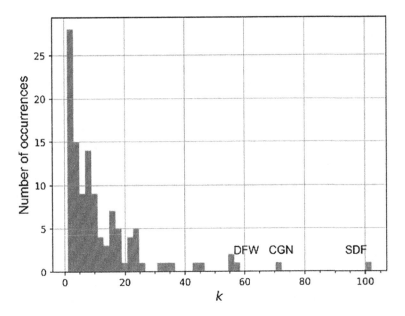

Figure 2.3 Degree distribution for the networks of FedEx, UPS and DHL. From (Bombelli, 2020).

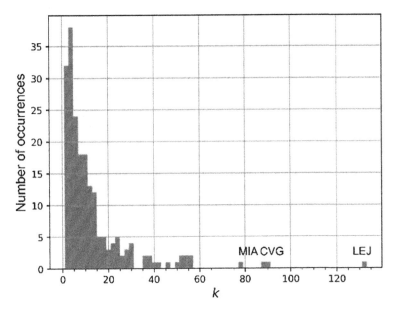

Figure 2.4 Degree distribution for the networks of FedEx, UPS and DHL. From (Bombelli, 2020).

the second one in Europe (FedEx and UPS) or vice-versa (DHL). Not surprisingly, the two American integrators are keeping their main hub within domestic soil, and so does the German DHL. Interestingly, all the six hubs (apart from CDG), are relatively small airports for passenger operations. This was indeed a driving force to establish a hub for cargo operations due to less congestion, restrictions, and more freedom and flexibility to operate a freighter fleet. Going back to the network analysis, all three networks are small world networks. This means that, although each network is characterized by only a fraction of edges with respect to the fully connected version of the same network of airports, the average number of stopovers to go from every airport to every other airport is generally small. More specifically, the characteristic path length for all three networks is around a value of 3, meaning that, on average, it takes two stopovers to go from a random to a different random airport in the network.

A careful reader might have identified the absence of Asian airports in Figure 2.1, which might sound counterintuitive given the relevance of (North-East) Asian airports in air cargo operations. This is mostly due to three intertwined factors. First, data used to generate those plots might be incomplete. Second, Asian hubs were only recently opened by each of the three integrators (e.g., the hub in CAN was established by FedEx in 2009). Third, a degree analysis highlights how many connections an airport might have but gives no indication on the strength of such connections, for example, measured in terms of frequencies or Freight Tones Kilometres (FTK). Overall, there is a set of airports that might score lower when degree is considered but would score much higher if FTK or potential transportable capacity is considered. An explicative example in this sense is ANC, which serves as the main transshipment airport for cargo flows between North-East Asia and North America (the largest air cargo trade line overall). ANC receives flights from a small set of airports from North-East Asia, and those flight rotations continue to serve an equivalently small set of airports in North America (mostly MEM, SDF, CVG and a handful of other airports). Notwithstanding, frequencies are high and large full freighters are generally used to serve these itineraries, hence making ANC a crucial node in integrators' networks.

The aforementioned insight was also identified when robustness to airport removal was assessed. Robustness was measured by eliminating from the network, in sequence, the airport that scored highest according to a specific criterion (e.g., degree) and by computing the size of the giant component of the updated network. In complex network theory, the giant component of a network defines the largest subset of nodes belonging to the network where every node can be reached (directly or indirectly) from every other node belonging to the giant component. While the removal of the major hubs proved to reduce the size of the giant component not very significantly (meaning that itineraries between airports were still available, although probably at the cost of more stopovers), the elimination of an airport such as ANC proved to reduce the size of the giant component by more than 10% for the

UPS network. In principle, removing ANC disconnected part of the Asian network from part of the North American network. This result stresses even more the relevance of cargo transshipment-oriented airports, as opposed to major hubs that serve both as sources/sinks of demand and as transshipment points, in case of disruptions.

Finally, the analysis of robustness and other performance indicators highlighted that, while all three networks are multi-"hub-and-spoke" networks, the nature of DHL leans towards a more balanced network without a single airport (MEM for FedEx and SDF for UPS) dominating the scene. For DHL, LEJ, CVG and HKG to a lesser extend manage most of the cargo flows in a more distributed way.

Future Challenges and New Players

While the passenger air transport network was brutally hit by the COVID-19 pandemic, and a full demand recover is not expected to happen anytime soon, integrators were the biggest winners of the pandemic, with FedEx, UPS and DHL all increasing their market share. In Figure 2.3, a comparison of the average daily package volumes for FedEx and UPS between 2019 and 2020 is provided (Figure 2.5).

This increase comes with its own challenges. On the one hand, the growth of e-commerce, which was fostered even more by the pandemic, implies the need for more infrastructure for inventory and sorting and, potentially, an increase in the fleet size. On the other hand, the call for a cleaner aviation clashes with the aforementioned needs if they are tackled using current technology. For example, FedEx has committed to reach carbon-neutral operations by 2040 (FedExb, 2021).

As it concerns air operations, it is stated that "since 2012, the FedEx Fuel Sense and Aircraft Modernization programmes have saved a combined 1.43 billion gallons of jet fuel and avoided over 13.5 million metric tonnes of carbon dioxide (CO_2) emissions." Notwithstanding, full freighters are not known to be the most fuel-efficient aircraft, and the need to keep up with the increased demand does not easily pair with air carbon-neutral operations. On the other hand, electrification of ground pickup and delivery vehicles, reduction of waste products along the supply chain, and investments to make warehouses more sustainable via renewable energy seem more realistic goals. Note that UPS (UPSb, 2021) and DHL (DHLb, 2021) are headed towards a similar direction as well.

Together with keeping operations up to speed while making them more sustainable, new players have also entered the integrator competition in recent years. First and foremost Amazon, with the creation of their own fleet Amazon air, became a de-facto enhanced integrator. The reason why it was defined enhanced is that, differently than FedEx, UPS and DHL, shippers generally buy products directly via Amazon, hence incorporating the purchase part in the supply chain. Note that this different business strategy

FedEx, UPS package volume

FedEx and UPS both saw residential volumes surge as the COVID-19 pandemic led people to stay at home and order more packages.

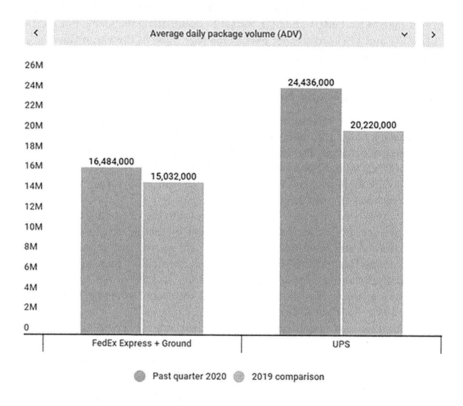

Figure 2.5 Comparison of average daily package volume for FedEx and UPS between 2019 and 2020.
Source: eu.commercialappeal, 2021.

makes Amazon not so much a competitor for FedEx and UPS on American soil. Amazon currently does not offer shipping and logistics from consumer to consumer destinations or businesses that do not store their products at an Amazon warehouse. Hence, it might be argued that the market targets of FedEx and UPS on the one hand and Amazon on the other hand do not overlap substantially. In addition, Amazon's fastest guaranteed time for products not stored in local fulfilment centres in 2 days, as opposed to the overnight delivery of integrators. Hence, as it concerns domestic operations in the Unites States, FedEx and UPS will remain the two main competitors as testified by the many similarities of their business strategy (location of the main hub, overnight option as the fastest delivery option, etc.). On the other hand, Amazon Air will centre its operations on CVG, hence conflicting with DHL. This might pose a problem if flight or capacity restrictions (especially during night hours) are in place at the airport.

The other integrator we are highlighting is SF Express, which was founded in Guangdong, China, in 1993. While operations were initially mostly domestic (in accordance to what seen for the other integrators), SF Express is quickly establishing as a worldwide integrator thanks to several factors. First, money availability that fostered the growth of the fleet, now counting 60+ aircraft, and heavy investments in optimization of the network and logistics operations (GaTech, 2021). Second, a careful strategy of partnerships to expand internationally, as testified by a partnership with DHL to create overseas warehouses that will facilitate e-commerce. Third, a constant growth within Asia (especially South-East Asia) and the Unites States and New York in particular, with a schedule comprising three flights per week from Hangzhou (GLDPartners, 2021). Lastly, projects are in place for the construction of the "Hubei International Logistics Key Hub Project" in Ezhou, the nation's first cargo airport that will serve as the hub for overseas operations. As it concerns domestic operations, Ezhou is roughly equidistant from Shanghai (East), Beijing (North) and Guangzhou (South). In addition, it is an hour's drive from Wuhan, a key location of the Belt and Road trade initiative (NikkeiAsia, 2021). While SF Express is facing harsh competition nationally, due to the presence of other companies backed by the Alibaba Group Holding, it might be argued their expansion worldwide might directly affect FedEx, UPS and DHL operations more explicitly than what Amazon Air would. Only time will tell.

Conclusions

While this section only scratched the surface of what integrator operations and business models entail, a historical and network-centred analysis of the three main integrators FedEx, UPS and DHL was presented. Similarities and differences were identified that reflect both the different path each integrator witnessed from its infancy until now, and the different ownership. In addition, an overview of the future directions has been provided. Similarly to passenger operations, a call for sustainability has been the main driver when it comes to operational changes. Unlike passenger operations, integrators rely on massive ground transportation and warehousing/inventory systems which, according to the author, seem to be easier to translate into (quasi) carbon-neutral in the decades to come rather than full freighters. Finally, an overview of potential new competitors has also been provided. It might not be surprising that, instead of pure competition, the future of integrators will naturally steer towards a coopetition (portmanteau of collaboration and competition) framework, where agreements might be stipulated between integrators as long as the extra profit exceeds the profit each integrator would make on its own. In addition, the skyrocketing growth of drone operations might revolutionize last-mile deliveries. Hence we might be witnessing drastic changes in ground transportation for integrators in the years to come, especially in those areas that allow seamless drone operations. All in all, the future for integrators seems bright in terms of demand growth, but technological advancements and changes in business strategy (possibly with inter-integrator agreements) will need to smoothly accommodate this demand surge.

Bibliography

Bombelli, A. (2020). Integrators' global networks: A topology analysis with insights into the effect of the COVID-19 pandemic. *Journal of Transport Geography*, 102815.

Bowen, J. T. (2012). A spatial analysis of FedEx and UPS: Hubs, spokes, and network structure. *Journal of Transport Geography*, 419–431.

DHLa. (2021, September 28). The history of Deutsche Post DHL group. Retrieved from https://www.dpdhl.com/: https://www.dpdhl.com/en/about-us/history.html

DHLb. (2021, September 22). Excellence, simply delivered, in a sustainable way. Retrieved from https://www.dhl.com/: https://www.dhl.com/global-en/home/about-us/sustainability.html

eu.commercialappeal. (2021, September 28). Here's how much FedEx, UPS are shipping of late amid COVID-19 volume surge. Retrieved from eu.commercialappeal.com: https://eu.commercialappeal.com/story/money/industries/logistics/2020/08/05/fedex-ups-covid-19-volume-spike/5574550002/

FedExa. (2021, September 28). FedEx history. Retrieved from fedex.com: https://www.fedex.com/en-us/about/history.html

FedExb. (2021, September 22). FedEx commits to carbon-neutral operations by 2040. Retrieved from newsroom.fedex.com: https://newsroom.fedex.com/newsroom/sustainability2021/

GaTech. (2021, September 22). Researchers from ISyE partner with China's SF express on data-driven design of logistics networks. Retrieved from ISyE website: https://www.isye.gatech.edu/news/researchers-isye-partner-chinas-sf-express-data-driven-design-logistics-networks

GLDPartners. (2021, September 22). SF express emerging as a global force in air cargo logistics integrator. Retrieved from http://www.gldpartners.com/: http://www.gldpartners.com/sf-express-emerging-as-global-force-in-air-cargo-logistics-integrator/

Hesse, M., & Rodrigue, J. (2004). The transport geography of logistics and freight distribution. *Journal of Transport Geography*, 171–184.

NikkeiAsia. (2021, September 22). Courier SF holding readies China's first cargo airport. Retrieved from asia.nikkei.com: https://asia.nikkei.com/Business/Transportation/Courier-SF-Holding-readies-China-s-first-cargo-airport

Reddit. (2021, September 28). The first FedEx air package was delivered by this plane, on display at the Udvar Hazy Air and Space Museum, in Virginia. Retrieved from Reddit: https://www.reddit.com/r/pics/comments/4h8m10/the_ first_fedex_air_package_was_delivered_by_this/

UPSa. (2021, September 28). Our history. Retrieved from https://about.ups.com/: https://about.ups.com/us/en/our-company/our-history.html

UPSb. (2021, September 22). UPS sustainability statement. Retrieved from about. ups.com: https://about.ups.com/us/en/social-impact/environment.html

3   Ground Handling

On the Ground

Within the entire air cargo supply chain, as cargo spends on average only up to 20% of its time within an aircraft, the ground handling part of the process demands excellent and efficient planning and execution. The potential for delays and mistakes and mis-communication is considerable. The process is impacted by a variety of factors – flight delays, bad weather, Customs examinations and road traffic pro and warehouse congestion. The industry is working hard to streamline the process and is using emerging technology to achieve better performance which eventually means happier customers in a highly competitive sector.

It has always been the challenge of air freight that however fast and efficient the flight itself, it is on the ground where the delays accumulate. Today, there are many techniques and systems available for handlers to streamline their operations, but at the same time, new security and dangerous goods regulations (DGRs), cargo screening and Customs rules must be factored into the handling process.

Ground or shed handling involves accepting cargo into the warehouse from the shipper. It may also include trucking cargo from the shipper or another airport. The handler must prepare cargo for shipment by building it into pallets or loading into containers Unit load devices (ULDs). The necessary documentation and Customs clearances must be obtained before handing over to the ramp handler. Inbound cargo is treated in reverse, by breaking down the pallets and containers cargo for eventual delivery to the customer. In this fiercely competitive sector, high standards are vital in order to keep the airlines' contracts. At the same time, handlers are under pressure to keep prices down. Costs of equipment and staff training make this constantly challenging. In some airports there may be a quality standards programme in place where key performance indicators (KPIs) are measured against actual performance. Within the handler's buildings, some special facilities would be required – cool storage rooms, a border inspection office, animal hotel and strong room. Handlers work very closely with airlines, general sales agents (GSAs) and forwarders in combining and maximizing their efforts to achieve the best possible results.

DOI: 10.4324/9781003167167-3

The ramp handler's job is to take the palletized cargo from the ground handler, load it into the aircraft and to deliver inbound cargo to the ground handler. In some cases, it may be the same company doing both tasks, as well as passenger handling.

It is perhaps surprising, given the technological sophistication of the aircraft, handling equipment and warehouse inventory control systems, that the air cargo industry was until very recently dependent on the filling in and exchange of paper documents. According to International Air Transport Association (IATA), each air cargo shipment carried with it as many as 30 paper documents as it made its way from shipper to consignee, via the forwarder, haulier, terminal operator, airline, ground and ramp handlers and customs authorities. The organization calculated that the industry generated 7,800 tonnes of documents annually, equivalent to the carrying capacity of 80 B747 freighters (Figure 3.1).

Even where there was a growing use of computer-based message systems, most of these were developed independently and often in-house by the major airlines, with the result that ground handlers were forced to use a mix of disparate legacy systems to communicate with their airline customers. The

Figure 3.1 Paper document.

arrival of IATA-led initiatives, such as Cargo 2000 (C2K) and e-freight, coupled with the development of the Internet into a universally used business tool has done much to remove the pen-pushing drudgery from the offices of ground handlers.

Electronic air waybills (e-AWBs) are now commonplace and in most countries mandatory, as are status updates and information on special cargo, such as dangerous goods or express shipments. Ever-more stringent security controls mean that more pre-arrival, or pre-shipment, data must now be sent to the airlines and on to Customs and other authorities in the country of destination.

Customs authorities are now demanding entries, as well as security information, in electronic format. In Europe, the most recent customs development is the Import Control System (ICS). Although the airlines are responsible for submitting ICS data to Customs, most have appointed handlers as their agents, and it is now down to these ground handlers to ensure that the correct information is obtained in time to make a submission to customs.

The computer systems can now alert handlers if ICS data has not arrived; if there are problems with the data, such as errors or inconsistencies; or if Customs has rejected an entry for any reason. The EU's Export Control System (ECS) tends to be more straightforward as it deals with master air waybills (MAWBs), while ICS deals with house air waybills (HAWBs).

IATA E-freight

The IATA launched its e-freight project with the aim of taking the paper out of air cargo and replacing it with cheaper, more accurate and more reliable electronic messaging.

Benefits of e-freight include

- lower costs, with an average annual saving of between $3.1 and $4.9 billion for the industry, depending on the level of adoption;
- faster supply chain transit times – the ability to send shipment documentation before the cargo itself can reduce the end-to-end transport cycle time by an average of 24 hours;
- greater accuracy – electronic documents allow auto-population, allowing one-time electronic data entry at the point of origin, which reduces delays to shipments due to inaccurate or inconsistent data entry. Electronic documents also have a lower risk of being misplaced, so shipments will no longer be delayed because of missing documentation;
- regulatory compliance – where it is implemented, e-freight meets all international and local regulations relating to the provision of electronic documents and data required by customs, civil aviation and other regulatory authorities.

Cargo IQ (previously Cargo 2000)

Cargo 2000 (C2K now reborn as Cargo IQ) defines quality standards for the supply chain, improving the efficiency of the air cargo industry, improving customer service and reducing costs for all participants through the implementation of a programme of agreed business and automation standards which are measurable and promote quality competitive performance.

The C2K Master Operating Plan (MOP) has been developed based on detailed customer research and with the assistance of leading IT companies. It sits at the heart of an air cargo industry-wide process control and reporting system that in turn drives data management and corrective action systems.

By reducing the number of individual processes in the air cargo supply chain from 40 to just 19, C2K is less labour-intensive and improves the processes for managing shipments in a paperless environment. It substantially reduces time spent managing irregularities, such as service failures, cuts the time required for manual track-and-trace procedures and leads to a reduction in service recovery costs.

Since 2010, C2K has been offering open access to its standard processes as part of its continuous initiative to improve quality management for customers and service providers across the air cargo supply chain.

C2K's quality management system is being implemented in three distinct phases. The key to the MOP is the creation of a unique "route map" for individual shipments that are monitored and measured throughout the delivery cycle of each shipment.

Phase 1 manages airport-to-airport movements – shipment planning and tracking at the MAWB level. Once a booking is made, a plan is automatically created with a series of checkpoints against which the transportation of every air cargo shipment is managed and measured. This enables the system to alert C2K members to any exceptions to the plan, allowing them to respond proactively to fulfil their customers' expectations.

Phase 2 is responsible for shipment planning and tracking at the HAWB level and provides interactive monitoring of the door-to-door movement.

The third and final phase of C2K manages shipment planning and tracking at the individual piece level, plus document tracking. This provides for real-time management of the transportation channel at the piece level. It will also control the flow of information, which will be vital for current and future security requirements. In Phase 3, the control of information is most important as the need for paper will be limited to the bare minimum required by law. In the attempt to operate in a paperless environment, the IATA e-freight initiative and C2K complement each other (Figure 3.2).

The introduction of the ULD (UNIT LOAD DEVICE) during the 1970s, helped airlines to maximize the use of their capacity and to save time when loading and unloading aircraft. The containers are made of aluminium and various composite materials in order to be as light as possible, but tough enough for everyday handling and flight duties. If treated carefully, these

Figure 3.2 Pallets.

containers can last for 10–15 years, but this is rarely the case as they are in constant use every day all around the world and handling personnel are more concerned with speed than caring for the equipment.

The pallets and containers are built up (a term generally meaning that they are carefully packed as tightly as possible with revenue-earning freight) by cargo handlers, whose skill is vital in order to achieve the maximum density possible. Pallets are covered with plastic sheets and nets before being loaded onto an aircraft. On arrival at the destination the reverse process is followed. This is termed "break-bulk" by the industry – a much-better revenue-earning ploy than just unpacking the ULD or pallet. New lightweight materials are now being used to reduce weight even further.

The cargo is then either handed over to the consignee when a representative calls at the airport, consolidated into truckloads for delivery or repacked into another ULD for onward carriage by air to its final destination.

The basic types of maindeck containers are

- LD1 (covers half the width of the aircraft), with a capacity of 4.59 cubic metres;
- LD2 (half-width), 3.4 cubic metres;
- LD3 (half-width), 4.5 cubic metres;
- LD6 (covers the full width of the aircraft), 8.9 cubic metres;
- LD8 (full-width), 6.88 cubic metres;

- LD11 (full width, rectangular), 7.16 cubic metres;
- LD3, LD6 and LD11 are designed for B787, B777, B747, MD-11, IL-86, IL-96 and L-1011 aircraft, as well as all Airbus wide-body aircraft.

While ULDs are as light as possible to save weight on the aircraft, they are often handled very roughly in the cargo terminals and at forwarder warehouses. Repatriating containers for maintenance is expensive, and there is always a problem of having the right amount of containers in the right place at the right time. These issues have given rise to the ULD pool – a method by which dedicated companies have sprung up that provide multiple solutions to the problems facing an airline.

Two leading companies in the ULD pooling business are Germany's Jettainer, a wholly owned subsidiary of Lufthansa Cargo, and CHEP Aerospace Solutions, which integrates the aviation industry experience of leading ULD pooling provider Unitpool with Driessen Services, a specialist in the outsourced repair and maintenance of ULD equipment. These companies will usually agree to purchase the existing ULD stock of a carrier joining its pool and add the equipment to its dedicated fleet. This outsourcing move creates an immediate cash flow for the airline and removes its need to add more capital cost for the purchase and maintenance of its ULD fleet. The airline then leases back exactly the amount of ULDs it needs to meet actual demand. This reduces the cost caused by unproductive ULD overstock at any station and the hassle caused by understock situations and removes the maintenance headache from the airline.

The pooling provider will look after repair and maintenance costs, capital expenditure, extra costs driven by new technologies or changes to the aircraft fleet, directly and indirectly associated with lost and unreported ULDs, and any problems associated with managing peaks and troughs in demand at any of the airline's network stations.

Loose Cargo

Large freighter aircraft such as the AN-124, the B747F and the MD-11 are frequently used to transport outsized items including vehicles, helicopters, locomotives, bridge sections and oilfield equipment. Such items are loaded by cranes, ramps and by hand, depending on the load and aircraft. They are then fixed to the main floor with heavy-duty ties (Figures 3.3 and 3.4).

Dangerous Goods

Ensuring that undeclared dangerous goods do not get on board an aircraft is one of many key objectives of the dangerous goods programme implemented by the IATA.

Figure 5.8 Dangerous goods sign

Figure 3.3 Sodexi express handling facility paris cdg.

By defining standards for documentation, handling and training in its DGRs, and by actively promoting the adoption and use of those standards by the air cargo industry, a very high degree of safety has been achieved in the transportation of dangerous goods by air.

Working closely with governments in the development of the regulations, including International Civil Aviation Organization (ICAO) and other national authorities, the IATA ensures that the rules and regulations governing dangerous goods transport are effective and efficient. The goal is to make it just as easy to ship dangerous goods by air as any other product, so it removes any incentive to bypass the regulations.

Dangerous goods are articles or substances that are capable of posing a risk to health, safety, property or the environment and which are shown on the list of dangerous goods in the IATA DGRs or which are classified according to those regulations.

Dangerous goods and their maximum quantities, packaging, handling, marking and documentation requirements are specified in detail in the DGRs published annually by the IATA. These regulations are based on those laid down by ICAO, which in turn are derived from United Nations recommendations concerning the transportation of dangerous goods for all modes of transport.

When a shipment contains one or more of the dangerous substances from the DGR list, the carrier requires the shipper to complete and sign a Shipper's

Figure 3.4 Dangerous goods signs.

Declaration for Dangerous Goods. This is a legal document declaring that the shipper has complied with all relevant regulations and instructions. It must be completed in duplicate and strictly follow the detailed instructions given in IATA DGR 8.1.6.

In practice, the shipper may use a specialist freight forwarder to handle the goods, but it remains the shipper's responsibility to provide the right information at the origin of the shipment. Completing a dangerous goods note is an effective way to do this for international shipments.

The following are examples of dangerous goods:

- Dry ice (also carbon dioxide, solid carbon dioxide, solid [dry ice]): This is produced by expanding liquid carbon dioxide to vapour and "snow" in presses that compact the product into blocks. It is used primarily for cooling and due to its very low temperature (about −79°C) can cause severe burns to skin upon direct contact. When solid carbon dioxide (dry ice) converts (sublimates) directly to gaseous carbon dioxide it takes in heat from its surroundings. The resulting gas is heavier than air and can cause suffocation in confined areas as it displaces air. Packages containing solid carbon dioxide must be designed and constructed to prevent the build-up of pressure due to the release of carbon dioxide gas.

- Flammable liquid: This category comprises liquids, mixtures of liquids or liquids containing solids in solution or in suspension (e.g., paints, varnishes, lacquers, etc.), but not substances otherwise classified on account of their dangerous characteristics, which give off a flammable vapour at temperatures of not more than 60°C (140°F) in a closed-cup test or not more than 65.6°C (150°F) in an open-cup test, normally referred to as the flash point.

- Blood samples: This relates to infectious substances which are known or are reasonably expected to contain pathogens. Pathogens are defined as micro-organisms (including bacteria, viruses, rickettsiae, parasites, fungi and other agents such as prions), which can cause disease in humans or animals.

- Corrosive substances: These are substances that by chemical action can cause severe damage when in contact with living tissue or, in the case of leakage, will materially damage or even destroy other goods or the means of transport – that is the aircraft itself!

- Gas: Definition 3.2.1.1: a gas is a substance which (a) at 50°C (122°F) has a vapour pressure greater than 300 kPa (3.0 bar, 43.5 lb/in^2) or (b) is completely gaseous at 20°C (68°F) at a standard pressure of 101.3 kPa (1.01 bar, 14.7 lb/in^2). Definition 3.21.2: the transport condition of a gas is described according to its physical state as (a) compressed gas, which is a gas which, when packaged under pressure for transport, is entirely gaseous at −50°C (−58°F); this category includes all gases with a critical temperature less than or equal to −50°C (−58°F), and (b) liquefied gas, which is a gas which, when packaged under pressure for transport, is partially liquid at temperature above −50°C (−58°F). A distinction is made between high-pressure liquefied gas (a gas with a critical temperature between −50°C [−58°F] and +65°C [+149°F]) and low-pressure liquefied gas (a gas with a critical temperature above +65°C [149°F]), and (c) refrigerated liquefied gas, which is a gas which, when packaged for transport, is made partially liquid because of its low temperature.

- Flammable gas: Gases which at 20°C (68°F) and a standard pressure of 101.3 kPa (1.01 bar, 14.7 lb/in^2) (a) are ignitable when in a mixture of 13% or less by volume with air or (b) have a flammable range with air of at least 12% points regardless of the lower flammable limit. Flammability must be determined by tests or by calculation in accordance with methods adopted by ISO (see ISO Standard 10156:1996). Where insufficient data are available to use these methods, tests by a comparable method recognized by the appropriate national authority must be used.

- Non-flammable, non-toxic gas: Gases which (a) are asphyxiates (those which dilute or replace the oxygen normally in the atmosphere) or (b) are oxidizing (those which may, generally by providing oxygen, cause or contribute to the combustion of other material more than air does. The oxidizing ability must be determined by tests or by calculation in accordance with methods adopted by ISO (see ISO Standard 10156: 2010).

- Toxic gas: Gases which (a) are known to be so toxic or corrosive to humans as to pose a hazard to health or (b) are presumed to be toxic or corrosive to humans because they have an LC50 value equal to or less than 5,000 ml/m^3 (ppm) when tested in accordance with subsection 3.6.1.5.3 of the DGR.

- Matches: Also known as safety matches, book, card or strike-on-box, are matches intended to be struck on a prepared surface. Strike-anywhere matches usually contain phosphorus sesquisulfide, potassium chlorate and other ingredients. The strike-anywhere matches are readily ignited by friction on almost any dry surface. When a closed package of strike-anywhere matches is ignited on impact or by friction, the head composition burns off the matches, and the fire then usually goes out unless the package is broken. If the package is broken, allowing access of air, the fire will continue. Packages of these matches that have been wetted for any reason and subsequently dried should be handled with extreme caution.

Reducing Flight Risks

Having the correct information easily to hand is key to any safety programme, no less for dangerous goods in air transport. Through its DGRs and a comprehensive and effective training programme, IATA ensures that shippers, forwarders and carriers have the tools and resources to ship dangerous goods safely.

It is a requirement in law that comprehensive and approved training must be given to all staff involved in the packaging, documentation or handling of dangerous goods destined for transportation by air, whether in the belly hold space of passenger aircraft or on full-freighter aircraft.

Through a network of IATA-accredited training schools, the association provides training worldwide through local partners. These warrant that the high IATA training standards are maintained and that local regulations are fully complied with. There are many independent training schools around the world.

DGR Print Manuals

The 2013 IATA DGR manuals are available in five languages: English, French, Spanish, German and Russian, as well as a spiral English version for frequent usage. For information on the Chinese or Japanese versions of the DGR, contact cutserv@iata.org.

DGRs Manual

Published each year in several languages, the global reference for shipping dangerous goods by air is the only reference recognized by the world's airlines in regular bound format. Each copy includes a quick-reference card. Now available online

Compliance with Regulations–Specific Training

The successful application of regulations concerning the transport of dangerous goods greatly depends on the appreciation by all individuals concerned about the risks involved and on a detailed understanding of the regulations. This can only be achieved by properly planned initial and recurrent training programmes.

The regulations covering the transportation of dangerous goods by air are issued by ICAO.

IATA Course

The UK Civil Aviation Authority (CAA) requires that staff responsible for the shipment and packing of consignments of dangerous goods for air transport be successfully trained on a course approved by them and be retrained every 2 years thereafter. IATA publishes an annual Dangerous Goods Manual which is recognized as the industry standard and is used on the course. All students who pass the examinations are registered as internationally approved to sign for dangerous goods consignments. It is also a requirement of law that revalidation training be carried out every 24 months.

Cargo training international trainers are approved by civil aviation authorities. The full 3-day course enables students to

- apply the information given in the ICAO and IATA regulations to dangerous goods shipments;
- check that packing, marking and labelling meet ICAO/IATA standards;
- interpret dangerous goods lists;
- recognize prohibited items;
- recognize marking and labelling;
- understand the shipper's and carrier's responsibilities; and
- complete dangerous goods documentation.

On completion of this course – which includes a written examination – candidates receive a certificate. All certificate holders are registered with the Approval Authority.

Revalidation

The 2-day revalidation course will enable students to

- check knowledge of the regulations and
- update on amendments and new rules.

Depending on the respective responsibilities of the person, the training must be in line with the scope of the applicable staff category. Download or view subsection 1.5 of the IATA DGRs for further information.

DGR Training Books

IATA's training programmes are designed to be used in conjunction with the DGRs to familiarize students with various sections of the dangerous goods manual and how and when to apply them. The training workbooks are based on practical application of the IATA DGRs, which includes all ICAO requirements.

Dangerous Goods Incidents

In a cargo hangar, a container that had been stuffed in a container loading area some miles away was sitting on the loading dock prior to being loaded onto a passenger aircraft. The cargo burst into flames. Airport emergency services were called to control a fierce blaze. One item of cargo in the container was, it was later learned, an oxygen generator – undeclared as dangerous goods. These devices produce oxygen through a chemical reaction which creates significant heat. The fire services made several attempts to extinguish the fire, but it kept on erupting and burned almost the entire contents of the container. It was fortunate that it did not erupt 4 or 5 hours later over the Pacific Ocean, as in spite of the firefighting facilities in the aircraft cargo hold, this fire would have fed on the oxygen it was creating.

It is easy to draw some parallels here with an aircraft that crashed into the Indian Ocean some years ago as a result of what is strongly suspected to be undeclared bottles of nitric acid. They broke and caused a severe fire by igniting other organic material in the vicinity. Another recent accident which also involved these oxygen generators highlights the need for declaration and proper packaging of all dangerous goods.

In another incident, undeclared dangerous goods described as "laundry products" loaded about 2 hours earlier almost caused the loss of a passenger aircraft. By the time the aircraft landed, the floor had started to sag from the heat generated by a fire caused by a mixture of a hydrogen peroxide solution, an oxidizer and about 12 kg of a sodium-based orthosilicate-based mixture (a corrosive solid). Because the consignment was not declared as dangerous goods, no labels or orientation markings were on the package. It was loaded on its side in the cargo compartment and the liquid leaked onto the solid, causing a very hot fire. It was estimated by aircraft accident investigators that this aircraft could have broken in two within another 10 and 15 minutes.

In another case an aircraft crashed due, it is thought, to a leakage of flammable liquid, probably contained in a passenger's stowed baggage. An ignition source ignited the liquid, causing the explosion which caused the aircraft to crash, resulting in the deaths of all on board.

The following list indicates known incidents of dangerous goods:

- Leaking/spillage of acid from wet cell batteries – three incidents
- Spillage from fuel tanks on motor mowers, chainsaws and other internal combustion engines – at least four incidents
- Explosives (1.4S – Article or substance so packed that any hazardous effects arising from accidental functioning are confined within the package unless the package has been degraded by fire) – two incidents
- Aerosol pressure packs – at least four incidents
- Flammable paint/thinners – at least four incidents

Investigation

It is interesting that in a number of these incidents, the investigation has revealed that not only was the shipper at fault for not declaring the dangerous goods, there was a sufficient number of tell-tale signs that should have alerted the cargo acceptance staff that there may be something wrong. For example in one case the shipper described the consignment as "paint" on the consignment note – yet it got through. It is difficult to understand how a chainsaw or a motor mower with fuel in the tank can be accepted without question.

There is an underlying problem with ground handling in general which is cost. Airlines are forcing handlers to work for ever-decreasing prices but expect more service. Ground handlers must train staff and invest in equipment and technology. This is a difficult equation when coupled with increased security.

For full details of IATA PROGRAMMES VISIT WEBSITE www.iata.org

The Importance of Cargo Claims and Loss Prevention

No matter how well and efficiently managed you are, events have a habit of finessing you sometimes, resulting in a claim against your company. A proper Cargo Claims and loss prevention programme is of great importance to meet the customer expectations in the unfortune event something goes wrong with shipments during air cargo transportation. Clear and responsive communication with the claimant during the process of damage investigation as well as an efficient claims recovery cycle in the event a claim resulted from loss, delay or damage. As there might be many stakeholders involved in the transportation process of shipments such as trucking companies, ground handlers and local forwarders, the claims and loss prevention process can often be a complex and time-consuming part of the business.

The Airlines Perspective

All airlines attempt to provide the best service possible for air cargo customers, from origin to destination, providing communication and shipment status updates, and achieving fast delivery of shipments in good condition. A vital part of the quality of the air cargo product offered by carriers is the prevention of damage or loss, which can result in poor relationships with customers. Loss prevention is ideally achieved by all the appropriate parties involved, combining efforts to accomplish the safe movement of a cargo from point of origin to point of destination. Working jointly with all involved logistic business partners involved in the transportation of shipments under the contract of carriage is vital to reduce or mitigate any loss suffered by any party.

In relation to cargo claims and loss prevention the main focus is to implement measures designed to minimize losses while a shipment is under Carrier's care and control.

Risks for Cargo Storage and Risks for Goods in Transit

Cargo Claims handling comes with a lot of stress, and the correct procedure needs to be followed to ensure the losses are covered properly and in a timely manner.

Receiving a Cargo Claim and Some Crucial Steps to be Considered

Collect Evidence

Efficient handling of cargo claims requires knowledge about logistics, cargo types, operational procedures methods of carriage, contracts, applicable law and jurisdiction, etc. In addition to knowledge in all these areas, efficient claims handling requires strategic and tactical skills, overview, patience as well as the ability to communicate and negotiate effectively and professionally.

When loss occurs, all parties should try to mitigate the loss. This is the right thing to do, literally it is an actual step in the claim process. Most of the time it is pricey and time-consuming to obtain evidence and pursue a claim, but it is necessary to collect all the evidence possible for speeding up the claims handling process and ensuring that everything is actioned correctly. Some crucial evidence that can be located are the reverse side of the AWB Conditions of Contract under which the Carrier transports the goods, proof of delivery and irregularity report. It is vital that the Carrier obtains a properly completed proof of delivery and an irregularity report to be retained in case of any action is brought against it. Any addition data showing the internal environment within the container, e.g., temperature, humidity or any kind of irregularity during the carriage, can be useful to establish the Carrier's liability.

Reviewing the Formal Claim

Once all necessary information and documents have been collected, the claim is considered ready for review. In most cases, a cargo claim is subject to a time bar. As soon as Claimant provides necessary documents/information to the Carrier, the quicker the investigation begins. Such investigation should allow Carrier to establish whether or not loss occurred during the period when the cargo was in his care and control. However, the Carrier will not be liable to compensate the claimant if the loss is caused by circumstances for which he is exonerated from liability by force of law or contract. Furthermore, even if the Carrier is liable, he may have a right to limit liability.

Digital tools are now available which allow claimants to register a claim quickly and easily, as well as enabling the carrier to collect all the necessary documents in a timely manner via a centralized channel and also optimize processes. Experience has shown that claims can be reduced or resolved at a much lower cost to the Carrier due to good customer service.

Closing the Case

When the claim has been investigated and the Carrier already identified whether the Carrier is liable or not liable to the loss of and/or damage to the goods the case is considering closed. One of the main goals of the Carrier is to identify any areas of service failures, ensuring that all claims are processed fairly and in timely manner in accordance with applicable conventions and do its best to avoid the similar failures in future.

Mitigating Cargo Claims

It's inevitable for loss to be occurred. Even with the best-laid plans, cargo damage mitigation strategies, and careful handling even in cargo storage facilities, cargo may still arrive damaged

The storage of unattended cargo in warehouses brings the added threat of theft and damage. Therefore, measures such as strengthening warehouse security and Close Circuit Television (CCTV) can greatly improve security by monitoring 24/7 the progress of cargo movement, starting from arrival and storage in warehouse and later to monitor any kind of loss until the shipment is released to the customer. Independent cargo monitoring data allows for faster and more efficient claims management processes, while reducing costs. The CCTV records can also provide evidence when analysing liability and establishing the Carrier's liability.

Mitigating of risks for cargo in transit can be enhanced by identifying alternative storage facilities. Carriers should identify alternative storage facilities in case to existing facilities being already full. Carriers should also make efforts to identify the amount of cargo in transit and obtain status updates from appropriate departments. Such measure will help to prevent any kind of loss during prolonged storage of the cargo. In case of claims being made against a Carrier due to improper storage, it will be able to prove that all reasonable measures to protect the cargo had been taken.

The Carrier should also consider review requirements for perishable cargoes, especially considering additional security requirements while cargo is located in temporary storage locations.

The recent pandemic situation has impacted risks of damage to cargo due to extended storage periods in transit, especially to high value and temperature sensitive goods have significantly increased. Temperature-sensitive cargo associated with the response to the coronavirus outbreak has been given priority for temperature-controlled capacity.

Cargo Claims and Loss Prevention Programme (CCLP)

In early 2021, a new CCLP programme was introduced by Amsterdam-based Cargohub, to simplify and control the cargo damage reporting process between ground handlers and airlines.

Traditionally, once damage to a consignment is caused or discovered, a report would be drawn up in Word or Excel or generated by a WMS system. The CCLP programme offers handlers a simple to use mobile app to create, control, validate and (semi) automatically send damage reports to the airline representatives involved in the process. In this way, the damage reporting requirements stipulated in the service level agreement with the airline are easily met. At the same time airlines are offered access to the CCLP platform to access the assigned reports, enabling the carrier to swiftly anticipate the customer service requirements and to monitor shipment quality performance within their network.

The fully customer centric focuses on CCLP solutions, identifies risks and provides loss prevention management insights to both the handling company and airline. I also provide a fully integrated quality assurance programme to investigate root causes and to classify corrective actions. This new solution has successfully been tested in Amsterdam by Menzies World Cargo and Airbridge cargo Airlines.

Personal Comment by Gerton Hulsman

Almost a decade ago I attended an IATA ground handling workshop. In separate working groups, we discussed quality in air cargo handling, warehouse, ramp issues, etc. At the meeting, we also touched on topics such as automation, robotization and artificial intelligence. Every topic was tabled, from improving quality to saving costs. The new process-thinking was born, and the customer would be served much better than before. That was the key outcome of the meeting, applauded by all participants, ground handling staff must earn more and shown more respect.

During one of these sessions, I raised my hand to comment. I said that the future would bring many changes and certainly lead to demanding challenges. During these processes of change, however, in my view, those who do the practical work on the floor should not be neglected. Without their commitment and dedication, improving quality is almost impossible. One precondition to keeping them on board is to pay handling staff decent wages and, at the same time, to train them better. Employers must give them the feeling that a big part of rendering good work/good service is in their hands, in spite of all the modern technology they work with. Motto: the heavy, physical work is still carried out by humans day after day.

This comment was met with laughter, and a VP Cargo from a major airline even asked me whether I was a communist or a trade unionist!

I am neither a commie nor a trade unionist, but someone with long experience in air freight handling. I have seen people who could not make a living with the money they earn, let alone properly feed their children and provide them a safe future, which, after all, is also our objective. In recent days, we are all reading and hearing that hardly any staff can be found to fill vacancies at warehouses to keep handling quality at proper levels. This particularly applies to low-skilled personnel deployed in freight handling.

Little Pay, No Respect

Take the United Kingdom that is hit by a worsening shortage of HGV drivers, leading to empty supermarket shelves, and gas stations that have to be supplied with fuel by British Army soldiers due to the absence of drivers. Brexit has surely worsened the situation, but across the Channel, continental Europe is facing similar problems, jeopardizing the distribution of foodstuff, technical equipment, pharmaceutical products, and so on.

Finding capable staff willing to work "for a few bucks" day in, day out, in distribution centres or cargo terminals, has become a growing challenge. This development has negative effects on the entire economy. The industry should ask itself if it is still attractive for people without academic degrees to work in transportation at cheap rates? I think not. According to my observation, the vast majority of these people lack not only sufficient income, but also respect.

For instance, it is a shame that truck drivers have to struggle to get a parking space overnight on European highways. They have to park their vehicles in insecure places along roads offering no sanitary facilities or shopping opportunities. Night-time robberies are frequent and increasingly violent. We need to re-think the whole labour element in the supply chain for securing the future of this vital industry.

4   Airports

The Vital Connection

There are more than 8,500 ICAO-designated airports throughout the world. Most of these are very small regional airports that support local and regional traffic, but little or no cargo except for some mail. It is difficult to qualify what is a significant airport in terms of cargo, as in some instances, like a sub-tropical country exporting seasonal fruit, cargo might well be the main traffic. Most airports handle some postal and courier traffic in addition to passengers.

All airports have one basic purpose, to connect passenger and air cargo traffic with the market. They may be the very large hubs, such as Frankfurt, Miami or Hong Kong, but at the other end of the scale small airports such as Ostend in Belgium, Hannover in Germany or Châteauroux, south of Paris, perform their own specialist functions. In addition special platforms such as Memphis, Atlanta and Leipzig handle the increasing volumes of freight for the big integrators.

Some airports also act as logistics centres, handling road traffic and distribution as well as assembly and repairs, often within duty-free zones. Globalization has introduced the concept of multi-source manufacturing with products, such as cars, becoming reliant on air cargo transportation keeping the assembly lines fed on a just-in-time (JIT) basis with components from different sources.

Historically, as you would expect, the provision of airports and ground services was developed in parallel with the expansion of the airline industry. Before the 1920s, the lack of suitable ground facilities was one of the factors that severely limited the progress of this industry. Airlines cannot carry passengers, mail or freight unless there is safe navigation with landing beacons and lighting, as well as a base for loading, unloading, fueling and onward transportation. At present, around 80% of all air cargo in Europe is trucked, and in the United States the percentage is even higher. The connection between flight and destination is the essential function of any airport. In today's aviation world, airports have become the economic drivers of business and industry and the service on the ground for both passengers and freight

DOI: 10.4324/9781003167167-4

has become very competitive, especially when customers have alternative choices.

For air cargo, it is the minimum time spent on the ground before and after the flight that can make a particular airport attractive and will play a role in the ultimate selection by the forwarders and consolidators, who will mostly determine how much cargo is directed to and from a particular airport.

Cargo requires warehouses with access to the aircraft, plus a good road network nearby. Within the buildings there will be cool rooms, an animal hotel, a phytosanitary office, Customs and security, as well as skilled handling staff. Their job is to build and break down pallets as efficiently and quickly as possible. Truck-loading bays integrated into the warehouse aid both speed and security.

The provision of modern and well-equipped handling warehousing facilities is essential, as is easy access to an efficient surface transport infrastructure. Despite the congestion on the roads, especially in Europe, a large proportion of road feeder services (RFSs) move during the night, thus having a reduced impact on traffic congestion. In less developed countries, airports are more basic and the provision of facilities such as cool storage is top priority when the main exports are perishable goods. In many cases, retail chains may operate their own farms and handling facilities within a specific country to ensure the integrity of their produce.

Airports fall into several broad categories which often overlap: large-scale international hubs, where many different carriers operate for both passengers and cargo. These tend to be capital city or major regional hubs such as Dubai, Paris, Frankfurt, London, Amsterdam, Hong Kong, Singapore, Sydney, Toronto, Tokyo, Atlanta, Chicago, New York, Los Angeles, Miami and many more. In each case, these are located in major catchment areas – conurbations with large concentrations of industrial and commercial activities.

The impact of the 2019–2021 COVID world pandemic has yet to be accurately analysed but figures from mid-June 2020 indicate the main trends in volumes. The figures are also distorted when they include major integrator hubs (Memphis, Louisville, Leipzig):

Ranking (Million Tonnes): Pre-Pandemic

1 Hong Kong (HKG) 4.8 m
2 Memphis (Fedex) (MEM) 4.3 m
3 Shanghai (PUG) 3.6 m
4 Louisville (UPS) (SDF) 2.8 m
5 Incheon (ICN) 2.8 m
6 Anchorage (ANC) 2.7 m
7 Dubai Int (DXB) 2.5 m
8 Doha (DOH) 2.2 m
9 Taiwan Taoyuan Int (TPE) 2.2 m
10 Tokyo Narita (NRT) 2.1 m

11 Paris (CDG) 2.1 m
12 Miami Int (MIA) 2.1 m
13 Frankfurt (FRA) 2.1 m
14 Singapore Changi (SIN) 2.0 m
15 Beijing capital (PEK) 1.9 m
16 Guangzhou (CAN) 1.9 m
17 Chicago O'Hare (ORD) 1.8 m
18 London Heathrow (LHR) 1.7 m
19 Amsterdam Schiphol (AMS) 1.6 m
20 Suvarnabhumi (BKK) 1.3 m

Other airports also have substantial passenger and cargo businesses, like Guangzhou, Milan, Munich, Barcelona, Geneva, St. Petersburg, Seattle, Montreal, Caracas or Houston. These also play their part in the air cargo supply chain by feeding local businesses with the raw material they need and taking the finished products to the marketplace.

Latin America and the Caribbean region are especially dependent on airfreight mainly due to the need for access to the U.S. market and beyond. This region accounts for around 5% of global air cargo trade. The largest based on 2018 figures, are as follows:

El Dorado International Airport (BOG)

Bogota, Colombia

Bogota has by far the busiest airport with exports of global healthcare products, cut flower

Benito Juárez International Airport (MEX)

Mexico City, Mexico

Moving into second place for air cargo volume, Guarulhos International Airport (GRU)

São Paulo, Brazil

Accounts for about 10% of all LATAM airfreight traffic.

Arturo Merino Benítez International Airport (SCL)

Santiago, Chile

SCL is South America's main gateway to Oceana destinations such as Sydney and Melbourne. Chile exports Salmon, fresh cherry, blueberries, asparagus and cut flowers.

Jorge Chávez International Airport (LIM)

Lima, Peru

Peru is the world's second-largest exporter of asparagus as well as blueberries. Other exports include cacao, nuts and textiles, while leading imports include hi-tech, spare parts and pharmaceuticals.

Viracopos International Airport (VCP)

Campinas, Brazil

Fruit exports, beef and fresh fish.

Mariscal Sucre International Airport (UIO)

Quito, Ecuador

Ecuador is the third largest exporter 0f flowers plus shrimp and prawns
Ministro Pistarini International **Airport (EZE)**
Buenos Aires, Argentina
Air exports include agricultural products, perishables, and chemicals, while imports include electronics, machinery and auto parts, and pharmaceuticals.
Luis Muñoz Marín International Airport (SJU)
San Juan, Puerto Rico
Pharmaceuticals, textiles, petrochemicals, and electronics (Figure 4.1).

Cargo-friendly airports, where the airfreight business is likely to outperform passenger activity, include Huntsville and Kansas City in the United States, Paris-Vatry in France, Hannover in Germany, Liege in Belgium and Vitoria in Spain.

Normally such airports can accommodate and handle any type of aircraft and cargo (general cargo, charter flights, humanitarian, perishables, hazmat, oversized). Open 24/7, they often have no curfew, no night restrictions, high-speed turnarounds, low-cost landing fees, technical assistance, cargo handling, parking on-site plus all related services: 24/7 customs, veterinarian and phytosanitary services, freight forwarders, trucking companies…with all the appropriate administrative certifications. They are also directly connected to highway network for the immediate distribution of the goods.

Whatever the size or location, all airports must operate with runways of over 3 km in length, plus suitable electronic navigation equipment, radar, beacons and perimeter fence security. Various international organizations, as well as national ones, such as the Federal Aviation Administration (FAA)

Figure 4.1 Athens international airport.

in the United States or the Civil Aviation Authority (CAA) in the United Kingdom, govern these basic requirements.

Round-The-Clock Access

All-night, 24-hour access is ideal for freighter and express traffic, but this is becoming more difficult due to political and environmental pressures. For example, Cologne (the European hub for UPS), Vitoria (the Spanish hub for DHL) and Hong Kong (with over 50 international cargo operators) are all able to operate 24-hour schedules to accommodate freighter and integrator flights. But today most airports enforce night curfews around which the airlines have to plan their schedules very carefully.

An airport is deemed to be a hub when airlines operate an interchange of flights on a hub-and-spoke system with a high proportion of both passengers and cargo being in transit. This is a highly efficient way of maximizing the energy and investment of the airlines and the airports. A perfect example of this would be Dallas/Fort Worth (DFW) in Texas, the main hub for American Airlines, a gateway with a network that covers a wide range of value-added services such as inventory management and order processing.

Gateway between Two Continents

Miami International Airport in southern Florida, which is currently ranked number 12 in the world in the amount of cargo handled annually, is a fine example of a hub that treats its passengers and cargo with equal enthusiasm. Miami is unique in the Americas as it links North and South America, the Caribbean and the rest of the world, and the airport continues to invest in new facilities and develop new ideas for increasing world trade.

Thanks to its unique geographical and historical situation, Miami is often referred to as the Capital of Latin America, with the airport connecting to the whole of the United States and beyond. The airport and its support infrastructure dominate the flow of trade between North and South America, Central America and the Caribbean, handling over 82% of air imports and 81% of the air exports from the whole region. Goods traded through Miami include perishable produce, high-tech and telecoms, textiles, pharmaceuticals and machinery.

Further afield, Miami connects to markets in Europe, the Middle East and Asia, as well as Australasia. Sophisticated packaging and marketing techniques, such as labelling flowers and fruits directly at the grower for specific retailers, speed up the process and increase the shelf life of these delicate items. A total of some 2 million tonnes of air cargo, worth around $61.5 million, of which around 88% is international, passes through Miami, much of it being in transit. Within this figure, around 650,000 tonnes of perishable goods are imported into the United States each year, some 70% of which goes via Miami. Of all the fruits and vegetables imported to North America, 72%

pass through Miami; for flowers this is 89%, and for fresh fish, 54%. This is also the only airport in the United States which houses veterinary services, import and export operations, an inspection station and an air cargo unit all in one complex.

A corridor has been built which links the cargo area to the warehouse district and to the interstate highway system. An estimated 200,000 separate truck journeys are made annually to and from the airport.

Around 90 air carriers, including charter operators and 38 all-cargo carriers, are in business at the airport, serving around 150 cities on five continents, with freighter flights connecting to 94 global destinations. Cargo facilities comprise 17 warehouses, providing 2.7 million square feet of space with 64 parking positions for cargo aircraft, most of which offer airside to landside access. Construction is underway for a new 895,000 square feet of cargo warehouse/office/storage.

Miami's cargo route development programme is aimed at stimulating overall cargo traffic between the airport and new global markets. This includes further development of European and Asian routes and the establishment of new trade routes to Africa and the Middle East. Miami International Airport also conducts business expansion and promotion throughout its stronghold markets in Latin America and the Caribbean.

Munich: The Southern European Gateway

Bavaria's Munich Airport in southern Germany reflects a strong regional operation for both passengers and cargo. Again, being built only 20 years ago this is a comparatively new project and its airfreight services concentrate on the regional strengths of modern Germany.

Bavaria is home to several famous brands of automobile and a fast-growing electronics industry, as well as being a major tourist centre. The fact that the airport is in a vibrant manufacturing zone also helps combat one of the major challenges facing operators of freighter aircraft – the need for return loads, as the aircraft is likely to run at a loss unless this is possible.

The growth of its freight segment is a major priority and the airport is planning a great deal of expansion. The national airline, Lufthansa, is developing Munich into an intercontinental hub in tandem with Frankfurt, as well as a central node of its European trucking network. A new freight forwarders' building opened in September 2012. The 16,000 square metre building has the annual capacity to handle 160,000 tonnes of cargo. A second phase is planned that will be 240 m long, 65 m deep, with an interior height of 12 m. It will be linked to the air cargo centre via a covered track for forklifts and dolly ULD trains direct from the tarmac. During 2014, the airport handled 291,000 tonnes of mixed cargo.

Following the opening of the new Border Inspection Office and Small Animal Station in 2007, the airport is examining the options for expanding this facility. There are plans at Munich for an increase in its temperature-controlled facilities and studies on its perishables and pharmaceuticals capabilities are in hand. The airport will need these extra facilities to remain competitive in the future.

Medium-Sized Airports

Apart from the capital city hubs, there are many regional and medium to small airports serving their local catchment areas for both passengers and cargo. In most cases cargo plays a minor role but is still important to the airport's bottom line. For example, Düsseldorf International Airport is situated in the North Rhine Westphalia region, the traditional home of Germany's industries. In recent years it has been chosen by Chinese and Japanese companies as a base for their European offices. Thanks to its central position, it is an ideal base for distribution for the whole of northern Europe. Furthermore, the regional universities are graduating large numbers of scientifically trained young people needed by these companies, as well as the high-tech and environmental industries that are springing up in the region.

The airport is the third-busiest passenger gateway in Germany, with 70 airlines serving over 180 destinations worldwide. It serves as a secondary hub for Air Berlin and Lufthansa, as well as benefiting from multiple daily flights to and from the Middle East. Main-deck freighter traffic is relatively small, but belly-hold cargo represents over 100,000 tonnes of air cargo capacity per year.

The airport has become a busy hub connected to a growing number of intercontinental destinations, making it increasingly important for the big forwarders and logistics companies. Its ready access to a wide range of lower deck capacity, together with an independent trucking network based in a high potential catchment area, is stimulating Düsseldorf's further cargo growth.

Cargo-Friendly Airports

There are a number of airports around the world where cargo plays a more important role than passenger traffic. There may be a number of reasons for it. The airport may have space for large-scale seasonal charter operations – for example, the New Beaujolais traffic at Chateauroux in France, seasonal produce imports at Ostend (Belgium). Each one of these airports has marginal low-cost airline traffic and they are all situated some distance from major passenger destinations. They are mostly open at night and can all handle large freighter aircraft such as an Antonov AN-124 or a B747F. Thanks to an absence of congestion they are capable of achieving a fast turnaround.

Located in northern Spain and connected by motorway to major cities on the Iberian Peninsula and in southern France, its long runway and 24-hour operations have made Vitoria a useful cargo centre. Over the last two decades it has specialized in fresh fish and seafood from southern Africa and Canada.

But due to the high cost of fuel and the effects of recession, the market for fresh fish in major Spanish cities, especially Madrid and Barcelona, could not sustain the prices. A large number of fish shipments, however, pass through London, Paris, Frankfurt and other major European gateways, and Vitoria is still useful as a trucking hub and distribution centre.

DHL has expanded its hub at the airport dealing with traffic from North Africa and the Iberian markets. Here, the ability to operate a large number of feeder aircraft at night makes Vitoria a good site for integrators.

In summary, modern airports around the world have become an essential factor in a country's economy. Passenger traffic combines with freight, express and mail, plus the expansion of aviation-related businesses around the airport perimeter to create a vital industrial component of the local, regional and national economy. In the world of the global supply chain, these airports are the key performance engines of the business world.

Europe has many airports large and small but due to the way that international carriers plan their routes, cargo needs to connect with main routes and hubs.

In France for historic and social reasons, aviation traffic of both passengers and cargo is based at Paris CDG and Orly airports with cargo travelling from the regions by road in order to connect to international flight networks. While in contrast, in Germany, due to historical regional structure, each state has its own economy, industries and airport. Thus Hannover, Hamburg, Cologne, Dusseldorf, Frankfurt, Munich and Stuttgart, all have thriving passenger and cargo side by side. In the United States, due to its size and state development there are over 300 airports which mostly serve the huge internal passenger market but the main cargo hubs are – Memphis (FedEx) Anchorage, Louisville, Chicago, Miami, Indianapolis, Los Angeles, JFK New York, Dallas Fort Worth and Cincinnati. Most internal national freight is moved by road while the integrators handle most domestic express and airfreight. The main carriers, both American and foreign are mostly international routes.

In China there are some 200 airports across 34 provinces, including Hong Kong, the biggest cargo hub in the world. Nearly all countries have a wide distribution of airports but very few will have the infrastructure and personnel necessary to satisfy the needs of the shippers and the airlines. An excellent example of a mixed passenger and cargo hub is Brussels. While being a major European passenger hub, its cargo department handles around 450,000 tonnes each year with pharmaceuticals and perishables being leading sectors. The two divisions work well together with the cargo zone at Zaventem, several kilometres from the passenger terminals. This airport benefits from traffic from the EU establishment and the fact that Belgium has become the leader in pharma shipments.

Right from the earliest days of aviation, the building of airports was the vital link between the flights and the market, for passenger, mail and cargo. Airports are business centres connecting people, products and services. Nothing has changed in that; only the scale.

5 History

Brief History of Air Cargo

Over a century ago, brave people took to the air in a variety of fragile, experimental machines, many of which crashed or even failed to clear the ground. Nowadays, we take air and, space travel for granted as part of daily life. We would not be in that situation but for the courage and forward thinking of those men and women. Here we take a brief look at air cargo's evolution.

The development of what we now know as the air cargo supply chain, has taken well over a century and during that time has been subject to drastic changes up to and including the latest 2020/21 COVID-19 pandemic. The true impact of this has yet to be assessed but it has certainly changed the aviation industry dramatically. Apart from some often-unsuccessful experiments with hot air balloons, it is generally agreed that true air freight was first employed to carry postal shipments in the United States. The initial U.S. airmail service was conducted during an aviation meeting at Nassau Boulevard, Long Island, New York the week beginning 23 September 1911. During this period Earle L. Ovington, with his "Queen" monoplane, was appointed as an airmail carrier flying the route between the temporary post office established at a flying field on Long Island and the post office at Mineola. Some 37,000 pieces were delivered by the service (Figure 5.1).

During the first decades of the twentieth century and between the two world wars, there were hundreds of projects and companies involved in the development of aviation both for passenger and cargo, which we cannot cover in this short volume. Here are some of the major events.

In August 1911, the first chapter in German air freight history began when the Berliner Morgenpost newspaper hired a biplane to fly from the Berlin-Johannisthal airfield to Frankfurt an der Oder. Its cargo consisted of a few bundles of newspapers, the latest edition of the Berliner Morgenpost. When pilot Siegfried Hoffmann landed, he also made media history: the newspapers fresh off the press arrived a whole hour earlier than was possible by rail. There was definitely no way at the time of being more up-to-date with the news of the day.

DOI: 10.4324/9781003167167-5

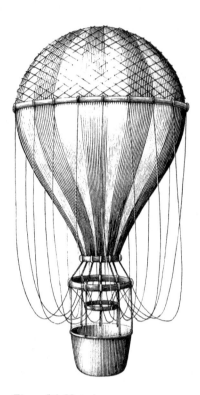

Figure 5.1 Hot air.

It is recorded that balloons were in use in China in the third century, but in Europe, the eighteenth century saw the development of gas balloons AD Gas balloons became the most common type from the 1790s until the 1960s. Pierre Testu-Brissy completed over 50 flights in total, including the first ascent on horseback on 16 October 1798 from Belleville Park, Paris. The Montgolfier brothers, Joseph-Michel and Jacques Etienne achieved the first recorded flight with humans in 1783 travelling some 5 miles while the Robert brothers launched and manned a hydrogen filled balloon from the Tuileries gardens in Paris, staying airborne for 125 minutes at a height of 560 m and travelling 36 km.

The first steerable balloon-dirigible flew in 1852 but its steam engine power source was not successful. The first attempt to fly in an untethered with an engine was made by Alberto Santos Dumont in 1898. A number of projects involving hot air balloons have been launched for carrying freight with very limited success.

Recent entries into this sector involve airships such as the Aeroscraft and Airlander which are more efficient and effective than many predecessors and could become a practicable air cargo vehicles in the future. Possible uses are, for example, access to disaster areas, and industrial area without traditional airport facilities. However, the infamous Hindenburg tragedy will always cast some doubt about the safety and reliability of any Balloon venture.

A few other similar experiments were made during the remainder of 1911, and the U.S. Post Office Department recognized the possibility of developing the aircraft into a practicable means of freight transportation. It made a recommendation to the U.S. Congress early in 1912 for an appropriation of $50,000 with which to start an experimental service. Congress refused to grant the appropriation.

After the First World War

The U.S. Post Office Department had already recognized the possibility of developing the aircraft into a practicable means of mail transportation. It took many years for this to become a really useful solution, as aircraft were very primitive with little weight capacity or range. However, the First World War generated more efficient aircraft and after the war many people, mostly former military pilots, attempted to start airline operations using ex-military equipment. Although very cheap to acquire, these machines incurred very high operating and maintenance costs, unaffordable for commercial operations. These planes, therefore, demanded modification, newer engines, and designs. The other severe limitation was that, in order to operate regular and reliable services, some basic but essential supporting ground and navigation services were needed. These included airports with proper runways, repair shops, connecting roads, handling facilities, as well as weather and flight controls. In most cases, these did not materialize for many years. Most important of all, sufficient paid traffic was needed, to achieve commercial viability. Mail delivery, domestic and international, accounted for over half of the nascent industry's income from 1918 to 1939. In addition, commercial aviation was not a profitable activity on its own and needed financial support from subsidies and high postal fees. Finally, it was impossible to overfly national territories, which imposed severe restrictions on developments. There was clearly a need for international cooperation both political and commercial, in order to take aviation into a global transportation mode to rival ocean freight (Figure 5.2).

Figure 5.2 Postal traffic Paris.

Regulations and Agreements

In order to meet these requirements, several conventions and agreements were introduced to cover the new aviation sector. The Paris International Air Convention, introduced in 1922, defined the sovereign control of national airspace. The principle of freedom to fly over a country's airspace was generally accepted. This treaty, containing nine separate chapters, also dealt with the nationality of aircraft, certificates of airworthiness, patents and permissions for take-off and landing. The International Commission of Air Navigation (ICAN) based in Paris, introduced a raft of legal, technical and meteorological services when representatives of 43 countries attended a conference in Paris in October 1925. Gradually, air travel was being accepted as a reliable means of transport.

During 1926, the newly formed German Lufthansa company transported some 1,000 tonnes of air cargo as well as 6,000 passengers. The new route network was soon followed by cooperation with the German National Railway System and in the year 1927 the over-the-counter market came into existence. While Lufthansa aircraft transported air cargo on its route network, the German railway took over the ground feeder services.

Another aviation milestone was the Warsaw Convention, which was signed in 1929 by 152 different parties and came into force in 1933 becoming the most important agreement of the Aviation industry at that time.

It set out to regulate liability for international carriage of person, luggage or goods performed by aircraft for reward. It defined international carriage, the rules concerning documentation, the liability limitations of the carrier as well as rules governing jurisdiction. In 1955, following a review by ICAO the Hague Protocol was adopted by the ICAO council. In 1955, the two conventions were merged into the Warsaw convention, as amended in 1955 and then in 1999 the Montreal Convention replaced it.

The Montreal Convention (formally, the Convention for the Unification of Certain Rules for International Carriage by Air) is a multilateral treaty adopted by a diplomatic meeting of ICAO member states in 1999. It amended important provisions of the Warsaw Convention's regime. The Convention sought to bring uniform and predictable rules relating to the international carriage of passengers, baggage and cargo.

The Second World War witnessed major improvements in aviation technology. The aircraft were vital for military purposes as well as heavy cargo transport. Most of these aircraft had little practical civil application; however, the capabilities of the manufacturers were tested and developed during this era. Having put their machines to the ultimate test, the resulting generation of aircraft was ready for a new reliable role in civil air transport.

Did You Know?

During the Middle Ages, food was liable to rapid deterioration caused by fluctuating temperatures, insect infestation and total lack of basic hygiene. Meat and fish could only be preserved by various curing, smoking and salting techniques, many of which are still in use today. Appalling breaches of basic health procedures such as the daily use of contaminated water and filthy hands, often resulted in death and the spread of disease. At London's Smithfield meat market, for example, animals which had been driven long distances would often be emaciated and diseased, but were still sold as fresh meat. Rotting carcases in the market were normal at this time. Then in the 1840s a miracle solution was discovered that changed things forever – preserving food with ice. In North America, some of the Northern fresh water lakes froze solid in winter and if this ice could be harvested to produce large blocks which when carefully stored, food could be preserved throughout the heat of summer. Lake Wenham in Massachusetts became famous for pure quality ice and a Bostonian named Frederic Tudor aided by Nathaniel Wyeth launched the Wenham Lake Ice Company to market the ice throughout America and beyond. By using sawdust to insulate the blocks of ice, it was possible to ship these blocks to far off places in Europe, South America and even India. It took some time for this idea to become accepted but eventually ice houses were built where the blocks could be stored. The Kennebec River in Maine produced even greater quantities and later the Norwegians also entered the European market. In the United States it was then possible to refrigerate railway wagons with blocks of ice and thus meat from herds in Texas and other Southern farmlands could be transported to the big markets in Chicago and New York. Ice remained the main source of refrigeration on railway freight cars until as late as the 1930s. The ability to transport fresh food over large distances revolutionized the American farming industry and changed the entire social structure. Similar patterns emerged in Europe.

The Pioneers

At first, cargo on long-haul international routes remained at a modest level and consisted mostly of priority airmail, which was light and did not require large capacity. KLM, Deutsche Lufthansa and Air France were the real pioneers, carrying newspapers, banknotes and gold bullion, perfume and fashion items, spare parts for machinery and live animals even including racing pigeons. KLM were the first in the transport of large animals, such as horses and cows, as well as fresh flowers. Most freighter aircraft used at this time were either converted passenger aircraft with the However, several important nations did not join, notably Germany, the Soviet Union, China and the United States. These nations formed the Pan-American Convention on Commercial Aviation, which was signed by 22 countries in Havana in 1928.

Throughout the world, different regions developed their own air services with varying degrees of success. In Switzerland, a service was initiated in 1919 between Zürich and Berne. Although this was initially restricted to transporting mail and some goods, including newspapers, it was later opened to passengers. At this time the air consignment note (ACN) was introduced, a highly complex document covering the entire transport process, which was later simplified into the Air Waybill (AWB), still in use today. These paper documents have been largely replaced by computer-generated docs which have speeded up the air cargo process out of recognition, but it was very slow to come.

In France, several airlines were formed, operating different routes within Europe, carrying passengers, goods and post. Compagnie des Messageries Aerienne (CMA) took over the Paris–Lille service from the postal administration, which was devoted only to mail and freight. This is generally regarded as the first genuine all-cargo service. The same company subsequently developed daily connections from Paris Le Bourget to London Croydon Airport. Aircraft Transport and Travel Ltd, which was launched in November 1919, offered regular airmail services between Paris and London. In April 1920, Handley Page Transport introduced a specially designed freighter aircraft with a tariff structure based on weight classification, still in use today. Many other companies emerged and vanished during the following era.

By contrast, in Germany, due to the social unrest, commercial aviation was somewhat chaotic with frequent fuel shortages playing a major role in restricting its development. However, an air postal network based in Hamburg operated successfully in the region consisting of the old Hanseatic League cities, to Scandinavia in the north and to Amsterdam and London in the south. It was the dirigible balloon that played a landmark role in increasing traffic. Between August and December 1919, the Bodensee model from the Zeppelin Company transported 2,250 passengers, 3,000 kg of mixed freight and 4,000 kg of mail between Berlin and Stockholm. Although many trials and experiments have been attempted over the intervening years to find a commercial use of air ships, no practicable formula has yet been developed. Several initiatives of varying success were launched in Africa, Australia, China, Japan, Thailand, South America and Europe with a view of setting up commercially viable air services, but it was in the United States that the main success can be seen.

Within a short period of time, air travel had established itself as a reliable means of transport. During 1926, the newly formed German Lufthansa company transported nearly 1,000 tonnes of air cargo and some 6,000 passengers. The new route network was soon followed by cooperation with the Deutsche Reichsbahn, the German National Railway System, in 1927. The over-the-counter market came into being during this period. While Lufthansa aircraft transported air cargo on its route network, the German railway took over the ground feeder services.

On 1 May 1926, Lufthansa established the first passenger night flight route in the world. Illuminated markings on the ground and on tall buildings and masts served as landmarks for pilots. Only the most experienced personnel were able to operate under these conditions.

The night flight service was organized by Hermann Kohl, who in 1928 would become famous because of his East to West crossing of the Atlantic. But the initial flights were often hazardous journeys into the unknown and the pioneers in the early days of aviation had to do without modern-day navigation standards, such as the artificial horizon on the instrument panel.

The worldwide air network was expanded continually during the 1930s. A huge milestone in the history of air cargo was the first trans-oceanic flight service on 3 February 1934, which inaugurated the airmail service between Germany and South America.

Because of falling air fares and low freight rates, some of the already established airlines came under pressure from these new competitors. Aviation as a means of travel and transporting goods experienced an unprecedented period of expansion. New types of aircraft were developed, starting with turbo propellers – and shortly afterwards came the jets. Again, it was the development of military aircraft that helped the civil sector to develop. Newly emerging quick-change or combi versions of aircraft allowed airlines to offer passengers and shippers the flexibility with which to operate at full capacity and profitably.

Fully automated processing of cargo, as it is today, is a far cry from the aviation practices of the post-war era, but many enthusiastic people dedicated their resources and energies to finding better ways of turning aviation into a vital part of the world economy.

Development of the Industry in North America

Between 1920 and 1940, the transportation of mail was the main activity of the aviation business, while railways were considered fast, safe and comfortable for moving passengers. Furthermore, the lack of airports and facilities discouraged potential travellers. The enthusiasm of both a few individuals within the U.S. Postal Administration and the pilots themselves enabled the creation of a serious airmail service. It was the U.S. Army that opened the Washington–New York service in 1918. After a moderately successful start, the military withdrew from the service. As a practical alternative to overnight on-time mail deliveries by train, the air service offered very little advantage. Initially, postage rates for airmail services were too high and then, with the eventual cuts in pricing to compete with ordinary mail charges, the service was commercially viable. Otto Praeger, originally a journalist by profession, persuaded his boss, the postmaster general Albert Burleson, to help develop long-distance flights to carry airmail. The De Havilland DH4, a wartime daylight bomber, was chosen to perform the task. After considerable modification, the aircraft came into service, but unfortunately required very high engine maintenance. With the addition of an exterior container under the fuselage, the aircraft could operate on the New York–San Francisco route via various intermediate stations, as well as the New York–Cleveland route. Conditions were hazardous due to bad weather, which resulted in a high death toll of pilots. In 1920, the service became truly established with a network of main and feeder routes like Chicago–Omaha–St. Louis and Minneapolis–Omaha–Sacramento.

The participation of rail was necessary as no night flights were yet possible. In 1922, when Paul Henderson was appointed as assistant postmaster general, his strategy was to prepare the routes of the U.S. Postal Service for transfer to private hands. He was determined to improve safety and to investigate how night flights could be introduced. To achieve this, huge light beacons were installed at Chicago, Iowa, Omaha, North Platt and Cheyenne with supporting lights along the route. Now with a delivery time of around 33 hours, compared with the 91 hours by train, airmail charges were again introduced. The results were disappointing and the commercial users, mostly banks with cheques to clear, demanded a true overnight service. Finally, in 1925, following a major improvement in equipment and infrastructure, the overnight service between Chicago and New York was started, allowing next-morning deliveries.

The development of South American air connections relied very much upon a French–German–American strategy and the American network of Pan-American Airways. After various disagreements and disputes, a well-organized air infrastructure was established in cooperation with various national airlines.

Growth in the USSR

The geography of the USSR – 13.7 million square miles – plus the harsh winters experienced in this vast country and the total lack of communication routes, cried out for some transport infrastructure. The Socialist government, with its 5-year plans, while admitting that the USSR faced more transport problems than any other country in the world, considered developing the railways as a priority. Once again, it was the postal service which opened the air network, but the initial flights were often hazardous journeys into the unknown.

Unrealistically, big government plans demanded an aircraft manufacturing industry populated by people, like Andrei Tupolev, who designed several passenger- and freight-carrying aircraft, including the Tupolev ANT-9 and ANT-6, a civilian version of the Tupolev TB-3 heavy bomber. In the late 1920s, the coastline of the Arctic Circle from Archangel to the Bering Strait was designated as an official target for air exploitation under the country's latest 5-year plan. The route was designed to serve isolated communities in mining areas, as well as scientific and weather stations. The flights had to endure appalling weather conditions with sub-zero temperatures, fog, snow and ice. To cope with these extreme conditions, aircraft were equipped with skis or floats.

The Global Market

Overall freight traffic on long-haul international routes remained at a modest level up to the start of the Second World War. This was largely due to the priority given to airmail and thus lack of capacity. KLM and Deutsche Lufthansa were the exception, carrying humanitarian cargo seats removed, or ex-military aircraft that had long proved to be suitable for the task.

Air travel started to expand and cargo capacity was needed to supply post-war re-building efforts. New types of aircraft were developed starting with turbo prop engines and then shortly afterwards came the introduction of commercial jet aircraft. Again, it was the development of military aircraft that influenced the development of the civil aircraft and support services. The aircraft could carry minimal amounts of weight and were severely restricted by navigational hazards and lack of landing sites. After the initial stages, the more lucrative passenger market began to develop, although flying was still extremely hazardous and full of various risks which some people were prepared to take. From that point on, cargo became an add-on to the passenger business. During the pioneer days of aviation, many small or one-man band airlines served markets in Africa and Latin America where road transport was and is in some cases, almost non-existent. Many heroic tales of bravery and deeds were created around the world over the years which have been part of the growing strength and vitality. Today's cargo market is very much an essential part of world trade.

The Impact of the Second World War

The Second World War brought about many major improvements in aviation technology. The aircraft played its biggest ever role, not only for wartime attack and defense in the shape of bombers and fighters, but also for the provision of heavy cargo transport. While most of these aircraft had no practical civil application, the capabilities of the manufacturers were honed during this period. Having put their machines through so much hardship and stress, the resulting generation of aircraft was ready for a new role in international transport. Consequently, the end of the war saw the start of a global network of flight connections. At first the large piston engines of the propeller aircraft shaped the industry. In the United States, the sale of a great number of Douglas C-47 Skytrain or Dakota aircraft – a military transport developed from the Douglas DC-3 airline, belonging to the U.S. Army – engendered a rush of airline start-ups. The reputation of this particular aircraft as an indestructible and reliable flying machine had become legendary. Very cheap prices for aircraft encouraged many former pilots to go into the aviation business for themselves. Small and even one-man airlines sprang up like mushrooms; initially, it was the passenger business that dominated as payloads were still low and lacking in revenue.

The Berlin Airlift

One of the major proving grounds for today's air cargo operators was the Berlin airlift (Figure 5.3).

One of the most significant milestones in airfreight progress was what became known as The Berlin Airlift. After the Second World War, the former allied forces – France, England, the USSR and the United States – shared the control of Germany. Berlin, which was within the overall Soviet territory, was also split as a city between the four powers. In the summer of 1948, USSR leader Joseph Stalin, feeling threatened by the U.S. presence in Berlin, decided to take control of the city and blockaded the western section, cutting off access to food and supplies. In what would become the first major confrontation of the Cold War, U.S. President Harry Truman made the historic decision to supply Berlin by air. In a heroic joint effort, the Americans and British delivered more than 2 million tonnes of supplies to the beleaguered city over the next ten?

The city of Berlin became the focal point of the post-war political standoff by the Western allies, the United States, France and Britain on the one hand

Figure 5.3 Map of divided Berlin.

and the Russians on the other. In order to supply the 2 million citizens of Berlin with almost everything necessary for their daily life, American and British pilots flew day and night to land urgently required supplies of food, coal, medicines and other essential necessities.

The runways available in West Berlin, especially at the Temple of airfield in the American sector, were not sufficient to land large cargo aircraft safely, so plans were made to build a new airfield in the French sector. All of the equipment and materials for the new runways had to be flown in. The United States provided a fleet of around 35 C-54 aircraft, the military version of the DC-4, with two squadrons of Sunderland flying boats based at Lake Havel in Berlin. When in full swing, around 260 American and British aircraft were ferrying the targeted 4,500 tonnes of supplies daily. This eventually rose to some 8,000 tonnes a day. The aircraft flew so frequently and were so densely scheduled that they often became stacked above the city in a dangerous holding pattern. The airlift moved a total of 2,325,000 tonnes of essential supplies during the 15-month period it was in operation. It is estimated that 621 aircraft took part in the airlift, operating 270,000 flights – with a total distance of over 124.5 million miles flown. The blockade of Berlin showed up the conflicting pressures of keeping costs down while fulfilling customers' needs, still present in the ever-changing challenge of successful air cargo operations in today's fluctuating world economy.

It is generally agreed that the Berlin Airlift was the first occasion when airfreight was employed to maximum effect. Aircraft, ground handlers and crews were forced to breaking point and many lessons were learned that were carried through into the next decades of commercial airfreight operations.

The Jet Age

The airfreight industry, as we know it today, was revolutionized by the arrival on the scene of a new generation of jet aircraft, the DC-8 and Boeing 707, capable of cruising speeds of around 550 mph with a payload in the freighter version of up to 40 tonnes. The Jet aircraft opened up not only international passenger services but the concept of efficient air cargo delivery. Freighter versions of these aircraft and the invention of the unit load device (ULD) engineered to fit the shape of the aircraft hull, allowed more efficient use of available space, faster loading and unloading of freight. Another refinement was the Combi, which carried both freight and passengers and was very popular with airlines such as KLM. But it was the legendary Boeing 747, the jumbo jet, which revolutionized flying (Figure 5.1). It took off for its maiden flight in 1969 this was a case of an original military design which was then adapted as a commercial aircraft. The B747 family of aircraft with its many different configurations and models has endured until today (**see special feature the queen of the skies**). The B747 freighter could carry 8' × 8' pallets side-by-side on the main deck. Lufthansa which was the first airline to operate the transatlantic flights with a payload of 114 tonnes. Although several carriers still employ the freighter versions, the aircraft has been mostly replaced by the more efficient B777 in its various configurations. In 1970 Air bus industries launched their first aircraft, the A300, but when FedEx started operating a fleet of 25 of these aircraft with a payload of 50 tonnes each, the aircraft became vital part of the industry.

The Freighter Market

The fundamental challenge of freighter operator is to be able to acquire return loads. Otherwise, the one-way flight becomes almost inoperable with the exception of special cases where a particular high value piece of freight such as a satellite launch is involved. As passenger aircraft have become bigger and able to carry significant freight in their bellies, the need for freighters has changed. The advantage of belly-hold cargo is that the aircraft will operate a passenger route and cargo can be acquired in both directions. Aircraft such as the B 747–8 or B777 can carry significant amounts of cargo, depending on the route and the passenger load. Unfortunately, the industry has traditionally treated cargo as a second level product and little attention has been paid to its relative importance in route planning. Cargo tends to be expensive compared with other modes of transport and it is also taking too long to process. From manufacturer to customer can take as much as 10 days whereas FedEx or DHL can achieve the same delivery within 48 hours. The price differential can often be justified by the amount of time saved. Similarly, if the cargo is moved by sea, the rates are much lower but the time taken is much higher. It is an ongoing debate that cargo such as fruit can be chilled for a sea voyage and delivered in good condition. Much research and investment goes into finding the best solutions (Figure 5.4).

The arrival of the pandemic in early 2020 has clearly devastated the aviation industry and it is probable that it will never return to its previous operational level. The increasing demand for cheap travel for tourism has been slashed and as a result capacity drastically reduced and this also applies to cargo. During this recovery period many of the wide-bodied jets normally in daily operation have been furloughed and planning for the next phase of aviation will probably involve much smaller aircraft. The whole industry is at work trying to find a solution and clearly much more transparency and greater use of available technology will play leading roles in this recovery. History shows, however, that the air cargo industry has an ability to survive and find new solutions and as we show in another chapter, a new business model will be necessary to achieve this. Now the aviation and airport sectors have commenced a new thought process. Whereas pre-pandemic routes were planned for mainly passenger traffic and airports designed around passengers' needs, cargo was relegated to a secondary importance. That has changed resulting in a more realistic approach to dealing with the needs of the air

Figure 5.4 Inside B747 freighter.

cargo operators. The arrival of large ecommerce operators such as Amazon is also changing the development of the sector.

The Modern Era

Many companies are having to reconsider their supply chains and look for alternative sourcing.

One solution is reshoring – moving manufacturing closer to home. This is easier said than done with manufacturing cost in some countries such as China, Vietnam, Bangladesh or Latin America being a fraction of home-based production, the original reason for the demise of textile production in the United States for example. A recent survey of North American manufacturers found 83% likely, or extremely likely, to r-shore sourcing, a leap from 54% in March 2020.

One main factor even before the pandemic was of course, the tariff war between the United States and China, which has continued for several years and has tested the ingenuity of all players in the supply chain.

A survey of more than 130 manufacturers published by technology and professional services provider Sikich and Industry Week, found that 93% of respondents had experienced challenges from COVID-19, and 76% reported that the pandemic had exposed gaps or weaknesses in their supply chains.

In addition to frequent supply chain disruption, extending lead times significantly, the higher costs of logistics are also causing companies to reconsider their options. The rising total cost of transporting goods is ruining the viability of importing goods from long distances such as Asia. Some smaller companies had dropped unviable product lines or gone out of business.

A recent report by The Economist Business Intelligence Unit concluded that more reshoring was bound to take place in Asia, arguing that North America was not a viable alternative owing to limited competitiveness. An article in a German news magazine reported that some European firms were returning to Europe and investing in increased automation and new plants.

Interest in near-shoring is also on the rise in North America. In March, Walmart pledged $350 billion to support this in six categories of manufacturing over the next decade, selecting 900 firms for support to enable production in the United States. Manufacturing in the United States must endure distinct disadvantages in terms of taxation and labour costs, but other countries in the Americas such as Mexico, Panama or Chile, with existing trade agreements with Washington offer real solutions. A November report by the Baker Institute for Public Policy of Rice University saw "a pivotal role for Mexico in a broad reshoring drive to the region," particularly for more labour-intensive products. While shipping costs will retreat from their vastly elevated level of today, they will not revert to pre-COVID levels,

The air cargo community is always under intense pressure from a myriad of directions. Has always managed to find and implement the next step and has become a vital factor in global re-generation after COVID-19.

The Queen of the Skies

No account of the history of air cargo can be complete without paying homage to the iconic B747-the Jumbo jet. The aircraft dominated the skies for generations (Figures 5.5–5.9).

On 9 February 1969, 53 years ago, the largest aircraft ever imagined, took off and flew into history. The queen of the skies, the B747, was born. It was the maiden flight of the jumbo jet, the famous Boeing 747. This iconic aircraft was to shape the future of both passenger and freight transport and revolutionized the air cargo industry. Today, despite its replacement by other types and models, the 747–8 as it has become, is still one of the top favourites of cargo operators. Forward thinking and courageous engineers, willing to risk all and make bold decisions, were led and inspired by Joe Sutter, who sadly passed away in 2016.

The darlings of the skies at that time were Boeing 707 and Douglas DC-8 – the first commercial jets which, while serving an increasing demand for international travel, also generated the specialized aircraft cargo container, the ULD.

Figure 5.5 First flight.

Figure 5.6 Crew of B747.

Figure 5.7 The queen.

Figure 5.8 Dangerous goos sign.

The Boeing team worked closely with Pan Am as the launch customer and some decisions were influenced by its first customer. The designers decided to have the same fuselage for cargo but the need for a large cargo door in the nose of the aircraft, required the re-design of the position of the cockpit to the upper deck.

When the Joe Sutter's project was close to bankruptcy, the Boeing management instructed him to lay off 1,000 engineers. He refused and subsequently went on to hire an additional 800. At Boeing, Sutter worked on many commercial airplane projects, including the 367–80 "Dash 80," 707, 727 and 737. He eventually became a manager for the new jumbo-sized wide body airplane, the four-engine Boeing 747. As chief engineer, he led the 747 design and build team from conception in 1965 to rollout in 1969. He would become known as the "father of the 747." Sutter's final job was as executive vice president for commercial airplane engineering and product development when he retired from Boeing in 1986.[5]

Sutter served on the Rogers Commission, investigating the Space Shuttle Challenger disaster. He was also selected as a recipient of the International Air Cargo Association's 2002 Hall of Fame Award. As of July 2010, he was a

Figure 5.9 22 Ready for first flight.

member of the Boeing Senior Advisory Group which is studying a clean sheet replacement of the Boeing 737 or to re-engine the current design.[11] For decades, he resided in West Seattle. In 2011, on his 90th birthday, Boeing's 40–87 building in Everett, WA, the main engineering building for Boeing Commercial Airplanes division, was renamed the Joe Sutter building. Sutter died on 30 August 2016 at a hospital in Bremerton, Washington from complications of pneumonia, at the age of 95.[12]

Aviation author and historian Jay Spenser worked closely with Sutter for 18 months to write his autobiography, entitled 747: Creating the World's First Jumbo Jet and Other Adventures from a Life in Aviation (ISBN 0-06-088241-7).

The Concept

The Initial designs of the 747 called for a twin-deck aircraft, but because of the requirement to evacuate two decks of passengers was found to be impossible within the recommended 90-second safety limit. Boeing opted for a single main deck.

The high bypass turbofan delivered twice the power of existing turbojets and burned 30% less fuel. Pratt and Whitney were also working on this concept and in 1966 Pan AM, Boeing and Pratt and Whitney agreed to develop the JT9D as the powerhouse for the 747.

Powered by General Electric GEnx-2B engines, the 747–8F is 16% longer than its most immediate predecessor, the 747–400, and offers 16% more cargo volume. And at 250 feet, 2 inches (76.3 metres), it is the world's longest commercial airliner.

B747 Version Progression

Model Series ICAO code[129] Orders Deliveries Unfilled orders 747-100B741 / BSCA[a]167167205—747-100B99—747-100SR B74R 2929—747-200BB742[b]22 5225393—747-200C1313—747-200F7373—747-200M7878—747E-4A33—747-E4B11—747-300B743565681—747-300M2121—747-300SR44—747-400B744 / BLCF[c]442442694—747-400ER66—747-400ERF4040—747-400F126126—747-400M6161—747-400DB74D1919—747-8IB74848471451747-8F107989747SPB74S454545—747 Total 1,5731,56310.

The 747–8F was launched in 2010 with Cargolux being its first customer. It is estimated that around 300 various 747 freighters are still flying, but the final deliveries are due for delivery to Atlas Air by the end of 2022. Despite being at the end phase of its life, the B747–8F offers unique cargo-carrying capabilities.

At 138 tonnes, the B747–8F has significantly greater payload than the next largest civil (new build) freighter – the B777F at 102 tonnes – and also offers the flexibility of nose-loading for outsize cargo.

The permanent retirement of the aircraft would leave cargo carriers facing a definite gap in the availability of new-build large capacity freighters.

Epilogue

Do we now wave goodbye to the QUEEN after over 50 years of service? It would seem that the jury is out on this issue. The increasing need for large capacity cargo lift, coupled with the temporary (we hope) grounding of the AN124 fleet, makes the iconic QUEEN more necessary than ever. The future of air logistics is moving fast and these wonderful aircraft still have a vital role to play. LONG LIVE THE QUEEN.

Note Camille Allaz, ex-chairman of Air France cargo, published a superb illustrated book "The History Of Air cargo And Mail" which covers the history of this industry up to the first jet era. It is presented in great and well researched detail.

6 Security

Security and Crime in Air Cargo

Everyone either remembers or knows about the horrendous terrorist attacks on the World Trade Centre in New York and the White House in Washington, known as 9/11. It was this event which made the world aware of the fragility and vulnerability of air transport, bringing about major changes in attitudes towards security systems and prevention methods. Attacks on both people and goods in transit are not new, from pirates and highway robbers centuries ago, to bullion heists on warehouses and trucks by armed gangs to missile attacks on aircraft in flight. The problem is becoming worse, and we have set out the most frequent and obvious types of crime here, as well as some of the methods of prevention. The COVID-19 pandemic has highlighted this weakness as we explain later in this chapter.

Goods in transit have always attracted criminal attention and modern supply chains are being targeted by criminal gangs. In addition to this menace, a number of other criminal activities are associated with air transport. Cargo's main advantage is that exact routes and timings are often difficult to anticipate, thus making it a less attractive target to plant explosive devices.

Theft Is a Constant Challenge

Air freight's main reason to exist is to move high-value goods around the world, thus providing ideal targets for possible theft. Every shipment starts and ends its journey in a truck or warehouse where it becomes most vulnerable. Cargo is at its biggest risk when it is stationary, on the ground or in a vehicle. For several decades, criminals have had easy access to cargo in general thanks to poor security and dishonest employees providing vital information to criminals. There have been some spectacular robberies over the years but today, companies and insurance companies prefer to keep quiet about their losses, not wanting to reveal possible opportunities for future incidents, as well diverging the negative publicity and confidence in the company. Costs to everyone in the supply chain, as well as insurance companies are eye watering, with accurate figures being unavailable due to security

DOI: 10.4324/9781003167167-6

issues. In the EU region alone, it is estimated that over 8 billion Euros worth of goods were stolen 2019 not including the costs of damage to vehicles, property and insurance companies.

The transport assets protection association (TAPA) was formed in 1997 to tackle the escalating problem of cargo thefts from the supply chain, TAPA has more than 800 members globally, including many of the world's biggest manufacturers and logistics service providers, freight forwarders and transport operators and other stakeholders. TAPA provides members with a wide range of security advice and technologies to help reduce risk and actual crimes. This in training includes unified cargo security standards, shared industry practices, technology, education, benchmarking, regulatory collaboration and the proactive identification of crime trends and supply chain security threats. One of the main problems facing road transport companies is the lack of secure parking for drivers on long journeys and with drivers being obliged to stop for rest after limited driving periods. Many thefts are carried out during these stops which are often in layby is or in unprotected truck parks. This is further exaggerated by the fact that many drivers are foreign and do not necessarily know the delivery areas or regulations as well as they should. One technique used by criminals posing as police is to "arrest" the drivers and demand either to inspect the load or even confiscate the entire vehicle. Physical attacks on drivers or breaking into trucks also make easy pickings for the gangs.

Although there have been some spectacular robberies in the past, the trend in increasing cargo theft continues to rise and very often the use of technology, while protecting goods in transit, can also exaggerate the problem when dishonest employees are involved giving out secret data. In 1983, following a tip-off, thieves broke easily into the Matt-Brinks security warehouse at London Heathrow airport. Expecting to find a haul of around £3 million in cash, they were astonished to discover gold bullion, jewels and cash worth £28 million (around £87 million at today's values), which with great difficulty, they managed to load the three tonnes of gold bullion into a small vehicle and remove it from the premises. The police, recognizing an inside job, quickly identified and arrested the most of a gang but a large proportion of the gold was never recovered. Unable to deal with the bullion, it is reported that the brothers brought in other criminals to help reprocess and distribute the gold to other international banks. It reportedly re-cycled into the jewellery trade. It was frequently rumoured that hundreds of newly wed couples were married with rings made from the stolen gold. The history of the next 20 years and it is so of a popular TV drama The Sweeny and has become a crime folklore saga.

In another incident in 2004 the police flying squad (the Sweeny, cockney rhyming slang-Sweeny Todd-flying squad) prevented another bullion robbery worth £40 million at the Swiss port cargo warehouse at London Heathrow airport.

In 2005, at Schiphol Airport in the Netherlands, a $118 million load of uncut diamonds was hijacked by uniformed criminals posing as legitimate officials.

All of these cases and hundreds more, share some common features. They were betrayed by dishonest employees with criminal contacts, which police usually quickly identified. Very often the culprits were disgruntled ex-employees. Security in every case was weak with easy access. In today's globalized society, the quantity and value of goods moving by air has reached an all-time high. Computers, mobile phones and electronics, fashion, pharmaceuticals and recently, large quantities of personal protection equipment (PPE) being flown, much of these goods are prime targets for criminal gangs. Unfortunately, violence is also becoming more usual, for example, the break in at the airport at Charleroi in Belgium, where a gang broke in and stole a consignment of 10,000 smartphones, injuring several workers. While the industry works hard to invent new technology to defeat these crimes, professional criminals are becoming equally more sophisticated and using the latest technology.

Unfortunately, organized crime is not without its victims. Such crime damages everyone in a long chain and is often backed by large international criminal organizations, funding fake products and drug trafficking and can often result in destroying legitimate businesses and economies.

Stolen goods in transit will also impact on retailers and cause them to lose their customers and push them further into the safety of online shopping. Governments, in turn, lose legitimate sales tax.

Security continues to challenge all stakeholders in the international supply chain, the air mode being no exception. Criminals of all disciplines recognize the importance of the supply chain, in providing access to goods and facilitating the movement of illicit goods. Criminals have heavily invested in developing a thorough understanding of the inner workings of supply chain models, to the point today where they could be considered highly skilled logisticians in their own right.

Security continues to challenge all stakeholders in the international supply chain, air cargo included. Criminals of all types know the importance of the supply chain, in providing access to goods and facilitating the movement of illicit goods. Criminals have heavily invested in developing a thorough understanding of the inner workings of supply chain models, to the point today where they could be considered highly skilled logisticians in their own right.

Digitalization has and continues to be a useful tool, for example, for transfer of documents, access to capacity data or fast communication. While legitimate use benefits business, criminals have the possibility to access systems. Infiltrating networks, disrupting supply chains and selecting target businesses. In the wrong hands, technology provides unrivalled access into the supply chain process.

Detailed information such as which cargoes are in transit, destinations and schedules. Do drivers regularly stop for rest breaks in a specific location? Will drivers park locally and insecurely if they are waiting for the loading gate? All such information opens the doors for the well-experienced criminal.

Technology supporting security has continued to evolve GPS, track, trace and monitor and other devices become ever smarter. Able not only to relay data to a central hub but to other devices. Locking devices, forensic solutions and tamper-evident security seals all serve to close security gaps. Similarly, for every step taken towards a truly secure supply chain, criminals are not far behind. Jamming signals, methods of working around security seals or placing GPS tracking devices on vehicles, providing them with the exact location of their target.

The legitimate supply chain has long been used to facilitate the movement of illicit goods and people undetected across borders. There are numerous opportunities including free trade zones that provide the opportunity for the introduction of illicit goods into the supply chain. Wildlife trafficking, counterfeit goods and illicit drugs are frequently transported through legitimate supply chains. Intricate knowledge of the supply chain allows criminals to disguise both the nature of the goods and the point of origin, by shipping through a series of hubs in less obvious locations.

Through the pandemic as capacity decreased, there was a definite increase in the volume of illicit goods, particularly drugs being shipped. While intercepted shipments historically consisted of a few kilos, it is not uncommon now to hear of several tonnes being discovered. A further demonstration of the criminals' agility and motivation to achieve their goals.

Supply chain stakeholders cannot rest on their laurels. For criminals, access to the legitimate supply chain is worth billions of dollars each year. Whether through theft of cargo or disguising and transporting illicit goods, the supply chain is critical to their business models. While localized efforts to disrupt criminal activity can be effective, one should always be mindful that the motivations are great and often the security challenge simply shifts rather than being resolved. Criminals will constantly strive to identify the next weakest link and opportunities which provide the least chance of apprehension.

Strategies around fraud are an increasing risk to legitimate actors in the supply chain. While the concept of fraud has always existed, the digital business landscape gives rise to unrivalled opportunity for criminals who are able to deceive with relative impunity. From less sophisticated business email compromise schemes to intricately planned schemes to infiltrate the supply chain and take control of valuable cargo. Criminals are highly motivated and amply resourced to deceive even the most security conscious operator.

Autonomous vehicles, land, ocean and air based will likely present a host of new security challenges. Without the deterrent of a physical person present there will undoubtedly be opportunities for criminals to intervene and interrupt the supply chain. It remains feasible that sufficiently motivated hackers could take control of vehicles, either hijacking and positioning for their own gain or to use in acts of terror. The cyber landscape has already become a battlefield for many businesses, while ransomware attacks are currently prevalent, criminals are extremely agile and will quickly adapt to take full advantage of emerging opportunities.

Drugs, Counterfeit and Illegal Goods

Other criminal activities are also eating away at the integrity and profitability of world trade. Drug trafficking, carried out by highly skilled and ruthless gang, will often place consignments in boxes of flowers or unsealed containers, in the full knowledge that if they are discovered the blame will fall on the airline and airport staff. A good friend of mine fell victim to this and served many years in prison. The drug gangs are so wealthy that they can bribe and intimidate almost anyone in order to clear the way for their trade.

Counterfeiting is also a major threat to the manufacturers of branded goods but can also be dangerous or even lethal. Fake drugs and pharmaceuticals, toys, cosmetics and sports clothing are examples of products frequently counterfeited, depriving legitimate manufacturers of hard-won markets and in the case of pharmaceuticals, cigarettes and cosmetics the results can be injury or even death. At one time these fakes were crudely presented and easy to spot, but today's fakers are very adept at duplicating packaging and presentation. Apart from the obvious damage to people's health and bank balance, this will have the effect of increasing prices throughout the supply chain and present Customs officers with even more difficult tasks. Thanks to security systems at airports, smuggling in general amongst airline passengers is becoming increasingly difficult and that includes the practice of carrying small animals and illegal food products.

Prior to 9/11, there was easy access to on-airport areas, warehouses and even the aircraft, and a wide range of unauthorized people, carried out their tasks on both passenger and freighter aircraft. Today, however, access is stringently limited and authorized by security officials. All employees undertake strict police background checks and identification procedures. This all makes the aircraft itself almost untouchable but as we have already stated the danger lies on the ground and on the roads.

What Are the Solutions Available with Which to Fight Back?

The practice of replacing the old paper trail for a cargo has been largely replaced by technology which in turn increases security. Bar-coded packages and pallets can be traced using GPS trackers and by adding high-quality alarms to the vehicles, some of the threat is diminished. Also, common sense and basic instruments and better locks can make a big difference.

Secure cargo identified with barcodes can be tracked throughout its journey with GPS trackers and alarm systems fitted to vehicles which can be immobilized. A range of hi-tech systems and solutions are available to companies. Low-tech solutions such as better locks and seals which are alarmed can also be effective. Any suspicious activity or person should be investigated quickly as outsourcing prospective thieves may be just testing the security system. For any company which outsources trucking all warehousing to outside contractors, extra care is vital so that no unknown vehicles or drivers are permitted without careful inspection. The screening and training of all staff should be fundamental to the entire security process.

The TAPA, mentioned before, attempts to unite manufacturers, logistics companies, carriers and law enforcement agencies with a common aim to reduce theft and subsequent losses from the international logistics industry. TAPA sets out to identify problem areas and develop solutions. With thefts increasing every year, companies which apply the TAPA standards are reporting significant reductions in losses. There are other organizations which also combat criminal activities in the supply chain including Cargo Security Alliance, Freight Watch, Security Cargo Network and many more, including insurance companies.

Cybercrime, which is becoming a global menace for everyone, is also part of the air freight security problem. The ability to hack into company systems, identify rich targets, track their location and even forge necessary documents and permits, frequently outwits the experts working on the inside for the operators. The European Cybercrime Centre, part of the EU's police body Europol, deals with billions of internet protocol addresses when attempting to trace possible criminal activity. Some intelligence services and large companies are being targeted to steal online data which could lead to illicit trading advantages.

Terrorism

Transport systems are very easily incapacitated by terrorist activities. Take the example of the Brussels airport bomb in 2016. The explosion of multiple bombs in the airport passenger terminal and Metro system, brought the city of Brussels to an almost complete standstill and in turn caused the entire Western world to rethink its aviation security systems. In this case, dedicated freighter aircraft were able to continue operations, but with more than 50% of air cargo travelling in the bellies of passenger aircraft, the significance and importance of Brussels as a vital trading hub became almost decimated for several months. As a leading centre for pharmaceutical manufacture, the attack had a profound effect on the delivery of vital medicines which fortunately could be moved by road to other neighbouring airports. Over several decades of disasters and a variety of problems, whether it is earthquakes, wars or pandemics, the air cargo industry always manages to meet the challenges and find solutions. Scanning cargo in the handling warehouse prior to flight has become accepted practice internationally but sniffer dogs have proved to be much more efficient and faster and certainly cheaper to operate than machines.

Corruption, the Invisible Disease

The real challenge of defeating the creeping curse of corruption is that in many countries it has been the practice for centuries for bribery and vested interests to run the wheels of government and commerce. The bribing of officials such as low paid Customs officers, government officials, petty bureaucrats, safety inspectors, police and many more, can often cause cargo to be tied up in red tape. This has been seen frequently in the delayed delivery of humanitarian aid where frequently the goods are stolen by local warlords and corrupt officials. This has certainly been the case in the 2020 COVID-19 delivery of PPE, where frequently shipments have been held up by Customs disputes. Alternatively, an official may accelerate the clearance of an illegal shipment. Drugs, which are the root of a large proportion of criminal activity, frequently need help to pass through inspections. Dishonest officials and managers can often expedite safe passage. Furthermore, such is the wealth and reach of the drug barons and local gangs, that people who accept a bribe once, live in fear of their lives. The drug trade is enormous and much of the product travels by air. The use of sniffer dogs and other methods had greatly increased the detection figures.

The real culprits are seldom identified and if they are, they are so powerful that arrest is very rare. Thanks to the enormous profits to be had, the trade grows continuously.

The Merchants of Death

No reliable statistics exist for the illegal global trade in arms. This is because most of this trade, legal or illegal, is conducted secretly with some countries defining arms in different ways, industrial machinery for example. The figure most accepted for the global market value of the arms trade was $80 billion (2013) but is probably more the various wars and small regional conflicts throughout the world that continue to blight our society, represents a huge profit for the arms manufacturers and traders both legal and illegal. Surplus weapons are easily acquired by these "merchants of death," but, in today's air cargo and ocean freight industries, such trade is mostly carried out by unscrupulous governments or gangs using unregistered aircraft and ships operating out of obscure airports and ports.

Sarkis Garabet Soghana, VICKTOR BOUT nicknamed **Merchant of Death**, is a Syrian[1] Armenian and Lebanese[2] international private arms dealer who gained fame for being the "Cold War's largest arms merchant"[3] and the lead seller of firearms and weaponry to the former government of Iraq under Saddam Hussein during the 1980s. Soghanalian's testimony exposed the role of American government officials in the illicit arms trade. Soghanalian (now exchanged by USA with Russia, December 2022). Gave a detailed description of official and unofficial American involvement in the enormous buildup of arms to Saddam Hussein.[11]

The character Simeon Weisz from the 2005 film Lord of War is a fictional character created as a composite of real life, middle-eastern arms dealers, including Soghanalian.

There are many other nefarious activities which we have not dealt with, but it is obvious that when you move high-value goods, you will be targeted by criminals. This brief summary indicates the breadth and diversity of the security challenges faced by air logistics operators. No matter how clever the protection systems may be, there is always someone equally willing and, skillful, capable of defeating such devices. If we wish to live in an open and free society, we must be prepared to accept the risks which surround us. Unfortunately, crime is an integrated part of human society and our beloved air cargo business will always fight its corner to protect international trade and its customers. Inevitably the powerful drugs gangs are involved in all areas of crime and much of those mentioned in this chapter have some involvement by these gangs. Some countries are far worse than others when it comes to corruption and involvement in crimes such as people trafficking, drugs counterfeit goods the list is endless.

Pandemics Encourage Crime

The recent COVID-19 pandemic has opened up even more opportunities for criminals to profit from the global chaos and emergencies. The old age that cargo stationery on the ground is the biggest risk. One of the main time sensitive categories during this pandemic has of course been medical equipment-PPE, medical equipment-ventilators, masks and miscellaneous sanitary goods as well as vaccines themselves. Due to the need for speed, the air cargo industry has responded with enormous flexibility and innovation, converting passenger aircraft into cargo carriers, bringing into service a variety of aircraft probably not usual for this kind of business. Handling companies have been stretched and with the limitations of national health barriers, shipments are more difficult to deliver than normal. However, the risk has shifted to warehouses, especially those that are outsourced and not normally part of the supply chain. This means that vast amounts of cargo are sitting in warehouses waiting for delivery.

Cargo Crime Focus Shifts To Warehouses

Thefts of freight in transit remain the highest proportion but dropped from 87% to 71% last year, while losses from storage facilities rose to 25%, TT Club-BSI study finds.

BSI publishes this report in coordination with TT Club. BSI Supply Chain Services and Solutions is the leading global supply chain intelligence provider, auditing services, audit and risk management compliance solutions and advisory services. BSI's charter is to help corporations, governments, and associations identify, manage and mitigate global supply chain risks and maintain world-class governance, risk and compliance programmes. BSI's holistic supply chain risk management suite is designed to predict and visualize risk and develop robust risk mitigation and compliance management programmes to protect global supply chains, brands and reputations. BSI's intelligence-infused supply chain solutions and global network empower the clients to understand global supply chain risk with unequalled precision. TT Club is the established market-leading independent provider of mutual insurance and related risk management services to the international transport and logistics industry. The Club's services include specialist underwriting, claims management and risk and loss management advice, supported by a global office network. TT Club's primary objective is to help make the industry safer and more secure. Established in 1968, TT Club has more than 1,100 Members, spanning owners and operators, ports and terminals and logistics companies, working across maritime, road, rail and air. Members range from some of the world's largest logistics operators to smaller, bespoke companies managing similar risks. The Club is renowned for its high-quality service, in-depth industry knowledge and enduring Member loyalty. It retains more than 93% of its Members with a third of its entire membership having chosen to insure with the Club for 20 years or more. TT Club is managed by Thomas Miller – an independent and international provider of insurance, professional and investment services.

Thefts of freight in transit remain the highest proportion but dropped from 87% to 71% last year, while losses from storage facilities rose to 25%, TT Club-BSI study finds

Cargo crime patterns have changed significantly over the past year, as criminals adjust to different freight flows due to the COVID-19 pandemic.

A cargo theft report for 2020 compiled by leading international transport and logistics insurer TT Club and global supply chain intelligence provider BSI highlights "significant new trends in risks both regionally and globally," including a shift in the focus of cargo crime to warehouses.

The report, which reflects whole-year data from 2020, notes that thefts of freight in transit remain by far the highest method of cargo crime, but the proportion dropped significantly from 87% in 2019 to 71% last year, while losses from storage facilities rose to 25%. But it noted significant variations from region to region.

Noting that last year was an atypical year due to supply chain threats from the pandemic, the report said these trends were "likely to be of continued concern well into 2021."

The report's authors said the most significant trend highlighted by the report "was the relative shift in the location of thefts, with in-transit incidents and those involving vehicles showing a decline, though remaining the most dominant threat, and theft from storage facilities increasing." It said the extent of the rise in the latter was variable from region to region, noting that this trend was "reflective of the disruption to supply chains brought about by radical changes to consumer buying patterns as a consequence of the pandemic."

New High-Value Targets

Other noteworthy findings include the observation of new high-value targets such as PPE, face masks and anti-bacterial gel, with vaccine supply chains expected to come under threat as their roll out expands. Meanwhile, the food and beverage sector remained the largest target last year at 31% of total cargo thefts.

TT Club's managing director for loss prevention, Mike Yarwood, commented:

The effects throughout 2020 of the COVID crisis threatened supply chain security, continuity and resilience. Not only did newly created high-value commodities such as PPE become targets for theft but bottle-necks in the logistics infrastructure at ports and warehouses brought increased potential risks. Temporary overflow storage facilities added to the dangers in loosening the grip of existing security systems.

Although specific incidents have not yet occurred, unless distribution plans for vaccines are perfectly executed within the expectations of any given population, challenges will arise in protecting the single most valuable cargo of all in the coming months, the report notes.

Regional Variances

It said regional variances were also worthy of note, including over the issue of crime against goods in storage. In Europe, for example, the stockpiling of goods meant these inventories came under particular threat, with 48% of 2020 reported thefts coming from warehouses and production facilities. This was in contrast with 2019 when only 18% came at such locations.

On the other hand, 54% of incidents occurred in rest areas and parking sites in 2019 in Europe, whereas the 2020 figure was 19%.

In Asia, the countries with the highest risk remain India, Indonesia, China and Bangladesh. The proportion of storage-based risk remains around 50% in Asia as a whole but in Southeast Asia the in-transit risk indicates the prevalence of bribery and corruption with a high percentage of thefts being facilitated by employees and customs or other officials.

North America continues to see theft coming almost exclusively in transit via hijackings or directly from a parked vehicle. The risk of social unrest, particularly in Mexico, arguably impacted the risk of cargo loss through most of last year.

The report noted that significant disruption to the Mexican rail freight industry, with protesters setting up blockades on train tracks, created a backup of cargo across the country. This disruption led to estimated losses of close to US$4.4 billion.

Brazil Hotspot

In South America, Brazil was a hotspot last year. A key driver of the high rates of cargo theft here remains the presence of major illegal drug smuggling gangs that need to fund their trafficking efforts, the report notes. Again, the dominant risks were from hijacking and theft from or of vehicles. These theft types accounted for 78% of the total losses reported. The extreme rate of cargo theft, however, did drop for the first time in several years, as continued efforts by police and industry contributed to a slight decline in incidents in 2020, the report found.

The Coming Year

In the coming year, disruption and the uneven resumption of international trade resulting from the spread of COVID will continue with imbalances in shipping container distribution that are likely to impact maritime, and through a knock-on effect air cargo capacity throughout 2021, the report noted, adding that "the added vulnerability of cargo will, therefore, continue."

The authors said the "key to mitigating threats in 2021 is to stay ahead of the risk," noting that BSI and TT Club "have once more collaborated to analyse the detail of these risks. In the report, the authors furthermore offer mitigation techniques so organizations can proactively understand their risk and build a supply chain that is ahead of the criminal tactics and emerging threats."

The full report can be downloaded free of charge via this link (HYPER-LINK TO: https://www.ttclub.com/news-and-resources/publications/tt-bsi-cargo-theft-reports/bsi-and-tt-club-cargo-theft-report/)

Views from TT Club

Dealing with inside correct large majority of thefts and frauds involving cargo originates from inside threats from either company staff or subcontractors. It can even be the action of disgruntled ex-employees or existing employees with a grudge against the company if these people have access to sensitive data concerning consignments of cargo security codes, route planning et cetera, they are in a position to help perpetrate theft or fraud. Such actions can be blamed squarely on poor recruitment techniques, checking of legitimate background previous employees et cetera, overall poor security and inadequate corporate governance pre-employment screening is a vital as well as the disclosure of sensitive information.

It is vital that anyone having access to computers with sensitive information must be very carefully checked on an ongoing basis as people's personal circumstances can change. For example, somebody develops a financial problem or divorce or major personal upheaval which provides temptation to acquire illicit funds. Selling such information to criminal gangs is where most thefts originate.

Employees can also be corrupted by illegally using fuel cards or selling cloned cards or having access to fuel bunkering. This must be audited on a regular basis. Warehouses: security in the warehouse is vital and all security devices such as locks and cameras should be checked regularly to ensure perfect function this demands the development of a security culture whereby members of staff do not become complacent or sloppy or inadvertently give away information to potential criminals for example uniforms can be cloned along with security badges. Today computer systems are so sophisticated that almost perfect copies can be made of any document. The recent survey by CPI showed that 47% of all incidents are based on financial gain whereas 6% can be based on revenge to mitigate against corrupt staff, again screening and updated information are vital check that staff are really who they say there are do not be too trusting credit checks can also reveal potential thieves loyalties can change if for example an employee is passed over for promotion or doesn't get an expected pay rise. Poor attitude can be caused by stress which again could relate to financial or marital problems. Vital information should only be given out on a need-to-know basis. Sensitive areas such as alarms, control boards and expensive equipment should be checked regularly and codes frequently changed. Keys to vehicles must be handed in after every journey; keep checking all this data.

Mandate fraud is often a problem. An invoice can be intercepted on email and reply giving a slightly different bank details the money is paid and lost all invoice payments must be checked carefully. It must be remembered that criminals have as much access to technology as you. They are constantly thinking up new ways to hack into security systems, emails, websites, etc., and lack of attention can allow them to penetrate your company. Be vigilant and aware of all at all times; many small incidents are overlooked by the police. Due diligence is vital; keep anti-virus systems updated.

Despite a downward global trend from 2020 to 2021, a step up in the proportion of organized crime, "internet-enabled" theft, shortage of secure parking and queues and overspill from new Brexit border controls could create "the perfect storm" for European road freight theft in 2022, warns TT Club.

Industry professionals have long suspected last year was likely to have been the highest on record for global road freight theft, had cross-border crime not been hampered by lockdown restrictions.

Thorsten Neumann, president and CEO of TAPA EMEA, said in April: "…it is difficult to give a meaningful comparison with previous years… however, while some criminal operations would have been disrupted by lockdown measures, 2020 still saw the second-highest rate of incidents in TAPA's 24-year history."

Much of this activity could be due to the accumulation risk from a spike in e-commerce cargo, according to TT Club's MD loss prevention, Mike Yarwood.

He also noted that TT Club's figures were down on those of 2020, adding: "At the moment, on the global picture, the frequency of cargo theft looks to have decreased so far this year, over last."

But there is worse to come, he warned.

"We are still desperately short of good parking facilities, especially in the UK in Germany and in other places," Mr Yarwood said. "More e-commerce, more consumables, more goods on the move – road transport is by far the most vulnerable mode of transport."

He warned that the shortage of drivers across Europe was likely to facilitate the risk of "insider threat," as companies relax their screening procedures with the hope of hiring more drivers.

> At the moment [companies] aren't blessed with time and choice; there's a shortage of drivers, trucks and availability and, when you look at the pay conditions, it is not beyond the wit of man to imagine criminals paying drivers to do something they shouldn't.

Meanwhile, as border requirements change in January and again in July, the likelihood is that conditions will improve for petty and opportunistic – as well as organized – criminals.

"It could be the perfect storm," Mr Yarwood said.

> There was a time where a lot of it was opportunistic – but those days are gone. Internet-enabled is the best way of describing it; it's not quite cybercrime, but the data we share and hold via the internet is accessible, and very valuable in the wrong hands. These guys are very organised, they know exactly what is moving and when – they are almost one step ahead.

Stephen Paul Bacot, landrisk manager at Risk Intelligence, agreed the lack of available parking facilities for trucks was a major issue.

"In Mexico, or Brazil – the MO is hijacking," he said. "But in Europe, it is much more common to wait until the truck is parked and the driver is asleep. Cargo at rest is cargo at risk."

Despite EU attempts to harden parking facilities, much more work needed to be done, Mr Bacot said.

> They need thousands more spaces – and of course there is cost to using them, which is especially challenging if you're working on a very low profit margin. We see a lot is problems with just-in-time supply chains; the drivers can't be late, so they arrive at 2 AM for an 8 AM delivery and park in an industrial estate. You find a truck from Europe has been 'turned over' 500 metres from the destination.

Long queues in France and the UK would most likely exacerbate the challenge, he said. "Anything that causes trucks to be delayed and parked up in non-secure areas increases the threat," he said. "There are active measures being taken by police in France, but organised criminal gangs are responsive and agile, and if the measures increase at Calais, they will simply move to other ports." Source loadstar.

Conclusion

As in most other human activities, criminals are enjoying a new rich era of comparatively risk-free crime. Anonymous computer-based fraud is incredibly difficult to detect and even when it is detected, legal measures are often impossible to apply. With the use of computers located in far off countries available, the need to carry out violent crime is lessened. In the case of logistics, it is clear that the weaknesses of the system lie in on the road risk, especially involving low paid employees, open to incentives. One can only assume that the recent conflict and violence in the Ukraine and its impact on international logistics is also opening new opportunities for the world's criminal gangs. The industry is responding to these threats and will continue to invest in new security.

7   Special Cargoes

Every kind of product imaginable is routinely delivered by air including, computer chips, telecon and mobile phones, household goods, clothes, day old chicks and ships' spares. This is the bread-and-butter diet of air cargo. However, there are several large-scale categories which usually require very special handling and sometimes specially equipped aircraft. Here are some of these cargoes.

In some cases goods that are required for emergencies or specific needs may demand a chartered freighter aircraft suitable for a specific task. Charter brokers who serve this market are expert in matching aircraft to shipment. The fashion industry, for example, employs a variety of transport modes from ocean freight for mass produced items such as jeans or tee shirts, to airfreight or even express for high fashion collections required for international fashion shows.

The transport of orchestras, music groups, art and museum exhibitions and even election equipment, all travel regularly by air and in the case of a world tour, may charter one or more freighter aircraft for the duration of the series. On the ground handling of these delicate shipments requires highly skilled experts.

There is the continuous movement of horses for racing, show jumping and breeding. Very specialized equipment and skills are essential for this high and sensitive traffic.

VIP Animals

Few members of the public are aware that a large variety of animals, birds, fish and insects are routinely transported by air, including even large animals such as tigers, Rhinos, pandas and even elephants. Animals require fast and careful expert handling and transportation, so although domestic transport is carried out on the road, for international transport flying is frequently the only option.

In dealing with live animals and associated products, airports are governed by strict regulations for quarantine and phytosanitary supervision. Although

DOI: 10.4324/9781003167167-7

restrictions on global transportation animals have been greatly eased in recent years, border inspection controls in all countries to ensure that the legal procedures are followed. In addition, it is equally important to guarantee the provision of a calm humane environment while the animals are in the care of handlers and airlines.

Animals of all types suffer considerable stress in these circumstances and it is vital that they be treated as gently as possible although some airlines will decline to carry animals it is a significant part of regular airfreight commerce and sometimes may impact on the profitability of a particular airline route or airport stop, for example, a busy airport that refuses to accept animals due to the lack of appropriate facilities, may lose passenger traffic as well. While most animals such as horses, cattle and zoo are transported in special freighters, together with their grooms and attendants, these will probably be delivered to an airport with the necessary facilities. In the case of racehorses; for example, they will need to be landed as close as possible to the racecourse in order to avoid additional long road links.

Regulations covering the transport of animals are applied from a variety of sources. Each country operates its own department of agriculture and health with some variations between countries while international row rules are also applied. The company shipping the animals will need to ensure that the appropriate documentation, licences and other necessary documents are obtained well in advance of the flight. Apart from domestic pets, animals travel in special aircraft with stalls and cages organized by the shipper or their agent, IATA has introduced its CEIV standards to raise the level of international practice and regulation.

Animal Diseases and Regulations

IATA publishes its *Live Animals Regulations* (LAR) that demonstrate how to transport animals safely, legally, efficiently and cost effectively. For more information see www.iata.org/lar.

One of the factors to have had the effect of decreasing the transport of farm animals has been the outbreak of several virulent and destructive diseases. These occur around the world, and strong efforts are made to contain and restrict their spread. Many animals are transported for breeding purposes, with the aim of improving conditions and stock quality in developing countries. The main diseases are rabies, foot and mouth disease, bluetongue, bovine spongiform encephalopathy, equine influenza, equine infectious anaemia, equine piroplasmosis, equine rhinopneumonitis, glanders, equine viral arteritis, classical swine fever and avian influenza. The impact of regulations, disease and extremism impact constantly on the successful transport of animals by both surface and air transport. The regulated companies and organizations involved in this business are dedicated to the humane and safe movement of this precious cargo. Stress is also a very important negative factor, as it can damage or even kill an animal in transport.

Animals are broadly classified as follows, although there is a cross-over between the various groups:

- Pets, which may include some laboratory animals;
- Agricultural, covering the full range of cattle, pigs, sheep, goats, poultry;
- Horses and other equine species, which includes racehorses, show horses, polo ponies and breeding stock;
- Zoo animals, including dolphins, sharks and whales. As most zoo animals cannot tolerate a long journey time, air transport is often the best or only solution.
- Exotics, which includes monkeys, lemurs, tropical birds, snakes and reptiles, insects, bees and a number of rare breeds. This is a highly controversial subject as in the past many rare breeds have been smuggled into Western countries illegally, often resulting in a mass death of the creatures in the consignment. This category will often overlap with zoo animals and pets such as mice and ostriches.

Moving Domestic Pets

Since the changes in international controls, it is now comparatively straightforward to either accompany pets on flights or send them separately. This has greatly increased the traffic of pets.

What is the definition of a pet? Normally airlines consider dogs, cats, ferrets, rabbits and hamsters as pets. However, some carriers will accept other varieties such as snakes, turtles, reptiles and amphibians, as well as mice, rats and guinea pigs. Most of the traffic, however, is for families taking conventional pets to new locations for work, retirement and so on. Many people, of course, make their own arrangements and are therefore responsible for organizing their own documentation and dealing directly with the airlines.

Regulations vary from country to country according to the national agricultural and health administration, which sets controls for vaccinations against rabies, etc. In the United States, for example, the Department of Agriculture (USDA) sets the requirements of the Animal Welfare Act. This covers not only air and road transport, but also pet shops and boarding kennels. In the United Kingdom, the Department for Environment, Food and Rural Affairs (DEFRA) does much the same thing. Each country has its own equivalent controlling body, but the rules are very similar. There is no accurate figure of the number of pets moving by air as no formal records are required, but a general estimate of 2 million pets are shipped worldwide in any given year. Some animals will be shipped independently of their owners, while many will accompany them on the same aircraft. The business of pet transportation tends to coincide with school vacations, particularly in the summer, as companies prefer to relocate personnel during this season to lessen the disruption. The busiest markets for pet transport are North America, Australia and Europe, but the rest of the world is still active.

Top Dog

Lesson in animal handling

By Gerton Hulsman

It must have been decades ago that I was working for a European Airline.

During that period, I was working in the Cargo Export Department where we were informed and trained to handle all kinds of merchandize to be air-lifted in the best possible way.

It was the beginning of the so-called verticals, where standard air cargo (general cargo) as a process was considered as the basis for airfreight.

Merchandize that needed extra attention like perishables, pharmaceuticals, automotives, etc.

The company was keen to develop the verticals in a proper way and everybody in the handling arena was trained and asked for the utmost attention for special cargo.

A very important vertical became the transportation of live animals. In the end this resulted in the transportation of expensive racehorses and zoo animals. However, at the beginning we had to deal with a lot of pets travelling with their owners to their destinations.

One day one of the colleagues who was very ambitious and tried to give the best possible service to the client picked up the phone and spoke a lady who wanted to take her Great Dane on a holiday trip to Spain. She had heard that this was possible to ship the dog by air to her holiday destination.

The colleague informed the lady that this was best possible and informed her about health certificates, rabies inoculation and the regulations.

He asked her the dates she wanted her pet to fly and made a booking in the cargo system for the requested flight. In order to give her an estimate of the costs he asked for the weight of the dog. She replied that it was a heavy one with around 90 kilos on the scale.

Everything was arranged and the lady received the details of where to deliver her dog at the airport and at what time she had to be there in order to prepare the paperwork and buying the necessary kennel in which the dog had to be transported.

On the flight day she delivered the dog promised to the cargo acceptance point and asked for the colleague who had made the reservation. He came with the airwaybill and she handed him all the necessary documentation. The dog was accepted and the kennel (the biggest one they had) was sold to the lady.

She paid and hugged her dog and wished him a good flight.

So far so good. The dog was picked up by the staff of the animal hotel and waited in the animal hotel till it was time to board the aircraft.

One hour before the departing time the colleague became a phone call of a shouting red cap (chief loader on the apron) and asked him why a Great Dane was underneath his aircraft? The colleague was very friendly to tell the man that this was his first pet he had booked and the animal was supposed to fly to Spain.

The furious red cap answered that it was all very nice to make bookings with pets but please observe the dimensions of the cargo holds of the DC 9. The dog could only fit in the biggest kennel (height 110 cms) and the belly height of a DC 9 is 105 cms! Red faces and Red Caps.

The dog returned to the animal hotel and his journey to Spain was by car.

He enjoyed it very much and was none the wiser.

The morale of the story – **size matters!!**

A Growing Business

The pet transportation business has grown tremendously in the past few years, largely due to the mobility of society in the modern age similar. Now that companies are including pet shipping as part of a good relocation package, the number of specialty pet shippers has increased, along with IPATA's membership. Approximately 50% of families have one or more pets, which means that this aspect of the transportation business will grow accordingly. Airport authorities have a big responsibility to providing inspection and border controls if international transport is involved. Both airports and the airlines risk losing passenger traffic if no facilities exist, thus forcing passengers to choose a suitable alternative airport. Following the rules on health, documentation is essential for individuals shipping their pets. The problems occur only when these are not respected.

Since the changes in international controls, it is now comparatively straightforward to either accompany pets on flights or send them separately. This has greatly increased the traffic of pets. It is important to clarify what a pet is. Normally airlines consider dogs, cats, ferrets, rabbits and hamsters as pets. However, some companies move snakes, turtles, reptiles and amphibians, as well as mice, rats and guinea pigs. Most of the traffic, however, is for families taking conventional pets to new locations for work, retirement and so on. Many people, of course, make their own arrangements and are therefore responsible for organizing their own documentation and dealing directly with the airlines.

Regulations vary from country to country according to the national agricultural and health administration, which sets controls for vaccinations against rabies, etc. In the United States, for example, the Department of Agriculture (USDA) sets the requirements of the Animal Welfare Act. This covers not only air and road transport, but also pet shops and boarding kennels. In the United Kingdom, DEFRA (the Department for Environment, Food and Rural Affairs) does much the same thing. Each country has its own equivalent controlling body, but the rules are very similar. There is no accurate figure of the number of pets moving by air as no formal records are required, but a general estimate of 2 million pets are shipped worldwide in any given year. Some animals will be shipped independently of their owners, while many will accompany them on the same aircraft. The business of pet transportation tends to coincide with school vacations, particularly in the summer, as companies prefer to relocate personnel during this season to lessen the disruption. The busiest markets for pet transport are North America, Australia and Europe, but the rest of the world is still active.

The International Pet and Animal Transportation Association

With **440 plus members** from more than **90 countries,** the International Pet and Animal Transportation Association is an **international network of professional pet shippers.** IPATA members are the Pet Shipping Experts™ who provide the **highest standard of care for animals,** providing constant attention to their security, safety, and well-being during travel. In accordance with IPATA's By-Laws, *Officers and Directors* serve three-year terms. *Assistant Regional Directors,* are not part of the Board of Directors but are appointed and responsible for working with the *Regional Director* in their region towards developing more interaction with members and **addressing industry concerns within the region**

Each Active IPATA member is an experienced **professional pet shipper,** registered with the United States Department of Agriculture (or its international equivalent, if applicable), and adheres to the rules and regulations of the Animal Welfare Act and the International Air Transportation Association (IATA) Live Animal Regulations as they relate to the **care and transport of family pets.**

Associate IPATA members are registered within their own industry, are experienced providers of goods and services to the pet transportation industry and actively support the safe and humane transport of the family pet. IPATA members are dedicated to the humane care and handling of the family pet as it is transported and/or relocate

IPATA has many different touchpoints with their members and the air logistics sector, including:

* Facebook Groups
* Email Information Groups
* The IPATA website
* Ongoing webinars and seminars

IPATA also has a committee that is dedicated solely to the interaction with airlines and industry partners. This committee meets frequently and is an immediate communication point if an airline needs to disseminate information quickly to the Animal Transport Sector.

The COVID Pandemic Impact on the Pet Transportation Business

Comments from the Committee

Not only has the pandemic affected our airlines, our agents, processes or systems, but it also has affected how our clients think and make decisions. Our clients are more "informed" however information overload has our clients more on edge and it sometimes leads to them making erratic decisions to keep their families together.

COVID-19 has taught us that sometimes we are playing the waiting game – for embargoes to end, to be off a red list, to have routings available, or finally get that long-awaited go ahead. One thing that clients are seeing is how different the passenger and cargo travel is and that they don't necessarily correlate or follow the same scheduling and timelines, which then adds to this waiting game. The greatest task for any agent right now is how to keep that one family happy and together while the industry settles into the new normal.

Technology Changes

Technology will always be a double-edged sword; we just love to hate it. While there is so much information available, sometimes the skill of working with an agent is how beautifully it's tied together with a bow. Sometimes clients expect the same experiences based on what they read, what they hear, or what the "media" is sharing. Technology is like a superhero and with power comes great responsibility. It is great for getting messages and information across the world, instantaneously! It is great for keeping up to date and keeping your clients informed. We can connect the world through technology and get the results needed for a successful relocation. Technology has changed the game because it makes managing client expectations that much harder due to the information overload.

Equines

Due to the increasing costs of air transport, only high-value animals are likely to warrant air transfer. Such value can be commercial, as with racehorses and equine competition horses moving to show events. There are also horses moving between champion breeders (Figure 7.1).

Horses for racing and events such as the Olympics, the Gold Cup, or the Kentucky derby, are the most frequent flyers but there are also other horses for breeding and preservation or special animals for disabled riders or children. All animals, especially horses, are extremely sensitive and easily distressed by travel and change of environment and therefore need careful handling and transportation in specially equipped aircraft with horseboxes and with accompanying grooms. Some individual animals may be extremely valuable and thus special treatment is necessary both on the ground and in the air. Some airports, such as Liege in Belgium, Kennedy airport, USA or SCHIPHOL in Amsterdam, have set up special facilities for expertly handling large quantities of horses. All the necessary phytosanitary facilities are of obligatory. For events such as the Olympic Games, as many as a hundred and 150 to 200 horses will be flown to the host country within the space

Figure 7.1 Show horses at Athens.

of a few days, moved to stables and after the event transported back to their original country. This operation requires enormous planning and careful handling and often at airports with no resident facilities, for example, Athens.

Cattle and Farm Animals

This business is mostly concerned with breeding stock required by countries wishing to improve domestic quality. In China, for example, now that the population has acquired the taste for meat on a regular basis, significant numbers of beef cattle are being imported in order to increase local herds. Over the years, pigs and sheep have been shipped from countries such as Ireland to Korea. The international traffic of farm animals is controlled and monitored by a set of regulations within the IATA LAR. It covers the basic conditions under which animals may be transported on an aircraft. It is the responsibility of the local competent authority to ensure that the rules are followed. Journey times, including transport by road to and from the airport, must be carefully planned and sufficient food, water and medication must be available at all times. Containers, pens or stalls must comply with IATA specifications, including the amount of space for each animal. Bad weather conditions or delays must be taken into account. Air quality is very important as some animals such as cows produce moisture and gas. The correct level of lighting will vary between different types of livestock. Some will be better in darkness, whereas others will need some low-level lighting.

On freighter aircraft with access to the animals, close attention can be maintained, but in the belly-hold space of passenger aircraft access is not possible so the animals must be carefully packed in safe and appropriate containers. The correct use of a recommended space for each animal avoids dangerous overcrowding. The staff involved must be trained and able to deal with emergencies including, in some extreme cases, the slaughtering of sick or badly injured animals. The entire animal transport process, which is routine for those in this trade, is carried out safely all over the world with few problems.

Zoo and Exotics

The old-fashioned entertainment purpose of zoos has been largely replaced by different and diverse functions. Modern Zoos while still providing family entertainment, now emphasize education, but also provide safety for threatened or rescued wildlife. They are centres of conservation, biodiversity and the preservation of endangered species. The world's wildlife is suffering badly due to climate and habitat changes, mostly caused by human behaviour which has pushed many species to near extinction. Zoos attempt to arrest the inevitable disappearance of our animal populations, by providing better breeding conditions and sanctity in the hope that some animals may be eventually returned to the wild when appropriate. Using specially equipped aircraft, it is quite normal to transport large animals such as rhinoceros, giraffes, big cats and prairie dogs and yes even elephants! (Figure 7.2)

The practice of smuggling endangered species of animals and birds has been largely curtailed by airport security and screening, but unfortunately there is still a great deal of such activity but mostly carried out by other modes of transport. Many airlines refuse to carry any animals or take only pets. Most smaller animals, such as dogs, cats, monkeys and fish, are usually moved in the bellies of passenger aircraft.

The control of traffic in live animals is governed by various conditions and international regulations, applying not only to animals themselves, for their health and condition, but also to the grooms and attendants with them in transit. Carriers of animals must be equipped with suitable stalls and boxes but they must also, ensure the safety of the aircraft. In dealing with live animals and related products, airports are obliged to provide quarantine and phytosanitary facilities. Regulations governing the transport of animals may vary from country to country, but international rules will also apply. Regulations are set by IATA and the protection of endangered species is governed by Convention on International Trade in Endangered Species (CITESs)

Figure 7.2 Elephant on the move.

regulations. Despite all the restrictions, there is still a significant trade in illegal species and animal body parts. WAZA – the World Association of Zoos and Aquariums – provides guidance, support and leadership for zoos and organizations involved in animal care, welfare, conservation of biodiversity, environmental education and global sustainability.

Animal Diseases and Regulations

IATA publishes its Live Animals Regulations (LAR) covering the transport animals safely, legally, efficiently and cost effectively. The transmission of animal diseases, which we now suspect can also cause human health problems, is a primary concern of regulatory bodies.

Many animals are transported for breeding purposes, with the aim of improving conditions and stock quality in developing countries. The main diseases are rabies, foot and mouth disease, bluetongue, bovine spongiform encephalopathy, equine influenza, equine infectious anaemia, equine piroplasmosis, equine rhinopneumonitis, glanders, equine viral arteritis, swine fever and avian influenza. While animal traffic accounts for about only 5% of airline revenue, it is still significant and is largely managed by dedicated carriers and airports.

Overall, because animals are living creatures, they are instantly more delicate to handle than other goods and products.

Humanitarian Relief

This is another sector where aircraft play a vital role. Lack of available landing sites is often a drawback and sometimes relief supplies must be dropped over the site, or drones are sometimes used especially for urgent medical supplies. However, some aircraft types such as the AN-12 and C-130 Hercules adapted from military aircraft are designed to operate on rougher terrain than standard civilian aircraft. A high proportion of disaster supplies are dropped or delivered by these aircraft and helicopters. Specialized logistics is an important factor in effective disaster-relief operations. Special organizations control where possible, the supply of good and storage of the supplies, arrange transportation to a disaster area and coordinate the teams participating in the operation (Figure 7.3).

Relief goods are stored in warehouses anticipating the mix of materials most likely to be needed. Distribution centres are positioned in strategic points accessible to disaster prone regions.

There is always difficulty to obtain data from operations, unpredictable working conditions, short lead time and unknown elements such as bad weather, inaccessible locations, political hostility and military conflict, the 2022 Ukraine war.

Data flows are helping plan and execute relief operations and contributions of funds and medical equipment raised by the general public need to be coordinated and protected against theft and corruption

When a disaster occurs, fast response to the emergency is essential and air transportation is often the quickest way to deliver supplies and services to save human lives are at risk. According to the International Federation of Red

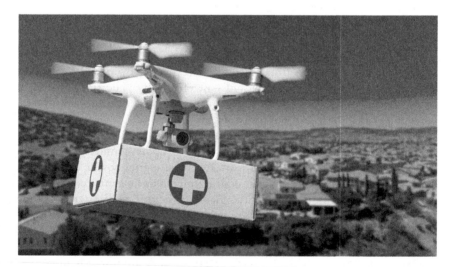

Figure 7.3 Drone delivers medications.

Cross and Red Crescent Societies (IFRC), in the immediate aftermath of a disaster, these primary aid items include food, water, temporary shelter and medicine, among other requirements. Many air freight operators willingly assist in such operations.

The role of the IFRC's Global Logistics Service is to ensure that the IFRC has a robust, competent, and efficient logistics capacity to effectively carry out its humanitarian assistance activities and achieve its goals. Its mission is to create a world-class service to support the core work of the Red Cross Red Crescent network and to share resources with other humanitarian organizations.

Art and Museum

The transportation of fine art between international galleries, outside the COVID restrictions, is a busy and on-going trade and some carriers are more focused on this. A good example is Air France/KLM Cargo, which regularly carries various paintings and museum pieces, between museums and exhibitions and back to its home museum some months later. Typical exchanges would be such as the "Musée du Louvre," or the "Musée d'Orsay" in Paris to the "Metropolitan Museum," or the "Guggenheim Museum" in NYC. This is also true for private paintings belonging to private galleries or owners. Although this traffic is routine business for the airline, experts from the museum or gallery will accompany and supervise the handling of the artworks which may be on board it is a Passenger aircraft or a Full Freighter, assuring the door-to-door safety of irreplaceable items. As for all fragile and valuable commodities, demand special attention and packaging which is done at the museum only by specialists under the permanent control of the sender.

Certain freight Agents who specialize in fine art and pieces are vital for this traffic regular destinations for this traffic include the United States (New York/Los Angeles/Chicago/San Francisco), Japan (Tokyo), Mexico, Beijing. This is a small but important slice of the airline's business but a high value contribution to the total cargo revenue bottom line.

On The Grid

During the COVID blockage of much international sport, nearly all sporting activities suffered financially and in many cases, emotionally. During the course of a normal year, many motor sport events routinely take place around the world. Many of the cars, motorbikes and support vehicles are flown to destination. Rallies, organized by the FIA in France and NASCAR stock car racing in the United States, historic and vintage rallies, Rallycross and Offroad are some examples, too many to mention. Many are purely domestic but leading international events will include entries from other countries.

Transporting F1 Equipment

In the case of the Formula 1 circuit, because the races are set so close together and in countries far apart on different continents, the planning and accurate timing of the entire season must be perfect. With events taking place in countries continents apart, cars, equipment, spare parts and technical teams, must be packed, flown and unpacked ready to prepare, practice and race within days. The supporting race teams travel more than 160,000 km each season. As a logistics operation it is extremely complex and time sensitive. The schedule includes destinations as diverse as Turkey, the United States, Brazil, Saudi Arabia and Shanghai. DHL is the chosen official logistics partner for the F1 World Championship managed by Formula one Management (FOM). Apart from the considerable task of organizing hotels, travel, local facilities and communications, when the events are "Flyaway," specially equipped freighter aircraft are used.

DHL continues as the logistics division of Formula One Management (FOM), FOM Cargo, in planning and moving the freight for the championship. The logistics specialist has transported race cars, fuel, oil, race team equipment and transmission technology around the world for Formula One's 23 planned Grands Prix in 2021 and 2022.

DHL provides air freight, ocean freight, road freight and express delivery services for Formula One shipments. The DHL Motorsports team works with the teams to book their freight for air and ocean transport to "fly-away" races, handling transport documentation, assisting with customs clearance, packing and carrier management.

Apart from this series of events many others also require specialized transport facilities such as

The World Rally championship, Dakar rally, Intercontinental, Historic Rally FIA World Rallycross, Le Mans 24 hours as well as motor cycle events in many countries. As well as the machines themselves, large quantities of spare parts, tyres and repair equipment are needed plus drivers and mechanics, altogether a massive logistics operation.

Music and Events

Whether it is a symphony orchestra on tour in several countries, a pop music group appearing at a festival or a stage musical on tour, a vast range of delicate equipment will need to be transported. If it is a multi-destination tour, the logistics become extremely complicated and require specialized and sophisticated supply chain management techniques. This industry is managed by specialist companies which have wide experience and knowledge for what is an extremely difficult logistics task (Figure 7.4).

A world tour is handled by hundreds of experienced and skilled specialists. Apart from the artists themselves, these will include the whole range of

Figure 7.4 Band equipment VIC.

personnel from forwarders, managers, roadies, lighting and set up experts, stage designers and logistics staff. Specially designed stages, lighting and other equipment, complex musical instruments and equipment are all part of the show. These cargoes accompany the main artists throughout their engagements and are often on tour. A surprising amount of equipment is necessary, for example, a recent tour by Lady Gaga required 3,747 freighters–a total capacity of around 300 tonnes. Entertainment Logistics is a very organized and precise business, where delays and breakages are unacceptable and can potentially put the event in jeopardy. Detailed planning and site inspection are vital to the success of this kind of shipment much of which needs to be dismantled after each performance.

When possible, the equipment will be moved by road but any international movement will be done by air charter. For example, Beyoncé's Formation tour of Europe, needed 7 Boeing 747 freighters. The freight agents handling this cargo will provide all the necessary Customs documents and carnets, which allow cargo to pass easily through national Customs areas.

Plane Fashion

Specialist freight forwarders equipped with suitably equipped vehicles, handle most of the shipments for this particular sector and are able to fulfil these needs (Figure 7.5).

Figure 7.5 Retail fashion.

In the distant past, using the air freight option was often the last resort for shippers. At as much as 30 times the price of its sea freight alternative, the high price was justified by top of the range pricing of the garments. Due to the highly sensitive nature of the shipments, a more stringent level of security is demanded plus speed of delivery, especially in the event of a major fashion show or product launch. The possibility of theft is a permanent threat which also can relate to the previously mentioned problem of counterfeiting. Furthermore, a sea container travelling from the Chinese port to a northern European destination such as Rotterdam or Hamburg may take up to 6 weeks to arrive in the customer's warehouse, where it will then be repackaged and undertake other journeys to final end user destinations. In a market as volatile as this, any design that is new is immediately under pressure to arrive in the marketplace. Changes in seasonal trends and demands for on–time deliveries demand well-managed supply chain systems.

However during the last few years, with the world's concern about global warming and environmental damage, there is a new resistance to buying more clothes and throwing away used ones, old in some cases being just a few weeks if there is a fashion change. The idea of remaking these rejected garments into new ones is catching on rapidly. The concern about the environment, which is very largely promoted by the younger generations as produced some interesting reactions. For example, the supermodel and event organizer Jessica Minh Ahn personifies this trend by insisting on holding fashion shows in unusual places such as a DHL warehouse or the deck of a solar powered ship. She emphasizes that she wants to cooperate with climate sensitive transport partners.

Following the economic turmoil of the COVID-19 pandemic many retail outlets large and small are disappearing, which will change the way in which the fashion industry operates. The dependence on cheap labour in developing countries to produce our clothes may well change with more manufacturing in home-based markets. Unfortunately, many of our highly skilled and traditional expert workers in textile and garment manufacturing have disappeared but our dependence on cheap foreign low-cost labour will certainly change.

Heavy-Lift Air Transportation

This chapter, with slight modifications, was originally published in the previous edition of AIR CARGO MANAGEMENT. Due to the conflict in Ukraine and the subsequent banning of many aircraft, the AN-124 fleet operated by ABC is partly grounded. The AN-225 (Mriya) has been completely destroyed. The industry hopes fervently that these aircraft will return to service when the peace is established. Some of these aircraft continue to operate from Leipzig Halle airport (Figure 7.6).

In the globalized industrial marketplace, there is an increasing demand for the transport of outsized loads by air. Heavy lift operators can handle almost anything that is needed including oil field equipment, heavy engineering, locomotives, yachts jet engines and satellites.

Figure 7.6 AN 124 at VIA.

There are relatively few freight aircraft that can lift heavy single-piece loads, and there is always an eager demand for their capacity.

The Antonov AN-124 Ruslan Condor was designed by the Antonov Design Bureau in the Ukraine, then part of the Soviet Union, as a strategic heavy-lift military aircraft capable of flying two fully loaded battle tanks, as well as the infantry and supplies needed to support them in battle, into unprepared airstrips on rough terrain. The aircraft featured a reinforced floor to support the weight it was designed to carry and had nose-door and rear ramps to enable drive-on, drive-off wheeled and tracked access to the main cargo deck. Externally similar to the American Lockheed C-5 Galaxy, it has a 25% larger payload and the capability to "kneel" on its retractable front undercarriage, allowing full utilization of its front ramp during cargo loading – or initially to unleash its cargo of battle tanks at full speed.

Manufactured in parallel by the Russian company Aviastar-SP in Ulyanovsk and by the Kyiv Aviation Plant AVIANT in Ukraine, the AN-124 is the world's largest serially manufactured cargo aircraft capable of handling heavy loads in its main deck cabin by virtue of a specially reinforced floor.

First flown as a military aircraft in 1982, civil certification for the AN-124 was issued on 30 December 1992. Twenty years later, 26 of the civilian aircraft were still in commercial use with various carriers in Ukraine, Russia, the United Arab Emirates and Libya.

Transportation of Oversized and Super-Heavy Cargo

By Vladimir Vyshehirsky head of engineering and logistics
Volga-Dnepr UK Ltd

Note this chapter was written some time ago before the Ukraine war. Although the ownership and operating criteria have changes, the essential facts about these aircraft remain largely unchanged.

We respect the authority of the author on this highly specialized subject

Air transportation of oversized and super-heavy cargo has been made possible by advances in global aviation manufacturing. Since the middle of the last century, the load capacity and dimensions of the cargo compartments of aircraft have greatly increased. The transportation of single pieces of cargo weighing 100 tonnes is no longer uncommon. In fact, the heaviest load ever transported by air is a turbine weighing 187 tonnes, which includes the weight of the load distribution frame and part of the special loading equipment. This particular transportation was carried out by the airline Antonov Airlines using the An-225 Mriya cargo aircraft from Frankfurt–Hahn Airport to Yerevan Airport in August 2009. Such remarkable capabilities of modern aircraft have enabled the development of the global market for the air carriage of oversized, super-heavy or unique cargoes.

Before talking about the logistics process, it is necessary to understand which cargoes are considered to be oversized and super-heavy shipments, henceforth to be referred to in this text as "unique." We assume pieces of cargo to be unique goods if they satisfy one or more conditions:

- Cargo whose transportation is not possible without the development and use of specialist engineering and design solutions;
- Cargo that requires loading and unloading to and from aircraft with the use of non-standard ground and aircraft loading equipment;
- The transportation of cargo requiring special preparation of the aircraft and training for the flight crew.

Usually, the transport of such cargo on the roads requires special permission from the police or other public authorities.

For example, a steam turbine rotor on a transport frame weighing up to 20 tonnes is not considered unique cargo in the case of the An-124 freighter aircraft, as it can be loaded using the standard onboard loading equipment. In this particular case, this would be achieved by simply using the onboard loading cranes. If the transportation is undertaken using the IL-76 aircraft, the shipment is considered unique because the load capacity of the onboard loading cranes is not sufficient to carry out the loading without the use of special ground loading equipment. In the case of an increase in weight up to 30 tonnes or more, this cargo will be considered unique for both the An-124 and IL-76. As a rule, the transport of industrial rotors, for example, requires a special transport frame that satisfies the requirements of air transportation. In general, this frame must be designed and constructed to ensure safe transportation.

Here are some examples of cargo classified as unique:

- A high-pressure gas column 17.36 m in length, 4.64 m in width, 4.14 m in height and weighing 63,400 kg;
- A special container with a satellite 11.2 m in length, 4.1 m in width and 4.2 m in height;
- A hydroelectric turbine impeller 6.25 m in diameter and 3.51 m in height weighing 97,600 kg.
- A rectifying column 38.4 m in length, 3.72 m in diameter and weighing 70 T

Other examples of such cargos include the aircraft fuselage of a C-130 Hercules, the Atlas family rocket carriers, marine diesel engines, metro train more than 30 m in length and there are so many other such examples. All of these goods were transported by plane at some time. However, the air transportation of oversized and super-heavy (unique) cargo in itself is only one part of the complex process of the delivery of cargo from door-to-door. Therefore, the logistics of the transportation of such cargo must be considered in its entirety, as a continuous chain of different interrelated processes.

The timely and high quality performance of complex transport operations or projects is possible only when each stage is executed on-time and with a satisfactory level of quality. At the same time, a failure at any point in the chain may cause the failure of the entire operation, or even lead to the complete loss of valuable cargo.

In terms of transport logistics for the air transportation of unique cargo, there are two main areas which can be identified:

1   The provision within the corporate technological supply chain to maintain mass production processes;
2   One-off transportation and implementation of projects for different branches of industry.

Let us consider two of these areas in more detail. In the first case, the technological development process initially envisages the use of air transport for the delivery of oversized loads from one industrial enterprise to another, within the terms of corporate and international cooperation. For this purpose, special planes are designed and upgraded, in small numbers. The dimensions of the cargo compartments and functionality of such aircraft, as well as ground-based infrastructure, are created for certain types of already familiar cargoes. Such examples are the organization of logistics needed to support the production of the Airbus family of aircraft and the Boeing 787. In its internal corporate and technological chain, Airbus uses aircraft of the type A-300–600ST Beluga, which has been specially designed for the transportation of oversized but relatively light cargo. Transportation is carried out between Toulouse, Hamburg and nine other European cities. Thus, the various large parts of the aircraft, which are manufactured in different factories of the corporation, are delivered to the place of final assembly. The cargo compartment of the A-300–600ST Beluga aircraft has a diameter of 7.4 m (24 feet) and a length of 37.7 m (124 feet). The maximum load capacity is 47 tonnes, and the maximum take-off weight is 155 tonnes.

The production of the various components of the Boeing 787 Dreamliner aeroplane has an even wider geography than that of the Airbus. The wing sections are manufactured in Japan, the fuselage sections in the south of Italy, and the final assembly is done in Seattle in the United States. In order to ensure the organization of uninterrupted assembly to tight production schedules, Boeing has designed and built four specialized Dreamlifter aircraft. The dimensions of the cargo compartment of this aircraft allow any fuselage sections, tail elements and two wing sections to be placed **"edgewise" (longitudinally with the chord section vertical)** inside it. Years of experience have demonstrated the success of the use of such air logistics for the organization of uninterrupted production processes. However, the use of the aircraft for projects and charter services outside the processing chain is difficult or even impossible for the following reasons:

1   The fleet of specialized planes is usually busy fulfilling internal corporate needs;
2   In most cases, the use of the aircraft Beluga, and in all cases, the use of the Dreamlifter aircraft require special ground infrastructure; special loading

devices and a tractor to support the tail lifting operation (in the case of the Dreamlifter). And this infrastructure is available only at the airports where the aircraft are operating.

The Airbus Transport International Company (ATI), the operator of the Beluga aircraft, has in the past provided transportation for some third-party clients. Such operations are completely impossible using the Dreamlifter as the FAA Certificate restricts the use of the aircraft to the transport of strictly defined types of cargo.

In aviation logistics, for the transportation of unique goods to a wide range of customers, it is mainly ramp-loading planes that are currently used, namely the An-124-100 (Ruslan), An-225 (Mriya) and IL-76. In recent years, the Boeing 747F aircraft has been increasingly used to carry super-heavy and oversized cargo too. However, their use for this purpose is significantly limited by the size of their cargo doors, low strength of the cargo floor in comparison with ramp aircraft, the insufficient numbers of mooring devices for these purposes and the load-carrying capacity of airport cargo loading devices.

The An-124-100 (Ruslan) has the following main freight characteristics.

Inner Dimensions of the Cargo Compartment

- maximum height   4.40 m
- the length with the front and rear ramp   43.45 m
- length of the loading floor without the ramps   36.48 m
- maximum width   6.68 m
- width of the floor   6.40 m
- size of the front and rear cargo doors   6.4 × 4.4 m
- maximum load capacity   120 tonnes

The An-225 (Mriya) airplane has an identical cargo compartment and front cargo door size to the An-124-100 but there is no rear cargo door on this aircraft. The length of the cargo compartment is 43 m and the load capacity is 250 tonnes. The maximum weight of it can carry, in terms of a single piece of cargo, is 200 tonnes.

At present, these two types of aircraft determine the capabilities of air transport logistics for oversized and super-heavy cargo and define the leading role of the companies exploiting them in the global air transportation market. In recent years, there has also been growth in unique transportation carried out by IL-76 aircraft. This aircraft has the following characteristics:

- size of cargo door 3.45 × 3.40 m
- length of cargo hold with ramp 20 m
- maximum load capacity 45 tonnes

The IL-76 aircraft is equipped with onboard trolley hoists capable of loading packages weighing up to 12 tonnes.

As mentioned previously, however, while the aviation component of the complete logistics process to transport unique cargo is the most impressive, expensive and complicated part of the delivery of cargo from door-to-door, it couldn't exist without the other preliminary stages and the existence of the complete logistical chain. Let's briefly consider the essential components of this system:

1 **Planning of transportation or project.** Sensible optimum planning of transport and logistics operations is the key to its successful implementation. At this stage, the possibility of air transport is assessed, the most appropriate type of aircraft for the transportation is chosen, the most convenient routes and airports of departure and arrival are chosen and the contractors are determined. For instant the nearest airport to the place of originating cargo or the nearest airport of the final destination suitable for air operation not necessary would be the obvious option. In some occasions we cannot use them just because for delivery of heavy or outside cargo by roads is impossible due to some bridges, flyovers or roads limitations.

2 **Technical development and preparation of cargo for transportation.** In practice, oversized and heavy cargo can rarely be transported by air without additional preparation. Despite the fact that the leading players in this niche market of air transportation, such as the Russian Volga-Dnepr Airlines and Ukrainian Antonov Airlines, have a diverse fleet of special transport devices and equipment, in many cases, additional packaging and transport devices must be developed and produced for unique cargo. For example, the An-124, An-225 and the IL-76 cargo floor can take up to 9.6 tonnes per linear metre of the cargo compartment. Let's suppose for the sake of simplicity that you want to transport a weight of 96 tonnes. In this case, the main weight of the load on the cargo floor should be evenly distributed on a length of no less than 10 m.

It is clear that cargo is not always able to satisfy this condition. Therefore, it is necessary to design and manufacture transport platforms for transportation which evenly distribute the load. Another common problem is the presence of cargo mooring points. At the technical development stage, engineering solutions are developed and produced, strength calculations are made and the conditions of transportation are agreed upon with the manufacturers of the transport equipment. It is necessary to consider not only the aviation requirements but also the requirements of other types of transport that will be used for the delivery of the cargo to the airport of departure and from the airport of arrival, up to the final destination.

3 **Ground delivery before and after air transportation.** The ground delivery of unique cargo is a highly specialized matter. For such a

delivery, it is preferable to choose proven transport companies with experience in carrying out such work. Particular attention should be paid to checking company licenses and insurance coverage. In the majority of cases, the delivery is done by road. In the preparation stage, the delivery of the cargo is worked out, transport routes are checked and permission to transport is obtained. Usually, such permits are issued by special police departments. When planning, it is essential to consider the time necessary for the issuing of permits. They can vary considerably from country to country. For example, in France the process of registration of a road permit should be given at least a month.

4 **Airport and terminal services.** When choosing the airport of departure, it is necessary to determine the possibility of delivery to the parking area of the intended aircraft where loading will be carried out, the suitability of the access road for the movement of the trailer with a heavy load, and the width of the entrance gate on route to the platform. It is necessary to check with the handling companies in advance regarding the time periods for obtaining permits for drivers and personnel involved in the loading process, and the aviation security requirements for persons who may be admitted onto the territory of the airport. Be sure to identify and provide the required documents within the necessary timescale. Particularly strict requirements exist in some Middle Eastern countries, for example. To move the cargo from the trailer to the extension ramp will require one or two cranes. Not all airports allow cranes to work on their territory. There may also be restrictions on the height of the boom used for the loading cranes. Particular attention should be paid to compatibility with aviation safety issues. Oversized cargo, in most cases, cannot pass the scanning procedure. Therefore, special aviation security procedures need to be applied to such loads. These procedures must be agreed upon with the relevant departments of the airport. In some cases, due to the impossibility of agreement with the airport authorities concerning conditions, it is necessary to change the departure or destination airport, which causes significant difficulties in the execution of the transportation process. A change of airport for any reason will result in the need to verify a new road route and obtain new permits for transportation. Therefore, the process of assessing the possibility of using an airport should start as soon as possible, particularly in cases where this airport has previously not been used for such traffic.

5 **Cargo Insurance.** Usually, unique cargo consists of engineering products, special containers with space technology, aircraft equipment and its components. It is obvious that such goods are extremely valuable. Often in these cases, standard insurance coverage is inadequate to cover any possible damage. Therefore, during the preparation phase, it is essential to agree with the insurance company and the client the value and conditions of insurance. In this matter, unambiguous and absolute clarity must be reached. It is clear that additional insurance coverage will increase the

size of the insurance premium. This should be considered when calculating transportation costs.

6 **Loading and unloading operations.** A variety of methods can be used for the loading of unique packages into an aircraft, with numerous types of special loading equipment. Let's consider the most common method of loading oversized and heavy loads into an An-124-100 aircraft. The airlines which offer unique transportation operating this type of aircraft have special loading equipment at their disposal. Whilst there are certain differences, this equipment has a common principle. Loading is carried out through the front cargo door (An-124-100 and An-225). At the same time, the plane "squats down" on the front landing gear, while the cargo floor is lowered into a 2.5°–3° position relatively to the tarmac surface. The front loading ramp is fixed onto the corner of the cargo floor by means of special supports. In front of the ramp, the extension ramp joins to the doorstep with the same slope. On the floor of the cargo compartment and front ramp, skate load-carriers or roller beams are fitted. The cargo is moved from the trailer with one or two mobile cranes to the extension ramp and loaded into the aircraft on the load-carriers or roller frames using onboard loading winches. When ordering cranes, it is essential to send a drawing to the crane company showing the centre of mass of the cargo and location of rigging components. This is necessary in order to develop a lifting and cargo handling plan. It is preferable to use two mobile cranes because this allows the cargo to be lowered onto the extension ramp at an angle parallel to the surface of the load bearing rolling elements or loading platform. To ensure the safety of the transportation operation, the total load capacity of the cranes should be no less than triple the weight of the transported cargo. It is preferable to have cranes of equal load capacities. The unloading of cargo is carried out using the reverse sequence with the same equipment. In some cases, the technology of loading and unloading directly from the trailer without the use of cranes can be undertaken at the airport. However, this method requires the use of special hydraulic trailers with adjustable height and angle, and extra loading equipment. Therefore, this technology is only feasible (or reasonable) for a programme with a multitude of flights between two airports. For example, such a programme was carried out by the airline Volga-Dnepr in Papua New Guinea.

7 **Airfreight Services.** When the cargo is painstakingly planned and prepared, air transportation takes place safely. During transportation, the cargo is held on either skate beams, roller platforms or intermediary platforms. Therefore, the airlines pay special attention to securing cargo. Mooring to the aforementioned ramp aircraft is calculated from the acceleration rate of 2.3 g forward, 1.5 g backward, right and left and 2.0 g upwards. In some cases, airlines reduce the weight of the aircraft by unloading easily removable equipment which is not required for that particular transport operation, and run special additional training

for flight crews performing unique tasks. Often, in order to undertake the transportation, it is necessary to obtain special permission from the design office to exceed the operating limits of the aircraft.

Given the complexity of the organization and execution of unique transport operations, the Volga-Dnepr Group of companies offers its customers transportation from door-to-door, including the engineering and design development and production of special transport devices and appliances. The advantage of this approach for the customer is the "one-stop shop" solution, elimination of the need to spread responsibility and, more importantly, reducing the cost of the implementation of air transportation and logistics projects.

A good example of the implementation of a large transport logistics project using aviation as the key carrier is the project to deliver gas extraction equipment in Papua New Guinea. The air transportation was performed by Volga-Dnepr Airlines from May to August 2013. In Papua New Guinea, industrial deposits of natural gas had been found. The discovery of the gas deposits had taken place some time ago, but the development was considered to be impossible because of the difficulties in delivering equipment for extraction and primary processing of gas into the high mountain areas where the potential deposits were located. The narrow, winding mountain roads, subject to yearly erosion, weak bridges, landslides, and other difficulties, made it impossible for the delivery of bulky and heavy equipment to the high mountain region. Therefore, the management of the gas extraction company took the extraordinarily courageous decision to organize the delivery of the equipment by air. The only type of aircraft capable of coping with this task was the An-124-100. The difficulty lay in the fact that it was necessary to build a completely new airfield in the mountains to achieve this goal. In 2008, on the advice of the flight personnel of Volga-Dnepr Airlines, the best place for the construction of the airfield was chosen. The design and construction of the airfield were worked on at the same time as the development and planning of the execution of the project. The manufacturers of equipment were located in different regions of the world: Korea, the United States, Italy, Australia, Malaysia, and Singapore. After comparing numerous options, the most suitable plan was chosen. All equipment by sea had to be delivered to Port Moresby, transported to the airport of this city, and then delivered to the newly built Komo airfield by an An-124 aircraft. In 2013, the construction of the airfield with its 3,500 m long and 45 m wide runway was completed. At the design and manufacturing of equipment stage, the transport components had already been taken into account. The conditions at Port Moresby Airport impose a weight restriction of 70 tonnes so no piece of cargo can exceed a weight of 70 tonnes nor have excessive loading dimensions. This work was carried out in close cooperation between the manufacturers of the cargo and the global freight forwarding company Deugro, with Volga-Dnepr providing continuous consultation and support. The aviation part of the project started in May 2013. The ground delivery was provided by Deugro International Spedition GmbH, and the air logistics by Volga-Dnepr Airlines. The order of delivery of the goods was synchronized precisely with the construction technology. For loading and unloading, the craneless loading method was used. To do this, Goldhofer hydraulic multi-sectional trailers were delivered to Port Moresby and Komo. The application of such a method of loading and unloading made it possible to make one flight per day in daylight, which is important for the security of flights in mountainous terrain. From 3 May to August 13 2013, 88 transport flights were made. Each flight had at least one consignment classed as unique cargo. During the implementation of this project, 5,877,877 kg of cargo was transported. It proved possible to minimize the number of flights, at the same time achieving the maximum possible load by utilizing the maximum cargo compartment volume on almost every flight. The average load on a flight was 71,449 kg, including an average of 6,500 kg of special loading equipment. The efficient implementation of this complex logistics project has allowed gas companies to extract deposits strictly according to schedule. In conclusion, we can say that the aviation logistics aspect of the transportation of oversized and super-heavy cargo is very harmoniously blended with the global processes of the world economy. In many cases, the use of air transport is economically profitable, because it reduces the implementation time of industrial projects. In some other cases, air logistics is the only possible solution for the delivery of certain large and heavy loads.

The SALIS Project

Ruslan SALIS GmbH is a 50–50 joint venture set up by Volga-Dnepr Group (Russia) and Antonov Design Bureau (Ukraine) in 2004 specifically to support the Strategic Airlift Interim Solution (SALIS) project in which member countries of NATO have pooled their resources to charter special aircraft that give the alliance the capability to transport heavy equipment across the globe by air.

The countries have committed to using the aircraft for a minimum of 2,000 flying hours each year and the capability can be utilized in times of urgent strategic or humanitarian need to provide NATO with the outsize and heavy-lift cargo lift it needs as an interim solution to meet shortfalls in its strategic airlift capabilities, pending the first deliveries of the Airbus A400M aircraft.

Under the terms of the agreement two AN-124-100s are constantly based on full-time charter for SALIS at Leipzig/Halle International Airport in Germany, but in case of necessity two more aircraft are to be provided on 6 days' notice and another 2 on 9 days' notice.

NATO has used the Antonov fleet to support its mission in Afghanistan with weekly flights, to deliver aid to the victims of the October 2005 earthquake in Pakistan and to airlift African Union peacekeepers in and out of Darfur.

Other than the AN-124, the next largest aircraft available for heavy-lift project work is the IL-76, a ramp-loading 40-tonne payload freighter that has become known as one of the most efficient aircraft when required to operate into and out of airports with undeveloped or underdeveloped infrastructure.

Since 2000, however, the use of the original IL-76 fleet has been seriously restricted by the introduction of a number of strict rules introduced by the ICAO.

Under ICAO's restrictions, numerous Russian-manufactured aircraft equipped with engines that did not meet the new international noise and emission standards were denied the right to operate in the world's largest airports.

Volga-Dnepr Group has been involved in the IL-76TD upgrading pro-gramme since 2002, which includes outfitting the aircraft with PS-90A-76 engines and modern avionics that meet the new international noise regula-tions and safety considerations. The IL-76TD-90VD aircraft has already been to all the countries from where the IL-76 was prohibited.

The transportation costs are estimated at half those of using the Hercules, the only immediate rival of the IL-76TD.

With market research showing a future demand for 15–20 aircraft of this type by 2015, Volga-Dnepr intends to meet the growing demand within a strategy to grow its current fleet of five IL-76TD-90VD aircraft to 15 aircraft in the longer term.

Other Heavy-Lift Aircraft

There is a range of heavy-lift aircraft operating in the lower weight sector of the market, offering specialized lift for heavy pieces of cargo. Many of these aircraft are now very old in commercial aviation terms and many of the mod-ern standard freighters operated by the world's airlines can easily lift heavier items on their main decks.

In November 2011, Emirates SkyCargo, the air freight division of Emirates Airline, set a new record for the heaviest recorded single item ever carried by a Boeing 777 freighter. Weighing in at just under 21.2 tonnes (including packaging), the item – a specialized valve used to seal, control and monitor oil and gas wells – was just short of the aircraft's 21.6-tonne limit.

The AN-26 can carry a 6.5-tonne load and is cheaper to operate than most similar aircraft; however, the Russian-built AN-26 cannot currently obtain traffic rights to fly into certain European countries, such as Germany and Italy.

Although over 900 were built in both military and civilian versions, the 20-tonne payload AN-12 aircraft is banned from operating in EU airspace and a lot of other world regions on the grounds of safety and emissions, severely restricting its use. In terms of configuration, size and capability, the aircraft is similar to the US-built Lockheed C-130 Hercules.

AN-225: the largest aircraft in the skies

Destroyed during the Russian/ Ukraine war 2022

Built in 1988 in order to transport the reusable Russian Buran Space Shuttle from its landing strip back to the launch pad, the original objective of the six-engine AN-225 was almost identical to that of the B747 aircraft specially adapted to piggyback the U.S. Space Shuttle.

Two aircraft were ordered, but only one was ever finished. The AN-225 is the largest commercially used transport aircraft in the world and it can carry ultra-heavy and oversize freight, up to 250 tonnes internally on its main deck or 200 tonnes fastened onto its upper fuselage. Cargo carried on the upper fuselage can be 70 m (230 ft) long.

Owned by Antonov Design Bureau and operated by Ruslan International, the AN-225 is powered by six Lotarev D-18 engines. It has a wingspan of 88.4 m (290 ft) and a main deck capable of holding 1,220 cubic m of cargo.

Based on the AN-124, the AN-225 has fuselage extensions added fore and aft of the wings, which received root extensions to increase the span. Two more Ivchenko Progress D-18T turbofan engines were added to the new wing roots, bringing the total to six, and an increased-capacity landing gear system with 32 wheels was designed, some of which are steerable to turn the aircraft within a 60 m wide runway.

The aircraft's first flight in commercial service departed from Stuttgart, Germany on 3 January 2002, and flew to Thumrait, Oman with 216,000 prepared meals for American military personnel based in the region. This vast number of ready meals was transported on some 375 pallets and weighed 187.5 tonnes.

The AN-225 had become the workhorse of the Antonov Airlines fleet, transporting objects once thought impossible to move by air, such as locomotives and 150-tonne generators. It has become an asset to international relief organizations for its ability to quickly transport huge quantities of emergency supplies during disaster-relief operations.

On 11 August 2009, the heaviest single-piece item ever sent by a commercial air freight service was loaded on the AN-225. At 16.23 m (53.2 ft) long and 4.27 m (14 ft) wide, the consignment – a generator and its loading frame for a gas power plant in Armenia – weighed in at a record 189 tonnes. On 11 June 2010, the AN-225 broke another record when it carried the world's longest piece of air cargo – two new 42-m (137.8 ft) test wind turbine blades from Tianjin in China to Denmark.

Reliable information on the second AN-225 fuselage has always been sketchy, unconfirmed and surrounded in myth and legend, but according to sources the second aircraft is 60%–70% complete, although it would require a large investment to complete construction.

Notable Shipments by Antonov Aircraft

These are some of the most notable shipments delivered by Antonov Airlines:

- An 88-tonne water turbine for the Tashtakumska Hydroelectric Plant from Kharkov to Tashkent;
- Civil engineering vehicles to deal with the consequences of the earthquake in Spitak, Armenia;
- Vehicles and systems for resolving the Persian Gulf crisis (mine clearance bulldozers, mobile electric stations, special mine and oil-clearing boats, humanitarian assistance);
- A 135.2-tonne Siemens generator from Düsseldorf, Germany to Delhi, India, airlifted by the AN-225;
- Nuclear fuel in special containers from Habaniya, Iraq to Yekaterinburg (Russia) under the United Nations programme for disarmament of Iraq;
- A 102-tonne locomotive from London, Canada to Dublin, Ireland;
- A 70-tonne generator to Lahore, Pakistan from Doncaster Robin Hood, UK for power station needs;
- A 187.6-tonne power plant generator from Frankfurt-Hahn Airport, Germany to Yerevan (listed in the Guinness Book of Records);
- A 95-tonne Putzmeister.

As of the time of writing, the part of the fleet of AN-124 aircraft remains grounded. After the grounding of the AN-124 fleet, due to the war in Ukraine, five of the remaining AN-124 freighters located outside the country were able to operate based at Leipzig/Halle Airport. Antonov Airlines already had a long standing maintenance facility at this airport. Some of these aircraft have been deployed on humanitarian duties

Coolchain Logistics

Part of Daily Life

The availability of unlimited quantities of fresh produce and medicines from around the world has become an accepted feature of daily life in most developed societies and is taken for granted by the public. In supermarkets and pharmacies throughout affluent economies everywhere, people expect to have access to out of season fruits, such as Mangos, vegetables such as asparagus, roses for Valentine's day and safe medication. Over the last 20 years, the industry has been developed to supply this increasing demand. Maintaining freshness of fruits and flowers and the integrity of pharmaceuticals, have always been a huge challenge for the suppliers, transporters, airports, handlers and distributors. These special supply chains must maintain and secure every link to the same impeccable standards throughout varying levels of temperatures, conditions, facilities and knowledge. The creation of systems and technologies which protect the products has evolved into what is collectively known as the cool chain. The logistics industry describes perishables as being shipments that, due to their nature, will spoil without proper care and handling. This includes, but is not limited to, fresh produce, seafood, floral products, fruits, berries and live tropical fish, medicines, drugs, cosmetics and some electronic elements.

Perishable products account for more than 10% of total shipments by air and are more seasonal than general cargo, making it difficult to calculate capacity needs. Consumers and markets define prices which determine the retail price which in turn impacts on. Due to the nature of most perishable products, there are directional imbalances of air cargo trade in most export markets. The industry has experienced modal shift as new container technology comes on stream, largely driven by costs. Another factor for growers and shippers is the impact of weather, which clearly does not affect the pharma sector. Then there is the problem of claims which can hit the bottom line. Largest perishable trade flows are at geographical proximity – Africa-Europe, South America-U.S. – Intra Asia and for basic perishables it is demographics rather than economics that define growth.

Those of us living in Western societies have, over the last few decades, become used to and indeed take for granted that when we visit a supermarket or a florist or the local pharmacy, that we will easily find and be able to purchase at a comparatively low price, fresh fruit and vegetables flowers and medicines. Do people have any idea as to how these products arrive at the retail counter? It is doubtful, because a massive and complex network of companies and technologies combine together to provide this service at an acceptable price. What is the scope of this cool supply chain?

The sector includes a wide variety of time and temperature-sensitive goods and products which demand different but strict regimes of temperature co, in order to maintain integrity and value. In the edible category it includes fresh fruit and vegetables from all over the world, such as asparagus, mangoes, melons, cherries, pineapples, lemons and limes, kiwifruit, avocados, Pak Choi and many more, seafood: live lobster and crab, prawns, shrimp, many varieties of and meats.

The non-edible sector includes flowers from tropical lilies, roses, tulips and carnations to Aloe VERA, Salvia, Anthurium and Ficus class plants and decorative trees and shrubs.

The medical sector demands an even greater detailed temperature control which varies, depending on the particular product. Medicines and vaccines, body parts and plasma, as well as samples, tests and experiments.

All these products, from their source or laboratory or a field to the customer, have one thing in common – they must be kept at a constant correct and specific temperature throughout a rapid journey and to make matters more complicated, different products require different temperatures. Any break in this temperature chain can cause damage to the product and in the case of sensitive vaccines, can render them not only useless but also potentially lethal. In the case of pharmaceuticals, from the moment that they are created in the laboratory until they are in use, they must be kept within this temperature bubble. All transport modes have concentrated on validating systems and methods to fulfil these temperature demands. In countries with unreliable or no electricity supply, or with transport difficulties, the challenge to provide temperature-controlled vaccines and medicines is formidable. Various solutions such as the use of drones are in full development but with products such as vaccines which demand extremely low temperature control, the industry is working hard to find viable technology.

The industry works continuously towards creating a better cool chain, possibly making the lives of millions of people better and more sustainable. During the COVID-19 pandemic, much of the normal belly-hold capacity became unavailable due to the severe restrictions on flying. The global shortage of dedicated freighter aircraft resulted in the adoption and temporary conversion of many passenger aircraft into freighters, especially for light cargo which can be loaded onto seats and floors. This practice was largely terminated in April 2022.

The cool chain is served with special facilities- refrigerated trucks, airport warehouses with cool rooms, insulated temperature-controlled ULD containers and various other specialized equipment like "cool dollies," used to move shipments between the cargo warehouse. We also consider the aircraft Temperature-controlled containers, electronic & control systems, equipment, electronic communications developed for cool chain operations.

Since 2000, general awareness of the importance of perishables and especially pharmaceuticals has grown within the air cargo industry. The COOL CHAIN ASSOCIATION (CCA) was founded in 2003 in an attempt to establish standards and a regulatory base for the handling of perishables of all kinds. Over the last two decades, the association has made an impact on the air cargo supply chain creating the Cool Chain Quality Indicators (CCQI), standards and processes for temperature-sensitive goods. The CCA is collaborating with the stakeholders in the air cargo supply chain and standardization for the transport of pharmaceuticals. The need for performance indicators has been implemented by IATA with the creation of the validation standard CEIV, which has become the industry standard for handlers, airports and carriers including RFSs.

Clearly the technology has evolved over the years, but unfortunately there is still some reluctance, among different stakeholders of the air cargo supply chain, to share information, transparency and visibility. As customers become more demanding for faster deliveries and lower costs, so the competition is becoming fiercer. Technology plays an increasingly important role in this trade. Over the last 15 years the use of active temperature-controlled containers has advanced substantially. These containers are expensive to operate and the very much used for high value goods especially pharmaceuticals. Although products such as fresh flowers, fruit, fish and dairy also require controlled temperature handling, they rely on fast transfer with as little as possible exposure to climatic pressures, heat. Handling and delivery warehousing and trucks require controlled temperatures facilities.

In sea freight, due to the much longer transit times, the use of active temperature containers is much more common than with air freight. In the maritime supply chain, there is therefore also much less handover to different agencies than with air freight, making the probability of temperature disruptions less common. Through the development of new technology, active temperature control has improved which has resulted even in a modal shift of cool chain products from air to sea during the last few years. However, due to severe disruption during the COVID-19 pandemic, there have been shortages of sea containers, plus severe congestion at many ports around the world. Such delays clearly pose a threat to the integrity of any perishable cargo with resulting price increases. This has resulted in a rebalance in the price differential with air transport and thus airfreight once again becomes the viable mode. In addition, customers look seriously at the reliability of sea freight with its delays, losses at sea, often caused by bad weather and incidents such as the blocking of the Suez canal which caused huge amounts of global cargo disruption over several months.

Common Need

Obviously, price and speed of transit are amongst the main selection criteria between air and sea, but previously, reliability has been better with sea, mainly due to the unbroken chain of containerization. However, since the outbreak of the COVID-19 pandemic, the impact on ocean freight has been considerable. The shortage of perishable equipped containers, the number of ships delayed at ports for unloading and the recent series canal blockage have made life very difficult for perishable shippers and the rising prices have pushed many suppliers back to airfreight. If something goes wrong with the sea transport it involves much larger quantities of potential waste than with air transport.

In practice, the needs of the pharma and perishable business are very similar. Both product types need to be shipped within a limited time frame otherwise the value will be lost, or lives may be at risk. Both groups need temperature control and special handling. The need for transparency is fundamental for both sea and air.

However regulatory control is much more present in the transport of pharma compared to perishable goods. This clear regulatory framework encourages pharma-related investments by logistics service providers.

Normally the cost of logistics, is a much lower proportion for pharma than for perishables, thanks to relatively high value for pharma coupled with low weight. Therefore, airlines and forwarders seek pharma traffic even though the total volumes of other perishables shipped by air is up to 7% higher.

It has been estimated that by 2050 the world's population will reach more than 9 billion. In practical terms, this means producing over 70% more food than now, less if the waste problem can be solved. This is covered later in this chapter. Advances in technology may well allow the production of different types of agricultural solutions but, there will still be a need to grow plants and certain fruits and flowers the natural way in different climates. Artificially heated greenhouses use a great deal of energy and create pollution. There is also the fact that millions of people in developing countries depend on agriculture for their livelihoods. In addition, severe changes in climate including drought, flooding and violent storms, are on the increase and we are warned time is running out to deal with the climate crisis. All these factors have implications for the production and delivery of the world's food needs.

Food Waste

According to the UN (FAO), about 30% of our food is wasted that is an amazing billion tonnes plus every year. Consider that equally, the corresponding amount of resources, energy and transport are also wasted, much of this ends up in landfills and creates even more CO_2 emissions. Why the waste? One of the major causes is overlarge content created by supermarkets plus zealous encouragement to discard by "use by" dates and health warnings. People are thus reluctant to keep or use the remainder in the pack. Agricultural activity accounts for approximately 14% of all global CO_2 emissions. Were the wastage to be removed, it would result in a substantial reduction in total global emissions as well as wasted land use and resources. Consider the amount of agricultural land that is created from forests and natural environments such as the rain forests of the Amazon basin or in Indonesia for cattle production or crop cultivation which cause severe damage to the climate The inevitable loss of animal and plant species follows, Clearly by limiting food loss and the improvement of the supply chain will lead to less global starvation, improved health and economic growth.

Serialization

The air logistics supply chain is vital for the pharma delivery and any form of interruption within the transport process may have disastrous results.

Serialization and labelling systems for makers of pharmaceuticals go some way to combat the burgeoning international market for counterfeit and illegal products. The European Union has brought in the initiative to combat dangerous counterfeiting of medical products, but this illegal and hugely profitable trade is increasing.

In order to protect the customer and the integrity of a medication, a unique serial number m assigned. This is linked to the individual production data–product identification, expiry date and batch, this takes the form of a data MATRIX code. The individual branding throughout the pharmaceutical industry in conjunction with sealed label on the packaging, ensures the authenticity and integrity are a particular drug. Traceability is an essential to safe and absolutely confident in the industry. Using this method, counterfeit drugs can be more easily identified. However, thanks to the increasing habit of online purchasing of almost anything, it is easy for fake products at low prices to seize the online market.

Measures for improving safety include

- Real-time monitoring solutions
- The application of technology such as wireless cloud monitoring solutions to improve product quality and compliance
- Data management, automated data assessment and release process
- Break down monitoring processes for time critical shipments
- In-storage monitoring
- Tracking solutions for special containers using cryogenics and dry ice.
- Reduce risk of false alarms and loss of product considerations.

Products require specific packaging. Today's customers require precise processes and innovative tools capable of moving their shipments in strict temperature ranges. This process is the "cold chain," and includes vaccines, biological samples and biologics, drugs with active pharmaceutical ingredients and other products with a strict timeline, including drugs intended for emergency therapy or those with low stability and temperature excursion tolerance.

A number of factors may threaten the successful final delivery of these precious products, often outside the control of the agencies involved. Factors such as bad weather, strike action, civil unrest, lack of transport capacity, delays at Customs and many more can result in unplanned temperature excursions and will finally affect the health of the patient.

Customers' trust in the complete integrity of a medication or treatment is supreme with the entire cool chain process included. The industry continues to work tirelessly to find new and better ways of protecting these highly sensitive and vital products of our modern society. The pharma industry's resilience and adaptability have been put to the most drastic test during the COVID-19 pandemic.

The Pandemic Impact

As in nearly aspects of daily life, the COVID-19 pandemic has had a massive impact on the entire perishables business. From exotic flowers to live lobsters from insulin to vaccines, fast transport has been a major challenge (Figure 7.7).

Logistics and transportation services working for the healthcare and pharmaceutical market have undergone dramatic changes during the COVID-19 pandemic as the pressure expanded. Providing logistics services in this sector has always been a challenge but with the massive drop in transport capacity, the industry has been forced to find innovative ways to respond to demand. The COVID-19 pandemic highlighted imbalances in the global pharmaceutical supply chain. According to Industry Standard Research (ISR), some 65% of the $ trillion pharmaceutical manufacturing business is outsourced. The demands of speed and special handling are mostly met by the air cargo industry which has had to adopt virtually overnight to accommodate this need. Many passenger aircraft were adapted in order to carry PPE and lightweight shipments which enabled deliveries to be maintained.

Prior to these events, the IATA had introduced its pharmaceutical certification – the Centre of Excellence for Independent Validators in Pharmaceutical Logistics (CEIV Pharma) which addresses a global standard for global consistency safety, security, compliance and efficiency. Pharmaceuticals,

Figure 7.7 Child vaccination.

which are temperature and humidity sensitive, require specialist packaging and technology and methods of monitoring any changes in transit. All freight forwarders and airlines that offer pharmaceutical logistics services offer such tracking and monitoring capabilities for all modes of transportation. Prior to the COVID-19 pandemic, ocean freight was considered less expensive than air transport, up for products that are not time sensitive.

Warehousing and Trucking

The Perfect Storm

The same handling standards apply equally in warehouses and airport handling facilities. National Government regulations apply in each country, for example, the U.S. Food and Drug Administration (FDA). These standards apply to warehouses, processes, and to the products themselves. Despite a downward global trend from 2020 to 2021, a step up in the proportion of organized crime, "Internet-enabled" theft, shortage of secure parking and queues and overspill from new Brexit border controls could create "the perfect storm" for European road freight theft in 2022, warns TT Club.

The transport Industry professionals calculated that 2021 was likely to have been the highest on record for global road freight theft, but for lockdown restrictions.

Thorsten Neumann, President and CEO of Transported Asset Protection Association (TAPA) EMEA, commented that it is difficult to give a meaningful comparison with previous years. However, while some criminal operations would have been disrupted by lockdown measures, 2020 still saw the second-highest rate of incidents in TAPA's 24-year history.

Much of this activity could be due to the accumulation risk from a spike in e-commerce cargo, according to TT Club's MD loss prevention, Mike Yarwood.

He also noted that TT Club's figures were down on those of 2020, adding: that at the moment, on the global picture, the frequency of cargo theft looks to have decreased so far this year, over last.

"We are still desperately short of good parking facilities, especially in the UK in Germany and in other places," Yarwood said. "More e-commerce, more consumables, more goods on the move – road transport is by far the most vulnerable mode of transport."

He warned that the shortage of drivers across Europe was likely to facilitate the risk of "insider threat," as companies relax their screening procedures with the hope of hiring more drivers.

> At the moment [companies] aren't blessed with time and choice; there's a shortage of drivers, trucks, and availability and, when you look at the pay conditions, it is not beyond the wit of man to imagine criminals paying drivers to do something they shouldn't.

Meanwhile, as border requirements change in January and again in July, the likelihood is that conditions will improve for petty and opportunistic – as well as organized – criminals.

"It could be the perfect storm," Yarwood said.

> There was a time where a lot of it was opportunistic – but those days are gone. Internet-enabled is the best way of describing it; it's not quite cybercrime, but the data we share and hold via the internet is accessible, and very valuable in the wrong hands. These guys are very organised, they know exactly what is moving and when – they are almost one step ahead.

Stephen Paul Bacot, landrisk manager at Risk Intelligence, agreed the lack of available parking facilities for trucks was a major issue.

"In Mexico, or Brazil – the MO is hijacking," he said. "But in Europe, it is much more common to wait until the truck is parked and the driver is asleep. Cargo at rest is cargo at risk." Despite EU attempts to harden parking facilities, much more work needed to be done, Mr Bacot said.

> They need thousands more spaces – and of course there is cost to using them, which is especially challenging if you're working on a very low profit margin. We see a lot is problems with just-in-time supply chains; the drivers can't be late, so they arrive at 2 am for an 8 am delivery and park in an industrial estate. You find a truck from Europe has been 'turned over' 500 m from the destination.

Long queues in France and the UK would most likely exacerbate the challenge, he said. "Anything that causes trucks to be delayed and parked up in non-secure areas increases the threat," he said. "There are active measures being taken by police in France, but organized criminal gangs are responsive and agile, and if the measures increase at Calais, they will simply move to other ports."

Extract From Loadstar

Traceability

Due to the huge amount of money involved, counterfeiting and theft have become a major health and financial problem, thus traceability and monitoring of pharma shipments are necessary to protect both manufacturers as well as the recipients or end users of the drugs themselves. Improvements in packaging allow individual, secure doses of different medicine to be delivered to the patient.

Distributors

Healthcare distributors link pharmaceutical manufacturers to pharmacies, hospitals, healthcare facilities and other care sites. Similar to freight forwarders, healthcare distributors have found themselves having to reinvent their offerings to remain a viable part of the healthcare supply chain. However, when the COVID-19 pandemic hit in 2020, their value was immense as they worked with their customers to obtain the necessary equipment and supplies

COVID-19 pandemic pushed digital transformation in healthcare organizations. During the pandemic, lack of visibility into healthcare supply chains resulted in delays and mistakes plus, shortages in medical supplies and equipment. Pharmaceutical and healthcare providers have subsequently introduced more transparency.

Artificial intelligence (AI) also has great potential in the healthcare market – to improve the speed and accuracy of diagnosis and screening for diseases, assist with clinical care, strengthen health research and drug development, and support diverse public health interventions, such as disease surveillance, outbreak response and health systems management. It can also empower patients to take greater control of their health care and bridge gaps in access to health services. The World Health Organization (WHO) cautions,

Pharmaceutical Counterfeiting

Pharma products have always been a target for criminals but during the COVID-19 pandemic. The opportunities for counterfeiting increased to an alarming degree.

What has proved to be basic solutions to combat this? The ability of counterfeiters to copy packaging almost perfectly encourages the online sales of "genuine" products at much lower prices to the unsuspecting customer. Apart from the lost revenue to the drug producers, people risk serious health risks and will even blame the failure of the medicine on the drug company from which they believe the product derives., the return on investment (ROI) is very attractive for counterfeiters without the need for quality research and developing active ingredients that are not included in the counterfeit product. Counterfeiters can access the same technologies, including high-level production and scanning technologies as pharma manufacturers. The counterfeiters are often able to get products onto the market quicker than the genuine companies.

During the COVID-19 period of developing vaccines and tests in early 2021, Interpol seized around 34,000 counterfeit and substandard masks, spray, and fraudulent "coronavirus medicine," making huge profits from a global health crisis. The expenditure required to ensure security measures across the supply chain are in place for an organization's product also impacts bottom line results, necessitating strict authentication measures, a very difficult, expensive and also time-consuming process. The down the line result can often manifest itself in negative reputation and brand damage for the genuine company. If, for example, an individual were to experience a severe reaction to a counterfeit medicine or even death, the impact on the real company, its reputation and even share value, would be very damaging especially in such a highly competitive market. Previously pharma manufacturers were willing to tolerate a small amount of counterfeit products but not anymore. By depending on reliable and well tested partners in distribution, much of the risk can be avoided and if litigation is involved, proof of a counterfeit copy drug exists. When transport process is interrupted by lack of capacity or buildup of stocks, shippers may be obliged to store transit goods in untested and reliable warehouse, taking risks that they would not normally take.

Cool Chain Logistics

Within the cool chain logistics sector, competition is always fierce with an element of risk. Because the harvesting of some produce can be irregular or seasonal, market conditions and prices can vary considerably. This means that business planning contains a strong element of unreliability. The margins may be very tight and thus short-term losses can be easily suffered which impacts directly on long term viability. Companies working in these perishable markets, however, know their business well and based on years of experience are able to sustain worthwhile profits. Violent weather events can of course cause rapid loss of product. On the other hand most pharmaceutical products are required and supplied on a more constant and sustainable basis, with less price fluctuation being manufactured and controlled throughout the supply chain to the point of delivery. Pharmaceutical products need to maintain an absolutely constant temperature throughout their complete supply chain cycle, and they are transported in specially developed containers with a constant temperature that can be individually set between −20°C and +20°C.

Perishables Logistics Sectors

The business is broadly divided into the following.

- Food – fruit, vegetables, live fish and shellfish, meat and meat products.
- Fresh flowers and plants
- Medical products, including pharmaceuticals, vaccines, body parts, plasma Breeding products such as bull semen, eggs
- Live insects and mammals
- Some hi tech goods and components

Creating Standards

Although to most people, out of season asparagus, strawberries for Christmas or insulin injections just come from stores or from the supermarket. But, behind the scenes, the logistics industry provides the vital link in the process backed by the necessary management and control systems, refrigerated transport and warehousing which together complete the cool chain. While a large proportion of perishables are moved by sea, air freight is essential for most time-sensitive products.

Back in 2003, the different players working in the perishables sector agreed that there was a pressing need to establish a global structure of industry standards and rules was broadly agreed. From this meeting the Cool Chain Association was created. Now well established it works closely with bodies such as IATA and TIACA in establishing industry standards and criteria and to promote more efficient perishable supply chains.

Since that era, there has been an enormous investment on the part of operators, in an effort to maintain high standards, provide cheaper safer transportation for perishables at low cost while reducing the impact on the environment. Considerable benefits pass to the local growers and their employees in some parts of the developing world from their ability to air freight valuable consignments of perishables to eager consumer markets in more wealthy countries around the globe. Kenya is a good example of this. The flower trade is one of the country's leading sources of foreign revenue, employing some many thousands of workers who are growing, picking, grading and packing cut flowers in a country with high rates of unemployment and few well-paid jobs. Fresh salad crops and green beans are also highly regarded for example, with many European retailers having their own dedicated suppliers in African countries such as Kenya. Similarly, asparagus is a major revenue earner for Peru, with the country having become the world's largest single exporter of the luxury food, bringing in more than US$400 million a year and providing thousands of valuable jobs.

Fresh food now flies every day from countries all around the world to the consumer societies that today regard previously regarded luxury goods as mundane. In many countries there is now no seasonal period when exotic fresh fruit and vegetables are available in the shops – they are there for sale 365 days a year. According to the IATA, airlines have developed very effective and cost-efficient handling techniques to look after chilled and frozen products in transport.

Economics and Social Responsibility

Is an unbroken chain with controlled temperature conditions to ensure the integrity of shipments of fresh fish, cut flowers or dairy products. The continuous upgrading of logistics facilities to handle the movement of vital pharmaceutical products to where they are urgently needed is attracting large investments from the operators. For perishables to travel successfully from their point of origin to the consumer requires the use of specialized equipment, the application of knowledge and expertise, and the implementation of a quality management system that allows the cool chain of any shipment to be analysed, measured, controlled, documented and validated.

Conversely, it is frequently argued that the transport of these goods is extravagant, polluting and depriving local farmers of supplying their own national markets. It is the fact that such production in colder climates is very expensive, largely due to high fuel, heating and labour costs and regrettably creates more emissions. Furthermore, in the developing world, populations depend on this trade for livelihoods and have the climate to grow crops naturally. The ethics and moral arguments are a subject of discussion in the context of the world's need to grow more food and cut down on waste and spoilage by exposure to high temperatures.

The debate has intensified with the increasingly concerns about climate change coupled with food shortages and the effects of the COVID-19 pandemic and the blocking of wheat exports from Ukraine.

Here we indicate some examples of products being transported within the cool chain. The sheer volume of products involved makes it impossible to include all but the significant message is that all grown produce has a very limited shelf life and rapid delivery without damage or spoilage is vital for growers, retailers, carriers and logistics companies. For the pharma business, although it is easier overall to work within a specified temperature environment, strict and accurate cool chain control is essential to guarantee quality.

Flowers

Despite severe worldwide recessions and other social problems which have occurred over the last 20 years, the market for fresh flowers has steadily increased. What could, by some, be classed as a luxury, individual people and companies continue to spend money on flowers and plants. Celebrations such as St. Valentine's and Mother's day more than treble the usual demand. In addition, weddings, funerals and hotel displays ensure the steady stream of flowers. However, the impact of the 2019/20/21 global COVID-19 pandemic impacted heavily on the flower production, transport and delivery and this is a highly complex and cost-conscious market where failure to protect the integrity of the supply chain can result in poor shelf life and retail performance, resulting in heavy losses. In this chapter you will find a snapshot of the international flower and plant logistics market, as every country has its own ways and means of selling these highly delicate and time-sensitive goods (Figure 7.8).

Figure 7.8 Alsmeer flower market.

Latin America

The main Flower exporters in Latin America are Colombia and Ecuador. For both countries, floriculture is a fundamental part of their economy, making it its first non-traditional agricultural export.

Colombia is the leading exporter of Flowers in Latin America. It has about 7,000 hectares of different types, most importantly roses, carnations, and chrysanthemums. The country has been exporting Flowers for over 40 years and its main export crops are located in the vicinity of Bogota, the Ri Negroarea in Antioquia.

According to data of Asocolflores, The Association of Colombian Flower Exporters, about 7,290 hectares of land is spent for flower cultivation in Colombia. Every hectare of flower farm's plantation is 15 people, whose life directly depends on growing and producing fresh flowers. Behind each of them are families with five children on average. Every plantation has from 200 to 1,000 employees. Colombian floriculture industry is almost 100,000 of direct jobs and more than 80,000 of indirect employment, including suppliers and producers of fertilizers, polyethylene, filters, agronomists, chemists, even kindergarten teachers and psychologists.

Ecuador is the second largest flower exporter of this product in the region, with about 4,000 hectares, with 2,500 dedicated to roses. The provinces where floriculture is centred are Pichincha, Cotopaxi, Imbabura and Azuay.

Temperature-controlled transportation and logistics are essential, since these fragile and heat sensitive products require the utmost care and quality control to properly maintain this product and can spoil completely if left unprotected in hot sunshine for just a few moments.

Sector which contributes 25.3% of GDP. 2.63% of the national GDP is from the horticulture sub-sector while 1.29% is from the flower industry. Horticulture is one of the top exports.

The market comprises large, medium and small-scale producers who have attained high management standards and have invested heavily on technical skills, production, logistics and marketing. Farmers utilize high levels of technology, for example, computerized drip irrigation and fertigation systems, computerized greenhouses ventilation systems, net shading, pre-cooling and cold storage facilities, grading and bouqueting, fertilizer recycling systems to prevent wastage, wetlands for waste water treatment, artificial lighting to increase day length, grading/packaging sheds, and refrigerated trucks have been adopted.

It is estimated that over 500,000 people (including over 90,000 flower farm employees) depend on the floriculture industry.

Europe

Although many flowers and plants are flown directly into each European country, a large percentage of flowers and plants are traded through the Aalsmeer Flower Auction (Bloemenveiling Aalsmeer) located in the Netherlands. Flowers and plants are delivered from all over the world for the daily auctions which supply wholesale florists and traders throughout Europe. This is the largest flower auction in the world whose building covers 990,000 m² (10.6 million sq ft; 243 acres). Flowers from all over the world, Europe, Ecuador, Colombia, Ethiopia, Kenya and many more countries are traded daily. Around 20 million flowers are sold each day with a 15% increase around special days such as Valentine's Day and Mother's Day. All flowers are subjected to around 30 checks for grading on a scale (A1, A2 and B). This operates as a Dutch Auction in which the price starts high and works downwards. Bidders get only a few seconds to bid on the flowers.

In 2008 the auction merged with its biggest competitor Royal Flora Holland, a cooperative, connecting growers, buyers and third parties on a digital platform with the unique combinations of ordering, delivery and payment services.

Royal Flora Holland is located in Aalsmeer, Naaldwijk, Rijnsburg, Venlo, Bleiswijk and Eelde. Together, the auction houses are home to the largest flower auction in the world. Well over 20 million flowers and plants are sold at

Royal Flora Holland every day. It is a non-profit organization which is a result of the merger between FloraHolland and Aalsmeer Flower Auction in 2007.

Sadly, During the COVID-19 crisis in 2020, Flora Holland's sales collapsed by over 70% due to the drop in global demand. In March 2020 alone, 400 million flowers had to be destroyed, including 160 million tulips. Prior to the pandemic, annual turnover was 4.5 billion euros and it employed over 3,500 employees with plant and flower sales of around 12.4 billion items per year. There are more than 4,500 members of whom approx. 600 are based abroad. The company has a customer base of around 2,400. This Greenport is, with Schiphol airport and the port of Rotterdam, one of the three economic "mainports" of the Netherlands responsible for some 250,000 direct and indirect jobs.

U.S. Flowers

The demand for cut flowers and plants in America is huge and thanks to air logistics, can be supplied from around the world. Although many flights, especially from Latin America serve major cities directly, the biggest flower market is based in Los Angeles entitled The Los Angeles Flower District. The District offers a "badge program" for member florists, event planners and others who qualify to purchase goods at wholesale prices includes around 4,500 members.

In the 1990s and early 2000s, many flower malls and shops moved to come close to the Los Angeles Flower District and consider themselves to be an integral part of it. The market is open to the public but concentrates on retail florists and wedding and event planners. While California itself supplies many types of flowers and plants, especially sunflowers and Lilies, much of the produce is flown in from Chile – carnations and roses, Colombia, Venezuela and Ecuador – carnations and roses, Costa Rica – chrysanthemums, Mexico – gladiolas, while chrysanthemums and roses are coming from Kenya, the Canary islands, Italy and India, Thailand orchids and South Africa protease and roses.

Some other districts such as South Florida are served by a number of large wholesale florists while in New York City is one of the largest and most diverse flower markets in the United States – the NYC flower district that spans out and around 28th St. at 6th Ave. Like the rest of the wholesale districts in the city, the flower district is comprised of individual wholesalers, each occupying a storefront along parts of 28th St., 6th Avenue, and 29th Street. Many specialize in one type of offering like greens/branches, potted plants, speciality cut flowers from Holland, tropical cut flowers and greens, silk flowers, or dried botanicals, to name a few. In addition there are suppliers that sell speciality floral supplies, everyday floral supplies.

It would be very difficult to operate this vast global industry without the use of air freight logistics.

Figure 7.9 Typical vegetables and fruit exports.

Fruit and Vegetables

Most countries are able to successfully farm and deliver crops to wholesalers, stores and supermarkets within their own national markets. However, despite much un-informed protest about unnecessary emissions caused by air and sea freight, It is often more efficient and cheaper to fly produce to markets. (See chapter Environment). Some produce has become very popular and is thus flown where road transport takes too much time (Figure 7.9).

Asparagus

Asparagus has become the main agricultural high value export by air from Peru, one of the most important producers and exporters of this crop world-wide. While the largest overall producer of Asparagus is China, Peru is the largest and principal exporter of fresh Green Asparagus, surpassing China and European countries. In Peru there are two types of Asparagus: White Aspar-agus, which grows underground and is used mainly for canning, although a small percentage of it is exported fresh, and Green Asparagus, mainly exported fresh by air to different markets. This product is grown in different sizes, the thickest being preferred by European markets, while the medium and thin sized is primarily exported to North America.

Peru's main target markets for the export of Green Asparagus are the United States (64%), Spain (11%), the Netherlands (8%) and England (8%). Other markets such as Australia and Asia have important seasonal demands.

Year Round Production

Peru has a significant competitive advantages compared to other exporting countries, since it has a uniquely favourable climate and geographical location producing high yields. The majority of crops are grown along the coast, especially in the regions of Ica, Lima, Ancash and La Libertad. This dispersion of productive zones allows year-round production, which becomes providing a significant advantage over other exporters of Asparagus.

Fish and Live Seafood

World sales of edible fresh fish and seafood are affected by several factors.

Over-Fishing

Availability of fish is impacted by over-fishing which has seen customers seeking further and further away to try to locate less fished areas. If trawlers continue to take smaller fish, often to convert them to fertilizer or animal feed, eventually the marine food chain will collapse. Fish farming is one solution and in countries such as Norway, farmed salmon is a huge export commodity. Altogether, Norway is the world's biggest fish farmer and accounts for about 50% of the global salmon trade, well ahead of world number two, Chile. The sector exports nearly $1 billion of seafood each month, including about a tenth of its salmon produce previously to Russia, which consumes nearly 7% of global salmon production.

Transport Costs

Long distance deliveries by air have been badly affected by the rise in oil prices. A good example is Spain which traditionally is the second biggest consumer nation for fresh fish especially hake, (merluza) a special favourite in Spain, was imported into Vitoria in Alava, northern Spain from South Africa and Chile, with lobsters from Canada. Two events, recession and high costs hit a weakening demand resulting in a drastic reduction to this trade.

Imported Seafood Products

China is the largest producer of seafood products in the world, and Japan and the United States are the largest importers of seafood products. Over three-quarters of the seafood consumed in the United States valued at several $billion is imported from other countries. Shrimp is the most important imported seafood product, Thailand was the leading U.S. supplier of shrimp followed by Ecuador, Indonesia, China, Vietnam and Mexico. Tuna was the second most important imported product, and an almost equal amount of canned tuna and fresh and frozen. Major suppliers of canned tuna are Thailand, Philippines, Indonesia, Vietnam and Ecuador. Freshwater fish fillets ranked third in volume for all seafood products imported into the United States. A major part of this product category is the Vietnamese fish species, called pangasius, basa or swai in U.S. markets. Other important products in order by volume imported include salmon from Norway, Canada, and Chile; ground fish species like cod, haddock, pollock and hake from Canada and Northern Europe, crabs and crabmeat from Southeast Asia, frozen fish blocks used to make fish portions and sticks from China, Russia, Canada and Iceland.

Live Lobsters

For successful live lobster transport certain key criteria are essential

*   Correct temperature,
*   Limited time in transit
*   Correct packaging and handling (Figure 7.10).

Lobsters are poikilotherms, taking on the varied body temperatures of their changing environment, and their metabolism is governed by body temperature. Low temperature maintains slow metabolism, which is key to a lobster being able to survive out of water for extended periods. High temperatures increase metabolism and therefore oxygen demand that cannot be met by their inefficient, aquatic gills while out of water. Although lobsters can be found in aquatic habitats in which the water temperature ranges from just above freezing to as high as 25°C, out of water temperatures above 5°C reduce their survival time to below 24 hours

With ideal temperature conditions, lobsters can be shipped out of water for up to 48 hours with little to no mortality. Beyond 48 hours, post-shipment mortality will occur, with the degree of mortality increasing exponentially with each additional hour out of water. This 48 hours shipment time is why airfreight is necessary to allow live lobsters to reach international destinations while maintaining their premium quality and strength. However, since cold chain logistics within and between airlines is inconsistent, lobsters must be packed in heavily insulated shipping boxes with self-contained frozen gel ice packs to maintain the ideal 3–5°C temperature inside the box during air shipment. Ice pack quantity is adjusted seasonally and by destination due

Figure 7.10 Live lobster.

to air temperatures >30°C that have been measured even during the Canadian portion of airfreight consignments in some cases. Significant cost is put into highly insulated, non-recyclable extruded polystyrene materials such as Styrofoam as well as gel ice packs that can comprise as much as 22% of the shipped box weight, adding significant shipment costs and inefficiencies. This system contrasts severely with ground transportation that has much better cold chain logistics solutions with little breaks in the cold chain parameters for the duration of the consignment. However, ground transportation is too slow and therefore only feasible for domestic, local shipments.

Product handling has a significant effect on the success of a live lobster shipment. Lobsters that are packed for air travel and left in a cooler on a shelf undisturbed can live for up to 120 hours without mortality. However, lobsters are sensitive to movements and forces that they do not normally experience while living in the aquatic world in which buoyancy negates any gravitational forces that are experienced while out of water. The forces of rough handling of a box of packed lobsters and vibrations from constant movement or jostling during transport cause the lobster's metabolism to increase above normal levels and shorten their survival time out of water. These delicate and valuable fish require viewer careful and gentle handling on the ground and on their long journeys in order to justify their high value and sought-after freshness.

Pharmaceuticals

This is the biggest and most profitable single sector in the growing cool chain market and the most temperature sensitive. The well-being of many millions depends on access to vaccine, insulin, blood plasma and other temperature-sensitive healthcare products. In the words of Sebastian Scholte, ex-Chairman of the Cool Chain Association. "There is a desperate need for standardization in handling pharmaceutical and healthcare products. Poor communication and training, skill deficiency plus cost pressures are affecting the quality of service."

The global pharmaceutical industry –or pharma business – is expected to be worth over US$1.1 trillion. One of the most effective ways to maintain the cool chain of goods in transit by air is to use the active temperature-controlled ULDs. Healthcare companies and regulatory authorities increasingly demand extremely high standards from their forwarders to properly handle their products, so that when they reach the patient they are just as medically effective and safe to use as when they left the production line. Some biotechnology and pharmaceutical products are potentially hazardous, so the shipper, forwarder, trucker, warehouse operator, cargo ground handler and air carriage provider must all ensure they are properly identified, packaged and handled, and that the special documentation required is correct and in good order.

The global pharmaceutical industry or "pharma" is estimated to be with many branded products passing out of patent protection resulting in the manufacture of generic versions. This new commercial market will drive expansion in the pharma cool chain business. The well-being of many depends on access to vaccine, insulin, blood plasma and other temperature-sensitive healthcare products. This has given rise to a burgeoning and image-conscious sector with a need to get goods to the marketplace on time, at an attractive price and ahead of the competition.

But apart from the need for fast distribution, the pharma products must mostly be kept at a constant temperature throughout their complete supply chain. A range of specially designed containers have been developed within which a constant temperature can be individually set between −20°C and +20°C. The ability to maintain a constant temperature control is vital, and it is especially required when delivering large consignments of extremely sensitive, high-value goods.

The production and distribution of temperature-sensitive pharmaceuticals, clinical trials, biotechnology products, high-tech materials and reagents have significantly expanded in recent years. The FDA estimates that 70%of drugs in clinical trials today are temperature-sensitive and the air cargo industry has had to learn how to cope with an increasing range of regulations for maintaining an unbroken cool chain in transportation. Healthcare companies and regulatory authorities increasingly demand extremely high standards in handling these products, to ensure that when they finally reach the patient they are as medically effective as when leaving the production line.

The Swedish cool chain logistics specialist Envirotainer is one company playing an important role in the transportation of pharmaceuticals with its range of active temperature-controlled air cargo containers that it rents to users when they are required. As long as the refrigerants are maintained, usually dry ice, and the batteries are powered, the temperature can be maintained as needed – no matter how long the journey, or whether cooling or heating is required.

When blood plasma, insulin, vaccine or other biological pharmaceuticals are being moved, transportation methods and modes must be carefully monitored. Envirotainer estimates that some 20% of temperature-sensitive healthcare products are spoiled during transportation due to an improperly maintained and/or broken cool chain.

Because the largest part of any air cargo freight chain is actually spent on the ground, it is where the biggest risks occur, thanks to wide variations in ambient temperature ranges in different parts of the world. Active sensors in the containers monitor the temperature in order to maintain the required conditions and data monitoring and documentation ensure that a shipper can follow up and verify the exact status of the shipment.

While most temperature-controlled supply chain systems rely on passive technology – cool packs or polystyrene insulation – to keep temperatures down during transportation, Envirotainer's active temperature control technology consists of a ULD container manufactured using high performance insulation material, with an internal fan and sensor. Warm air drawn into the sealed container by the fan passes over dry ice in a separate compartment and is cooled before being guided back out to the loading area. This convection process promotes a constant, regulated environment providing a stable pre-set temperature for up to 72 hours. The internal sensor helps keep the temperature within the required limits, which can range from -20°C to +20°C, depending on the product.

US-based CSafe is a similar company to Envirotainer, also provides a cold chain air transport container that meets the temperature and regulatory requirements for pharmaceutical cold chain management

With handling and quality standards that are uniform throughout the world, shippers, freight forwarders and the cargo-carrying airlines need specially trained and certified staff to handle pharmaceutical products during the supply chain and get them to their destination in impeccable condition.

Envirotainer offers its Qualified Envirotainer Provider (QEP) programme. The programme acknowledges service providers meeting the strict requirements of Envirotainer's Training and Quality Programme for Good Distribution Practices guidance documents, including the requirements of the Parenteral Drug Association (PDA) and the IATA.

Temperature Sensitive Ground Handling

To protect sensitive products from temperature fluctuations during offloading and transportation to the warehouse, staff in airports which process significant perishable traffic, the fast unloading or loading is essential as direct sunlight can quickly damage most products. In some airports such as Dubai, specially designed "Cool Dollies" ferry pallets to and from cool rooms in airport warehouses, also operated under the same stringent guidelines. Loading and unloading procedures involving the aircraft or air cargo trucks are identified as points in the supply chain where the integrity of the cool chain is most at risk. The conditions for pharmaceutical products should always be maintained within acceptable limits during the time the cargo spends in the warehouse.

Working to the premise in the air cargo business that urgent freight is not for storage, it is for immediate transshipment as quickly as possible, pharmaceutical shipments always move quickly through the airport warehouse – but even a small delay can be harmful to the maintenance of an unbroken cool chain.

Dangerous Goods in Pharma

Many goods used in biotechnology and pharmaceuticals are potentially hazardous, so the shipper, forwarder, trucker, warehouse operator, cargo ground handler and air carriage provider must all ensure they are properly identified, packaged and handled, and that the special documentation required is correct and in good order as IATA regulations state. Some types of goods are subject to particular rules, such as pesticides and biocides, where higher risks are associated with transportation, for example, flying chloroform by air rather than moving it by road where the container can be ventilated in an open atmosphere.

Insects and Eggs

Certain living creatures are accepted by air carriers, in special packs.

The following are accepted: bees, destroyers of noxious pests and other insects sent to or from officially recognized institutions, leeches and certain parasites, silkworms.

In addition the following may be sent to some destinations – caterpillars, earthworms, fish fry and eggs, lugworms, maggots, mealworms, pupae and chrysalides and rag worms. Large quantities of insects such as grasshoppers are sent to zoos for feeding some animals and birds.

IATA publishes a manual for the shipping of perishables including pharmaceuticals.

Perishable Cargo Regulations

The Perishable Cargo Regulations (PCR) provide access to the most current and efficient practices for perishable cargo operations and an integral tool to achieve cost savings and avoiding delays by guaranteeing shipments are problem-free and compliant with international or local regulations. The PCR includes:

Up-to-date airline and government requirements pertaining to the transport of perishable cargo, requirements on handling, marking and labelling, packaging requirements, information on the necessary documentation and a comprehensive classification of 100s of perishable commodities. The PCR is a necessity for everyone involved in the transport of perishable goods by air and is specifically geared towards: Commercial shippers, shippers of fresh fruits and flowers, pharmaceutical companies, ground handlers, freight Forwarders and airlines.

Conclusion

With some exceptions, importing the air-freighted fresh produce by sea freight from tropical countries to markets in Europe and North America is not an option with 10–20 days' lead time. In these situations, northern European and American consumers will always be reliant on produce imported from overseas. Customers demand out-of-season and exotic produce or alternatively would have to rely on frozen produce. Most people now have the appetite and taste for all these products that years ago would never have been available.

Packaging and Temperature Control

Because the various products being transported require different temperatures and packaging especially high value products including vaccines, biological samples, some drugs and other temperature-sensitive products. Bearing in mind the many causes of delays and problems which can occur during transport, efficient packaging is a vital factor in protecting the integrity of a shipment.

Cool chain efficiency is improving continuously coupled with stricter Government regulations and industry requirements such as CEIV standards. The COVID-19 pandemic has placed enormous pressure on security and product protection considering the high value of shipments, while innovation is a never-ending process.

During1990s to early 2000s Polystyrene and Polyurethane were the main packaging type for short transit with built-in insulation properties incorporating frozen liquids and, in some cases, dry ice. These packaging systems are still in use for fairly short transits even by post. This type of product can only be for one time use, which in today's environmental critical condition, creates more waste product.

During the 2020s other systems were evolving and temperatures down to −35°C or up to +25°C. These containers are made from plastics, vacuum insulated panels (VIPs) made from foam core and sealed with a tough metallic membrane; and most excitingly, phase change materials (PCMs). PCMs became popular with many customers, as this type of insulation technology is up to seven times more effective over long transits and offers greater product integrity.

PCMs are based on a salt solution or paraffin wax suspended in bricks, and store and release energy differently than water-filled blocks. PCM panels must be preconditioned in a refrigerator or freezer until they reach the correct temperature to allow the package to ship in range. Then, they are placed into a box typically fitted with vacuum insulated panels and sealed to prevent leakage. The energy released/absorbed by phase transition from solid to liquid, or vice versa, the heat of fusion is generally much higher than the sensible heat. Ice, for example, requires 333.55 J/g to melt, but then water will rise one degree further with the addition of just 4.18 J/g. Water/ice is therefore a very useful phase change material and has been used to store winter cold to cool buildings in summer.

By melting and solidifying at the phase change temperature (PCT), a PCM is capable of storing and releasing large amounts of energy compared to sensible heat storage. Heat is absorbed or released when the material changes from solid to liquid and vice versa or when the internal structure of the material changes; PCMs are accordingly referred to as latent heat storage (LHS) materials.

Although PCM technology is comparatively expensive in the first instance, it is far more economical in the long run. The advantages are

- PCM's weigh less than polystyrene or polyurethane and water gel packs combined, thus reducing costs especially for air freight
- They are more reliable and reduce the risk of damage.
- PCMs can be disinfected and reused after reaching their destination if required

Another technique is Evaporative Cooling packaging, a smaller and lighter solution for temperature-controlled packages that need to be kept between +2°C and +8°C taking less space with less waste. Preconditioning is not needed. A container of water is pierced and evaporates to absorb heat and cool the shipment for 2–3 days.

Liquid nitrogen is another option, especially for live samples and biologics. Biologics are drugs made from living tissue, from animals' plants. Liquid nitrogen makes it possible to ship these samples and others at −196°C. However, packages transported at such extremely low temperatures must meet IATA guidelines (some of the vaccines for COVID-19, for example). If the shipment is by air, a specially prepared dry shipper container.

It is also possible to t a "wet shipper" to ship their product using liquid nitrogen. Wet shippers allow for liquid nitrogen to flow between panels, less favoured for pharmaceuticals.

Monitoring

Of course, evolution in cold chain packaging is almost irrelevant without equipment to measure a shipment's integrity. The need for Monitoring became necessary to indicate the progress of a shipment and identify any incursions to help mitigate risks. It has been indicated that most temperature excursions occur within the last segment of a shipment's destination, where the containers are most likely to be transferred into delivery vehicles – thus the need is for technology capable of monitoring a temperature-controlled shipment from packing through transport, storage and delivery.

Packaging technology will continue to develop in line with global medical needs and considering the ever rising cost of producing products. The COVID-19 pandemic taught us many lessons about how to combat a world pandemic, in the knowledge that with the amount of international travel, we must be prepared for more such out breaks in the future. Furthermore, the pharma industry faces endless attack from counterfeiters, capable of accurately copying genuine package, costing millions of last revenue for the drug companies.

Reefer Vehicles

All cool chain products spend a significant part of transit time on the road from factory to airport, from airport to customer. Subsequently, the suitability of vehicles, refrigerated vehicles (REEFER) is a fundamental part of the supply chain. Climate change plays an increasingly demanding role in our lives and transport is often a key target. The fact is that certain produce or flowers cannot be economically grown in Transport in general accounts for around 14% of all emissions and opinions are changing and the more developed countries are having to measure their green credentials as well as just providing a service.

Apart from the highly sophisticated pharma sector, the growth of the big supermarkets has created centralized distribution hubs that rely totally on road transport supplies. Many of the developing countries supplying these fruits, flowers and vegetables still lack adequate cool chain facilities required to maintain integrity. In the past, due to temperature spikes and poor handling methods, the produce was often damaged at the very start of transport, much of which was invisible until its arrival at its destination.

More and more producing countries have grasped the nettle and installed modern facilities to protect the produce directly from the grower thus initiating the cool chain process from the start. A good example is in Colombia. In the 1990s I visited a rose plantation. The owner lamented that her beautiful long stemmed rose, lovingly grown and carefully patched, was left standing in the sub-tropical heat at the airport, often soaked in heavy downpours. As a result, up to 20% were damaged or crushed. Today, the airport's new cargo terminal is one of the best equipped in Latin America comprises: 207,000 m^2 of platforms and access roads; 71,000 m^2 for warehouses and offices; 63 docks for aerial operation; 25 parking positions for any type of aircraft that can be loaded or unloaded simultaneously; 50,000 m^2 in consolidation areas; 1,000 m^2 for quarantine areas of the Colombian Agricultural Institute, ICA, and 7,000 m^2 for the administrative cargo centre.

In today's new look post-COVID-19 society, the home delivery of food has exploded into a major lifestyle change. It is now possible to order by phone, any type of food service including fresh produce or partially prepared meals. Many people now will not even consider shopping for almost anything, at the detriment of the poor retailer. Many of these have adapted to providing this service. This movement has launched a tsunami of delivery vans, motorbikes and drones to provide the service.

8 The Multimodal Family

The world's transport networks, while being far from integrated, share the task of delivering goods to customers. Whether that might be a new bike for Christmas, a consignment of pharmaceuticals or offshore drilling tools, the process is much the same with obvious differences. Combined transport modes is an everyday function of the delivery process. However, a consignment may employ a number of transport modes – road, ship, air, river, rail and van, even drone or motorcycle. The use of combined transport modes is an everyday function of the delivery process.

In most cases when talking about inter-modality, it refers to the movement of containers between different transport systems for example from rail to truck or from ship to truck. As this book concentrates on the air logistics function of the transportation supply chain, this chapter presents a very brief view of other modes which may play a more significant role future. The fundamental difference between air freight and other transport types is of course weight to value, with air accounting for around 35% in traffic value, but less than 2% in weight. However, during the last decade, the ocean operators have successfully developed better equipment for handling goods such as perishables but there is always the time factor at work. If the goods are not time sensitive or urgent, ocean can be a much cheaper option. However, the longer the goods are in transit, the longer can be the realization of capital value. The comparative speed of air transport will always favour urgent goods.

The usual facilities offered by ocean freight operators include FCL (full container load) | Loading of full containers, LCL (less than container load), LCL express, Transport of conventional goods with oversized load, Ship charter (project logistics), Part charter and full charter.

The main advantages of ocean freight include Cost Effectiveness – transporting containers of goods by ship is the one of the most cost-effective methods and can help keep the price of goods competitive, Heavy goods – for items that are outsized or heavy such as project equipment or machinery. Many books, magazines and websites are dedicated to this mode of transportation, which in some instances competes with air freight, sometimes partners as in the various SEA-AIR hubs such as Seattle or Dubai.

DOI: 10.4324/9781003167167-8

Safety and reliability are two vital factors in transporting and delivering goods and whilst all transport modes suffer losses and damage, the loss of sea containers adds a significant risk as can be seen from the following.

Reliability at Sea

Aviation in general is a high-profile activity, whether it be a package holiday flight or wide-bodied freighter, if there is an accident, a problem on the ground or in the air, the publicity is invariably widespread and sensational. To consider accidents in general, the World Health Organization (WHO) reports that around 1.4 million recorded deaths occur on the world's roads every year, yet this is largely un-remarked. The general public appears to accept such losses. If one of the 5,220 container ships, plus bulk tankers, supply ships or ferries is involved in an accident, there is often little or no publicity outside the ocean shipping industry itself. The impression, therefore, is that shipping by sea is safe and reliable. A brief study of recent events shows a rather different picture. Frequently, delays and losses are nobody's fault but are the impact of bad weather or congestion at ports, such as the blocking of the Suez Canal in March 2021 by a massive container ship, which did hit the headlines, or another massive container vessel aground in Chesapeake Bay in 2022.

It is clear that with 95% of the world's global cargo travelling by sea, that there will inevitably be proportionally more incidents of unreliability thanks to the sheer volume of the traffic. Apart from damage caused by storms or collisions, the question of delay is also gathering more traction. During 2021/22 there were a number of port delays whereby ships were waiting several days or weeks to unload and load and in turn causing severe problems for the end customers of the products, many of them manufactured in the Far East. Of course, most cargo arrives without incident but it has to be considered as a value issue when dealing with very sensitive and high-value items.

As over 95% of all international cargo tonnage is moved by sea, clearly there is much risk involved, but if measured against the risk of accident or delays, it can be seen that reliability is not as great as you might think. Aside from bulk cargoes, the majority of goods are moved in sea containers (TEU) carrying an average of 12 tonnes). Here are a few recent examples of incidents involving containerships.

- In December 2020 the 14,000 TEU ONE APUS box ship from Japan ran into a violent storm resulting in the loss of an estimated 1,900 containers, 400 of which contained dangerous goods either lost overboard or severely damaged, a huge loss for the cargo owners' insurance company
- In 2020, the 13,092 TEU Maersk Eindhoven on route to California suffered a blackout and the subsequent loss of hundreds of containers
- The sister ship the Maersk Essen lost 750 containers whilst on route from Xiamen to Los Angeles

- In February 2021 the Phuc Khah a 672 TEU lost power in the Long Tau river near Ho Chi Minh City, causing a barge to crash into a crane at the base of the bridge linking Ho Chi Minh City with Dong Nai

Some of these recent incidents having caused by unusually bad storms which are thought to be due to the effects of increasingly violent climate change, but the big question is whether these vessels are in fact safe in these increasingly violent sea conditions. Due to the practice of piling containers on the deck, the question of securing them and their propensity to unbalance the vessel in heavy seas, the various Marine authorities such as the world's shipping Council, need to take a firm stance. A fire which broke out aboard the *Zim Kingston* was caused by a container collapse that damaged boxes containing dangerous cargo.

The 4,253 teu vessel, on charter from the Greek owner, was at an anchorage awaiting a berthing slot at the port of Vancouver when a storm caused a severe list. This caused the loss of some 40 containers overboard and it was reported that a fire then started.

Of course the vast majority of ocean cargoes are delivered safely and on time and losses incurred represent a small percentage of the overall tonnage, but more recently the concerns have been focused on port congestion and the lack of sufficient drivers to deliver the goods. This is an ongoing and worsening crisis. In addition, many of the lost containers float near the ocean surface and constitute a severe threat to small ships and yachts.

Damage and problems also occur with air cargo shipments and also in road transport. It would be impossible to transport millions of tonnes around the globe in total safety. The various authorities in all transport modes are working hard to improve safety and crew welfare as well as reducing emissions.

On The Road

Air cargo spends on average, 80% of its time on the ground, which in most cases includes road transport, an integral part of ground handling, it is clear that the opportunities for disruption are the weakest link in the chain. The road transport link between shipper, through the air freight process and finally to the customer, is one of the most critical, expensive and delay prone components of air logistics. As inter-Europe airfreight, for instance, mostly travels by road, this part of the process has to be addressed when viability and environmental issues are considered (Figure 8.1).

For several decades, Luxembourg-based Cargolux Airlines has been regarded as the example of efficient integration between the road and air. The company built its highly successful long haul air cargo business model by trucking all cargo to and from its base and operating a fleet of B747 freighters to many worldwide destinations. The company works with different trucking companies, serving over 40 airports. Cargolux is one of the outstanding success stories of the industry.

Figure 8.1 European road vehicle (Jan De Rijk).

The European sector includes thousands of truck movements between airports and customers, the vehicles involved frequently moving under airlines' AWBs. The factors which increasingly challenge the trucking process are

- Heavy congestion around major cities and airports such as Brussels, Amsterdam or London
- Emissions especially from vehicles waiting to load or unload at airports
- Poor security and lack of safe and secure overnight parking
- Increasing lack of drivers due to poor pay and working conditions. Younger potential new drivers are deterred by the high risk and frequent stays away from home, lack of decent washing and toilet facilities as well as danger from criminal gangs. This was exaggerated by the COVID-19 pandemic, resulting in a shortage of many thousands of drivers.

The problem came to a head in 2021 in the post–COVID-19 rush to re-start the economy and serious congestion and backlogs of goods. In the UK alone, it was estimated that around 90,000 driver vacancies had occurred. The pattern was repeated throughout Europe. Besides improved working conditions, lowering the age of new drivers one solution, integrating non-EU workers within the bloc's labour market and recognizing driving licenses from third countries would also add to the driver pool.

Industry and transport worker groups and unions have also called for more secure parking areas where drivers can safely rest or access basic services amid reports of increasing theft and violence. In the EU bloc there is an estimated 100,000 parking spots, but only 3% of existing parking spaces are certified safe and secure.

Ultimately, it comes down to making the job more interesting for potential new drivers, which means better pay, better working hours and condition with safe parking space. It also includes operators' investment in more technology for tracking, safeguarding and monitoring of truck movements. The recent COVID-19 pandemic has accentuated these daily challenges and coupled with the urgent need to reduce emissions and other climate change pressures, the truck manufacturers are working hard at innovations in electric vehicles and other technologies. With the exception of some integrator routes and some exceptional cargoes, all Inter- European routes are operated by road. Vast majority of air cargo in Europe travels on specialized tractor trailer units, specifically tasked for the efficient movement of complete ULDs, allowing a minimization of costs, almost entirely eliminating damage, and also ensuring in the case of perishable, a temperature controlled environment. Most RFSs crossing Europe operated or controlled by airlines even how vital trucking services are for keeping the global economy running and supplying retailers with goods was illustrated when the Icelandic volcano Eyjafjallajöekull erupted in March 2010, bringing air traffic in most parts of Europe to a complete standstill. "Unable to air freight our goods, we trucked our shipments from Germany and other countries of origin during those days to Istanbul where the ash cloud hadn't reached," said a DHL spokesman. Similarly in Iceland, where local carrier Icelandair had to relocate all flights from Keflavik airport near Reykjavik to Akureyri in the far north of the Atlantic island, whose local skies were not affected by the volcanic cloud due to favourable drifts. "Particularly many of our fish consignments bound to Canada and the USA had to be trucked all the way up north to Akureyri to circumvent the ash cloud and have them flown out," recalls Gunnar Sigurfinnsson, Icelandair's Head of Cargo. This highlights, like in the United States the integrators ensuring an efficient ground network reinforcing its air capabilities, trucking always will retain its close link to air cargo as a key component, or for the flexibility it to meet emergency circumstances.

The American Road Network

The United States has developed a fast interstate highway system consisting of around 77,000 kms, (478,000 miles). The interstate network handles most goods transported internally and is vastly cheaper than air. With the world's eyes on carbon emissions and climate change, this method will certainly come under much scrutiny. In a country the size of the United States with its comparatively weak rail network and huge distances, it will be a challenge to find alternative solutions. Goods for export or import are delivered and collected by truck to connect with international flights at major hubs employing specialized roller bed trucks, configured to handle ULD.

The integrators are thus handling the most urgent and express air traffic for internal customers, first for efficiency and cost, but also as a strategic tool especially in case of inclement weather. Miami Airport is an interesting example of both passenger and cargo traffic functioning in parallel. Known informally as the capital of Latin America. MIA is the busiest cargo hubs in the United States, especially for perishable goods. The flow of goods from South to Central America is largely channelled through Miami, including flowers, fruit and vegetables. Thanks to a comprehensive route network, goods which are not destined for the United States, are transited to other worldwide destinations. A road corridor links the airport cargo area to the warehouse zone and thence to the interstate highway system. To move the traffic, around 200,000 separate truck movements are executed annually. MIA handles 85% of imports and 80% of Latin American trade, some 2 million tonnes annually and one of IATA's registered (CEIV). Similarly Los Angeles (LAX) handles some 2 million tonnes of cargo each year, most of which is through Far East trade, mostly with Japan, China and South Korea.

In India, with around 3.8 million miles of roads, a series of high quality highways are under construction. As of 2020 705 were paved and over 85,000 miles of 4 or more lane highways were in use. But there is still much ground to make up in order to satisfy the needs of manufacturing companies. By 2013, some 21,000 kms of four to six lane highways had been brought into use. The poor quality of many unpaved rural roads, however, has made it difficult for farmers trying to transport their produce to distribution points, and perishables remain a key air freight commodity for exports. There is still a large proportion of rigid trucks with two or three axles capable of carrying between 9 and 25 tonnes on the three-axle vehicles, whereas the European five axles articulated trucks could carry 40 tonnes. DHL says that the 2,000 km run between New Delhi and Bangalore or Mumbai to Delhi takes around 35 hours while the same distance in Europe would average 11 to 12 hours and in China, 17/18 hours. The country operates 20 international airports but most cargo moves through Delhi and Mumbai. Road transport inefficiency has had some benefits for airlines operating freighters however, as direct services to key regional hubs or even direct to Europe can still demand premium pricing as the clients have little option to use alternate gateways.

The Specialized RFS Carrier

RFS companies continue to invest in training, sophisticated IT solutions, GPS tracking, safety and security and reliability, Jan de Rijk, one of Europe's largest RFS operators based in the Netherlands, deploys some 850 vehicles, of which 35% belong to subcontractors. These partners are screened thoroughly to maintain the company's own standards, including security training for their drivers. Due to cost reasons about 50% of Jan de Rijk's fleet is operating with a license from one of the Eastern European countries. Price pressure is enormous but again, if a customer insists on product quality, he is not well advised to choose the cheapest market player for performing his road transport. Cheap can become expensive very quickly in case of mistakes or drivers are not able to understand the contents of declarations on dangerous goods or other documents accompanying shipments (Figure 8.2).

Air freight accounts for 40% of the Dutch company's business, with 60% related to warehousing, rail transport and other segments. Jan de Rijk's three drivers for profitability, all must be met to end up in the black:

- high load factors throughout the year
- sufficient yields per kilogram and driven kilometres
- constant utilization of the rolling fleet asset.

Figure 8.2 RFS Jan de Rijk.

Predatory competition in this market forces the need to drive as many kilometres as possible to balance fixed costs. However, bottlenecks and slow throughput of shipments at major airports are increasingly hindering trucking firms from running their vehicles on schedule. The results are supply chain disruptions and reduced quality of air freight processes.

What RFS providers urgently need are fast turn-around times at gateways, enabling a seamless flow of shipments and a constant usage rate of vehicles.

For several reasons, waiting times getting longer, particularly at large hubs like Amsterdam, Frankfurt, Heathrow or Charles de Gaulle and the downtime of the vehicles is growing constantly, especially at peak times each Friday and Monday.

Low margins in air freight handling are a major contributory factor. Why, the manager also indicates:

> Because labour is the biggest cost factor for handlers, they don't increase their staff on days with heavy traffic in order to prevent additional expenditures in personnel. Even if they would like to hire more staff their capabilities are very limited due to the extremely low margins obtainable in this fiercely competitive field. Therefore, slower airfreight processing within the handling agent's warehouses is the obvious consequence. The entire case wouldn't be as harmful for trucking firms if the handlers would communicate any congestion or delayed pick-up times at an early stage, which most of them unfortunately do not. In that case we would be able to reroute our trucks and change their schedules at short notice.

The RFS trucking companies are crying out for efficiency improvements that would only benefit everyone in the supply chain.

In the meantime, hundreds of small and medium-sized players that are trucking goods from airport to airport are struggling to stay in business. Almost all of them lack the capacity and financial resources to challenge the big operators like Jan de Rijk, Arthur Welter, Wallenborn, DB Schenker, Panalpina and others.

They basically have three choices to survive:

- The independent: Deciding on standing alone as long as possible operating as a niche player,
- Becoming a subcontractor of one of the larger enterprises,
- Joining forces and forming their own alliances.

EU Commission's Mobility Package 1

The move represents "a welcome addition to the tool kit that targets road transport cargo crime and security," said Thorsten Neumann, president & CEO of TAPA in the Europe, Middle East & Africa (EMEA) region.

This new version of the SSTPA will replace the existing voluntary SSTPA scheme which was produced following a comprehensive study into EU parking needs. The availability of EC funding, alongside the new SSTPA, will help the industry to invest in projects that improve conditions for drivers and increase truck parking capacity.

Thorsten Neumann stated: "TAPA EMEA supports the introduction of the EU SSTPA because urgent action is needed to support the resilience of road transport supply chains in Europe, minimize the level of cargo crime, and, of course, protect the safety of truck drivers. The capacity for secure truck parking will not meet demand for many years but this is a positive step forward. TAPA EMEA estimates the industry has a shortfall of over 2,000 secure truck stops and over 400,000 parking bays in Europe."

> The EU Standard shares the objectives of TAPA EMEA's Parking Security Requirements (PSR) in promoting and facilitating the growth and use of classified secure truck parking. We, therefore, will actively support the adoption of either of the Standards. There are similarities in requirements between the two Standards, but there are differences in approach. So, it's not a case of which standard is best, but more a decision for each operator on which standard best suits their needs. The overwhelming priority – at a time when we are seeing severe driver shortages across Europe – is to deliver a safer and more secure operating environment for drivers, trucks and cargoes. On this, we all agree.

As a leading supply chain resilience and security Association representing Manufacturers, Logistics Services Providers and all supply chain security stakeholders, TAPA EMEA has played an active role in supporting the Commission's SSTPA Standard. However, the Association – which has been helping to protect its members' supply chains for over 24 years – has also recognized that businesses are cautious because the EU LABEL project, the predecessor to SSTPA, failed to attract many parking sites and certifications were not maintained.

TAPA EMEA's PSR Standard was created 3 years ago based on the Association's knowledge of the business reality facing supply chains as well as its understanding of what customers of secure parking places will accept.

> We support all initiatives, Standards and regulatory requirements which promote the safety and security of people, goods, equipment and services in the global supply chain as long as they are affordable, easy-to-adopt, fit-for-purpose and sustainable. We will progress faster if we all work together, Thorsten Neumann added.

While recognizing the long journey ahead, TAPA EMEA says its PSR continues to see strong growth and interest from Parking Place Operators and customers of secure trucking parking places. The TAPA EMEA secure parking database currently includes over 75 parking sites in 14 countries in the EMEA region, offering over 7,000 parking bays.

Conclusions

Although there has been much progress over the last decades on developing rail routes between China and Europe and other such links will follow in the future. Trucking companies, ground handlers and airports are working together as ground handling systems on behalf of carriers in improving efficiency, for speedier transit and lower costs. At the same time, significant reductions in emissions must be achieved. The examples shown from Europe will vary considerably in other countries and continents, local road conditions and networks, regulations, traffic flows and distances involved. In every case however the basic need is to transport goods to and from airports or sea ports and efficient and reliable road transport is vital, especially in the burgeoning E -tailing global marketplace.

Global Rail Freight

OTE: the 2022 conflict between Russia and Ukraine changes some of the operating conditions, hopefully on a temporary basis.
    By Kevin Smith, Editor-in-Chief, International Railway Journal

Operators Target Increased Share of Intermodal Market

Rail might be regarded as the ugly duckling of the freight world. While perhaps not living up to expectations in some regions, its ability to haul vast quantities of goods over long distances relatively quickly, and in many areas using electrified infrastructure, means there are vast opportunities for growth.

Bulk intermodal in particular is on the cusp of a significant increase in market share. With shippers seeking a green alternative to road and air transport, and governments determined to make good on environmental policy commitments through investments in new infrastructure, the railway renaissance is very much underway.

Rail's status inevitably varies depending on which area of the world you find yourself, while passenger trains take priority in Europe, in North America, freight dominates the rail landscape.

North America's 250,000 km network is privately owned, predominately by seven Class 1 railways, five of which hail from the United States and two from Canada.[1] The transcontinental network stretching from coast to coast, traversing mountains and the Great Plains, is arguably the backbone of the

---

1 The seven Class 1s could soon become six with Canadian rivals Canadian Pacific (CN) and Canadian Pacific (CP) currently bidding to acquire Kansas City Southern (KCS), the smallest Class 1 and the only railway with infrastructure in Mexico. If either CP or CN's bid is successful, the combined railways will create the first Canada-US-Mexico integrated freight railway.

North American economy. Indeed, the performance of the seven Class 1s is often a barometer of economic performance.

Deregulation of the industry in the 1980s, which rid the Class 1s of the burdensome legal obligations and pricing regulations that had nearly driven the industry to collapse, set the scene for a revival. Rapid consolidation from 56 Class 1s in 1976 to 13 in 1987 and seven today has laid the groundwork for stable and profitable businesses. Reform also served to reinvigorate short line, Class 2 and 3 railways, serving regional and rural America, helping to retain a dense network. That much of this network is able to accommodate 32-tonne axle loads reflects its importance for the heavy haul of the continent's vast quantities of natural resources, including petrochemicals, aggregates, fertilizers, grain and most notably coal.

Coal was the mainstay of the Class 1s, but especially the east coast railways, CSX and Norfolk Southern. However, more than 500 coal-fired power stations closed in the United States between 2010 and 2019 and coal now accounts for less than a quarter of all electricity generated in the United States compared with 52% in 2000. With the Biden administration seemingly intent on reducing this further, intermodal is a logical target for growth for the Class 1s.

The sight of double stack, 3,000 m-long container trains has been common across North America for many years. Growth of these types of trains was often three to four times that of GDP. But at the turn of the new decade, increases in intermodal rail freight flows out of west-coast ports bound for Chicago, Dallas–Fort Worth and Atlanta had slowed.[2] Railways were favouring longer mixed commodity trains as they embraced Precision Scheduled Railroading, an operating doctrine pioneered by Canadian National (CN) and now used by most of the Class 1s, which seeks to maximize asset utilization and cut corporate costs. This is the basis for reduced operating ratios and improved Class 1 profitability in recent years and has resulted in some railways walking away from intermodal traffic due to the perceived inefficiency of these services.

Yet the potential for further intermodal growth remains. For example, JB Hunt, a truck competitor but a major intermodal customer, was targeting the conversion of up to 11 million truck movements to intermodal before the pandemic. However, securing a significant modal shift will require rail to embrace digital tracking capabilities pioneered by its road competitors, an area where North American railways still lag behind.

Possible evolutions in the PSR model to develop better partnerships with other railways and related transport systems could improve the efficiency of these operations, increasing their attractiveness to both the railways

---

2 "Tough market set to persist in 2020," International Railway Journal, *The Railway in 2020*, January 2020, p. 28.

themselves and shippers.[3] The evolution of the shipping data and messaging platform provided by Railinc, a for-profit company owned by the Association of American Railroads (AAR), is an example of the ongoing work in this area.

Positive Train Control (PTC) also presents a major opportunity. This new federally mandated interoperable signalling system, rolled out at vast expense – some $US 15 billion – by U.S. freight and passenger railways over the past decade, was finally completed at the end of 2020. AAR's Train Control, Communications and Operations Committee is currently working on various subprojects to harness data retrieved from this new infrastructure with a view to improving network efficiency. Among the more exciting prospective developments is semi or automatic train operation, a sign that the sector is alert to the threat posed by automated trucking.[4]

Europe

In contrast to North America, in Europe rail freight is a low margin business with a static market share of around 18%. This is in spite of European Union (EU) targets instituted at the start of the 2010s to shift freight from road to rail to reduce carbon emissions and to ease pressure on the continent's congested road network.

Again, unlike North America, the European freight matrix consists of a mix of state-owned incumbents, and smaller more agile private operators. While predominant in their home markets, DB Cargo, a subsidiary of German government-owned Deutsche Bahn (DB), Rail Cargo Group (RCG), a subsidiary of Österreichische Bundesbahnen (ÖBB), and SBB Cargo, a subsidiary of Schweizerische Bundesbahnen (SBB) all operate in neighbouring countries.

European freight trains lengths are also limited to only 750 m, significantly shorter than their North American counterparts, which is a major hindrance on capacity. And while multi-system locomotives are now common, freight operators are struggling to swallow the costs of upgrading their stock to be compatible with the European Train Control System, Europe's interoperable signalling system.

The rollout of this platform, which was first conceived at the turn of the century as a universal signalling system to encourage cross-border operation, also remains painfully slow. Trackside ETCS was only installed on around 11% of the nine corridors that make up the core Trans-European Transport Network (TEN-T) at the end of 2017, the most recent available data.

Mindful that it needs to do more, a coalition of European freight operators joined forces at the end of 2018 to call for rail freight to account for 30% of all freight flows in Europe by 2030. The EU made a similar pledge in its

---

3 "Developing a scalable, digital PSR," International Railway Journal, *The Railway in 2021,* January 2021, p. XX.
4 "On the railroad to ATO," International Railway Journal, November 2019, p. 18.

Sustainable and Smart Mobility Strategy released in December 2020. The Rail Freight Forward coalition[5] is advocating for policy changes that make rail cheaper and more cost competitive than road and the adoption of new technologies that make rail more attractive.

Delivery of the Single European Area is another priority for rail freight operators. Completion of the core TEN-T, which the EU has pledged to do by 2030, is set to be reinforced in late 2021 by a recast of the TEN-T directive by the European Commission (EC). The network spans the European continent, and through the equipment of ETCS and a consistent 4 m loading gauge will guarantee interoperability. Completion of several big-ticket infrastructure projects by the end of the decade on key cross-border routes will also improve the viability of the network. This includes the Brenner Base Tunnel in Austria, Rail Baltica to develop a 250 km/h 1,435 mm-gauge line from Poland to Latvia, Lithuania and Estonia, the Fehmarn belt fixed link project to build a new rail connection between Germany and Denmark, and the construction of a new railway tunnel beneath the Alps to provide a high-speed rail line between Lyon and Turin.

Delivery of the TEN-T is a big opportunity for intermodal. Speaking on March 29 2021 during a launch event for The European Year of Rail, a EU policy initiative to highlight the value of rail and its contribution to the EU's Green Deal policy in 2021, Clemens Först, CEO of RCG and chair of RFF, said that with European heavy industry growth stagnating, rail must look to multimodality. In particular, he said rail must become more flexible and embrace small and medium-sized enterprises with smaller shipment sizes allowing trucks to be used only for Last Mile shipments.[6]

Both RCG and Polish state-owned incumbent PKP Cargo's corporate strategy reflects this changing market and mindset for rail freight operators. RCG has bucked the trend in recent years and become a profitable enterprise by positioning itself as a rail freight logistics provider. PKP Cargo has adopted a similar approach. Like the Class 1s, coal was mainstay of PKP Cargo's business, but changing demands for energy in Poland means it is diversifying towards intermodal as part of a major restructuring.[7] Among the key developments is the launch of PKP Cargo Connect in 2020, a new end-to-end intermodal service, which enables shippers to track consignments in real time throughout the entirety of their journey.

5 RFF members are: BLS Cargo, CD Cargo, CFL Cargo, DB Cargo, GreenCargo, Lineas, LTE Group, Mercitalia, Ost West Logistik, PKP Cargo, Rail Cargo Group, Renfe Meracnias, SBB Cargo, SNCF Logistics, ZSSK Cargo, The Community of European Railways and Infrastructure Managers (CER), German Railway Industry Association (VDV), International Union of Railways (UIC) and European Rail Freight Association (ERFA).
6 "European Year of Rail launches with reminder of the challenges confronting modal shift," International Railway Journal, May 2021, p. 5.
7 "Embracing Intermodal: PKP Cargo develops new strategy," International Railway Journal, June 2020, p. 18.

Deployment of improved tracking capability is also apparent in Internet of Things (IoT) and Big Data technology supplied as a software as a service application by start-up Nexxiot, which is enabling clients such as wagon leaser VTG as well as DB Cargo and SBB Cargo to make more informed decisions about their assets. VTG's Traigo platform offers clients real-time information on wagon and asset location and arrival times as well as supporting digital maintenance management tools.

Rail freight is also benefitting from a centralized research and development programme initiated by the EU, which aims to unearth the next generation of railway technology to help achieve modal shift targets. Among the key projects of the Shift2Rail joint undertaking of industry, railways, research institutes and universities are the Digital Automatic Coupling (DAC).[8] This technology supports the automatic connection of physical components such as the mechanical connector and air pipes as well as power and data connections, potentially ending the need for crews to walk the entire length of trains to manually check that couplings between wagons are secure, offering significant cost and time savings.

Shift2Rail researchers as well as teams at railways in France and Germany are also working to develop mainline automatic train operation (ATO), a potential gamechanger for rail operation. Running automatic and semi-automatic trains promises to improve network efficiency, freeing up capacity to run more rail freight services. Following encouraging progress in trials, the first commercial applications are expected within the next 5 years.

Asia

Single digital certificates for rail freight shipments are one of the factors behind the upsurge in China-Europe bulk intermodal rail freight flows, a major rail freight success story of recent years. The transformation of the Kazakh-China border post of Khorgos into a bustling inland port and city of 100,000 is the best visible example of the emergence of this market. It also again emphasizes rail infrastructure's Achilles heel.

Khorgos is a bottleneck on the network as it serves to transfer containers from 1,435 mm-gauge rolling stock used in China to 1,520 mm-gauge used in Kazakhstan, Russia and Belarus, for the next stage of the trains' journey to Europe. A further transfer back to 1,435 mm-gauge takes place at similar sites in Poland, Belarus and Ukraine as trains continue their journey to freight hubs across Europe.

While rail offers a significant time advantage over the sea and is substantially cheaper than air freight, the emergence of this market is not down to market economics alone. Chinese subsidies for these transcontinental rail

---

8 "Making the connection with digital couplings," International Railway Journal, February 2021, p. 32.

services continue to underpin their operation. And while there were indications that the subsidies would cease as the market was established, the onset of the COVID-19 pandemic in 2020 means the support is likely to continue for the time being.

In its latest study on Eurasian Corridor Development, published in February 2020, the International Union of Railways (UIC) says that active traffic growth experienced in 2016–2018 was expected to ease to more moderate growth in the coming years.[9] Its future forecast offers projections of 450,000 TEUs in more pessimistic scenarios depending on the recovery from COVID-19 and the decrease of Chinese subsidies, to more than 2 million TEUs in 2030 if anticipated digitalization developments, infrastructure improvements and support measures for rail emerge.

China's willingness to offer financial assistance for these trains is in line with its Belt and Road strategy. The Chinese government's revival of the Old Silk Road is considered as a means to both extend political influence and provide an overland network for the shipment of Chinese goods across the Eurasian continent and into Africa. Soft Chinese finance for rail projects that are or will benefit include new lines to Southeast Asian neighbours Laos and Vietnam, to projects in Pakistan, and even East Africa, notably standard gauge lines in Kenya, Uganda and Tanzania. However, uncertainty in China of the economic value of investing in some projects as domestic growth slows and concerns in states about China's geopolitical ambitions and the potential for corruption, is likely to see some changes in approach post-pandemic.

One direct beneficiary of China's desire to grow transcontinental rail freight is Russia. Russia accounts for more than 90% of Euro-Asian transit in both directions and state-owned behemoth Russian Railways (RZD) reported a 15.8% increase in container traffic to 5.8 million TEUs in 2020. This follows progressive growth since the middle of the last decade as RZD invested to improve infrastructure capacity on its transcontinental routes. The railway expects overall volumes to increase by 3.3% in 2021 as the economy embarks on a recovery from the pandemic.

The loosening of restrictions on sanctioned goods, which began to bear fruit in mid-2020, should also help to increase eastern freight flows. The UIC's study found a ratio of 67.6% westbound to 32.4% eastbound for loaded containers. This trade imbalance is a limitation of the service and the UIC says a balance of 42%–43% and 58%–57% between east and westbound traffic is likely to persist up to 2030.

Rail accounts for an impressive 88% of all freight transport turnover in Russia, excluding pipelines, and RZD is also investing in new technologies to improve performance. New high-capacity locomotives such as the

9 Eurasian Corridors: Development Potential, International Union of Railways, February 2020. Retrieved from: https://uic.org/IMG/pdf/uic-iec2020_eurasian-corridors-development-potential_exec_summary.pdf

3TE25K2M diesel unit introduced into service in eastern Russia in January 2021 are helping to boost capacity. This 9.3MW three-section unit can haul 7,100 tonnes trains compared with 5,600 tonnes by previous models, helping to improve the efficiency of export from eastern ports. The railway is also exploring the use of alternative fuels such as hydrogen and batteries for traction, mirroring a trend seen in markets across the world. Likewise, it is making significant progress with mainline automation projects on passenger lines in Moscow, which could conceivably transfer to freight operation as well as automatic shunting.

India is also on the cusp of a dramatic improvement in rail freight network efficiency. The inauguration of the first sections of the Dedicated Freight Corridors (DFCs) in December and January 2021 is heralding a new era for rail freight in the country.

The objective of the new 1,875 km Ludhiana, Punjab – Dankuni, West Bengal, Eastern DFC and the 1,506 km Western DFC from Dadri west of Delhi to Mumbai is to remove freight trains from lines used by passenger trains, helping to improve the efficiency of operation of both forms of rail transport. While they remain much delayed and well over budget, completion of the first two DFCs is expected in 2022. India is also planning to build four more DFCs to form a 10,000 km Golden Quadrilateral network of freight lines. The Western DFC was the first railway in the world to operate electrified double-stack container trains, a significant technical achievement.

Australia

Australia's Pilbara Region boasts some of the world's heaviest freight trains and most impressive railways. Mining giants Rio Tinto, BHP and Fortescue are continuing to push the boundaries of what is possible to maximize production and the efficiency of the region's iron-ore mines. Rio Tinto has even gone as far as to develop the world's first fully automatic railway on its 1,500 km network.

The company completed the transition to entirely automated operation of 2.4 km-long trains in June 2019.[10] The project has helped to increase train speeds by 6% while removing the need to change drivers two or three times has cut an hour from the journey. The cost of the project almost doubled to $US 940 m by its completion. But it is a landmark achievement and many other Australian railways as well as the North American Class 1s are looking to replicate the company's success.

The Australian government is also eyeing significant intermodal growth. Upcoming investments in expanded port facilities in Melbourne and Sydney are set to support the country's flagship freight rail project: Inland Rail. This

---

10 Rise of the Machines: Rio Tinto Breaks new ground with AutoHaul, *International Railway Journal*, August 2019, p. 14.

project of new and existing line upgrades on a 1,700 km corridor between Melbourne and Brisbane is targeting a sharp cut in transit times to less than 24 hours, helping to make rail more competitive with road and removing thousands of trucks from highways. The line will have the capacity to run double-stack container trains up to 1,800 m long, although these will not be able to access the port of Brisbane due to infrastructure constraints.[11]

At $A 10 billion the project is expensive and has courted controversy, with some questioning its economic benefit. However, the federal government, which is funding the project alongside investment from the state governments of Victoria, New South Wales and Queensland, seems intent to push ahead. Completion is scheduled for 2025.

The COVID-19 pandemic has slowed progress on Inland Rail slightly, as it has on many rail projects around the world. The associated economic slowdown has also impacted rail freight performance in 2020 and into 2021. However, the pandemic did highlight some of the advantages of rail. During the first wave, demand from Europe for fast delivery of personal protective equipment from China saw shippers turn to rail rather than the sea. Trains were also free to cross borders as countries instituted checks to curb unnecessary travel by road. And the use of significantly less people to carry and handle high quantities of goods also made rail a much safer option during the pandemic.

The sector faces numerous challenges if it is to deliver on its potential. However, as governments wise up to the challenges posed by the climate crisis, and an upsurge in economic activity is expected in the second half of 2021 as lockdown restrictions ease, there is growing momentum. Indeed, rail seems as well placed as at any time since it was superseded by road transport in the middle of the twentieth century to realize a significant upsurge in use and importance in global logistics chains.

---

11 Inland Rail: Nation building project or White Elephant?, International Railway Journal, October 2020, p. 22.

9 Technology in Air Logistics

It would be impossible to cover all the innovations, inventions and new systems which have been introduced and continue to improve the operation of the air supply chain. Every day new ideas are being coming online to streamline and speed up processes. We have discussed several of these in general terms and in this chapter, are some of the trends currently in hand. This is by no means inclusive. Also look at the chapter on Future thoughts. There is a continuous flow of cloud-based systems to streamline processes ranging from airport warehousing, to truck fleet control, from security to environment, all of which are changing the daily function of air cargo. However, one fact which is clear is that the air logistics business needs to recruit a substantial army of new thinkers, technicians, managers and entrepreneurs in order to take our industry forward for the next decades.

Technology for Air Logistics

Nowadays technology is more important than ever. In the last 20 years technology and especially digitization has moved at a fast pace. Information is the new gold, but information has only value when it is shared.

As the analysis in the image by PWC shows, we have become much more digitized, which again the COVID-19 crisis has only accelerated more.

The air cargo industry is lagging compared to other industries in terms of the adaption of technology. The challenge is not that much inventing new technology to optimize the process but more the adaption. Somehow people love to talk about the technologies yet not even adapted in more tech savvy industries instead of applying what is available now. We need to walk properly first before we start talking about how we can get to the moon.

Technology is there, but not always adapted as much in different industries. The air cargo industry has been very slow in adopting technological changes but is now catching up rapidly.

We need to be collective as an industry more Digital, Connected and Smart. It is great if for example an airline is completely ready to receive and purchase orders from its customers and suppliers. To work effectively, the entire supply chain must be connected. Nowadays it is a lot easier and cheaper

DOI: 10.4324/9781003167167-9

to connect. Application programming interfaces (API), which is a computing interface that identifies interactions between various software intermediaries.

Even if everyone is connected and digital, they still need to work in a smart way. Like they say: garbage in, garbage out. So, if we are digitally connected let us work in a smart way, meaning that we try to optimize the whole supply chain, making it more efficient.

Robotic process automation (RPA) aims to increase efficiencies, boost profits and automate manual and repetitive processes.

Also whatever is done internally or externally, it is crucial that the processes of a company are optimized. Internal processes should be looked at across the company, meaning over all departments, be it commercial, finance or operations. This implies a cross departmental optimization of processes. There are three ways to look at this:

1 Procure to Pay, where the flow of goods, information and money of the moment a service or products is ordered to when it will be paid, is being analysed. This process can be optimized by digitization and automation. However, it cannot be achieved just internally because you need to have all suppliers on board. The advantage of automating and digitizing the procure to pay process is that besides cost savings, also less errors will be realized.

2 Order to cash, where the process from the moment a customer orders a service to the time money is received is being analysed. The front-end interaction with the customer is extremely important and could potentially be a competitive differentiator. The easier it is to use for the customer the better. Bookings should go system to system or through portals.

3 RPA is a type of business process automation technology using software robots or on artificial intelligence/digital workers. It can take over simple administrative repetitive tasks between different (software) systems. The advantage is that an RPA does not get sick or goes on holiday, and it works 24/7.

Customer Satisfaction and Perception

According to IBM up to 65% of the value of a company's product or services are derived from its suppliers, according to a study by IBM. This is certainly also true for the air cargo industry. Most of the time cargo spends on the ground and therefore the differentiation is also realized on the ground services. The more reason to have a digitally interacted supply chain in order to replicate the seamless services of integrators.

Information is now moving at the same speed as the cargo which leads to inefficiencies in the air cargo supply chain. Information will move faster than the physical goods.

Most of the information on what is or will be on a flight is known for weeks. Mainly due to last minute few exceptions, like change in weight or change of carrier the information may change. But even then when the goods are for example being transported from the shipper or forwarder to a handling facility, the information on the goods, like how many pieces, what weight, what volume, what origin and destination and what kind of special handling is needed, is known. Unfortunately, this information is not immediately shared amongst the other players in the air cargo supply chain leading to an efficient suboptimal planning. Hence, the technology is there, but it is not adapted, and information is not always shared.

What are then the reasons why this crucial information is not timely shared? Basically, some people are still old fashioned and think like in the past that by keeping information to yourself you are in control and have the power. The other reason is the so-called "blame game" where certain companies do not want to share the information because it will show what the errors or flaws where. But each hick up in the chain will lead to more inefficiency further up the supply chain. Sharing information, even though it shows operational inefficiencies, is a strength and will help other companies react to it and adjust.

As an example:

If a flight will be delayed and that information is not shared, then the handling agent may have too much personnel at the wrong earlier time and when the flight arrived it may not have sufficient people to handle it resulting in delays. Subsequently the trucking company picking up the goods may think that the GHA is ready but due to congestion the documents take much longer resulting in waiting times and further delays. It could also be that the GHA is on time, but the trucker is too late.

One of the reasons for not sharing this information is because the GHA and trucker have strict SOPs (standard operating procedures) with the airline, where they are either rewarded or penalized for their on-time performance.

This is where it goes wrong. All this information should be available in a community system, with real life data shared with and by everybody. Companies should be rewarded for sharing their information real time, including delays and not for an on-time performance report that is made afterwards monthly, and mostly used to reduce prices instead of optimizing operations.

E-commerce is a major driver for technological change. Want to have information at all time in an easy interactive way. Moreover, what we are used to as a consumer, we now want in the business to business environment, like being able to have information in a digital way on mobile devices.

Digital Booking Platforms

Platform checking other platforms (like booking, pricewise, etc.). There are nowadays several digital booking platforms, making it easier and more interactive to book a shipment. Like with many other platforms, it is probably not the wisest decision for a forwarder to put all eggs in one basket, being a single booking platform. Obviously, that could work in a buyers' market where supply exceeds demand. However, when demand will outstrip supply, the forwarder may be better off with longer term price agreements with airlines. Therefore, the price mechanism of a booking platform should be used next to the traditional price agreements, which could also be booked through a certain platform.

There should be one standard in booking platforms and community systems, not necessarily one platform, which would lead to monopolistic situations.

Digital front-end customer interface could lead to competitive edge

Easy to use, interactive, informative, unburden, reports

The customer needs to have (i) a quicker interaction with its suppliers by going digital, it should be (ii) easy to use and (iii) provide her/him with data and reports which will help in the decision-making process but also in reports internally at the customer's company.

In an increasingly commoditized air cargo supply chain with many tenders dominated by almost on factor, the price, it is harder to differentiate yourself and to "lock in" the customer. By offering a great customer interface the users at the customer should be so satisfied with the system that they rather not switch from the supplier. That is how a lock in could be created.

AI, Predictive Analytics

With big historic data you could forecast the future a lot better. In the air cargo supply chain, there is repetitive work but also trends that can be forecast and acted upon accordingly. With these so-called predictive analytics, you could automate certain processes and decisions.

For example, planning of trucks could be automated and people could manage the exceptions. A Monday is not the same as a Friday and there are variations in months during the year as well. If based on historic data, these events and even waiting times at certain locations can be contemplated then a planning could be automated and customer expectations could be managed better.

The whole air cargo supply chain could be optimized using AI predictive analytics. Historic data on certain days or months of the GHA and RFS processes can help to predict the future and act accordingly. Yes, the customer wants to reduce the transit times from shipper to consignee, but also wants to have more information and predictability so she or he can plan better.

Robotics and Automation

Blockchain and 3D printing may be far away still.

There was much hype about the potential of 3D printing, possibly disrupting production processes globally. The impact on air cargo was foreseen that, by near sourcing production instead of producing in masse abroad, the volumes of global trade would decline and subsequently the air cargo volumes.

Nevertheless, this has not happened at that scale. 3D printing is ideal for samples and certain industries, like for example the dental and aerospace industry, but consumers will not buy an expensive 3D printer to make their own goods at home, nor will 3D printing be able to replicate mass production in terms of efficiencies, scale and time.

Technology is important, people even more

The cost of new technology is mostly change management, which is defined by people. If the people are not driving the change and implementation of new technology nothing will happen. Like in so many times, the implementation is more difficult than the ideas. The air cargo industry operates with low margins and therefore people are quite busy with their day to day activities and it is difficult to implement change projects that even are cross departmental.

The need for young talent is bigger than ever. Not only because of their skills but also mainly because of the drive for change.

Speak devices, touchless not paperless

Due to the COVID crisis digitization was accelerated mainly driven by the need for contactless interaction. Future will be through voice plus serious gaming to help with training

The enhanced reality helps pick and pack with images and voices.

Summary

This industry is slow in adapting technology because of traditional systems and unwillingness to change. However, change is inevitable. Technology can not only be used to optimize internal processes which leads to more efficiencies and less errors, but also externally with suppliers and customers. By applying the technology in the right way, companies might differentiate themselves and in this way gain market share and healthier margins.

The air cargo industry is by no means leading new technologies to be developed. It should embrace existing technologies, like AI, big data, IOT and robotics and automation a lot more and quicker. Information is crucial and therefore should be shared in the whole community.

The changes needed can only be initiated by people with the right skills and attitude.

It is of utmost importance that the air cargo industry attracts more young talent to drive the much-needed changes.

The Drones Are Coming

Safety and Regulation

The potential use of drones for commercial operations in the urban environment over the coming years is evolving rapidly. Operation in densely populated areas challenges the environment, as compared to more remote rural populated areas. In order to develop drone use, a wide range of factors must be considered. For example, personal injury and property damage, safety around existing airports and the control and management of air traffic in low-level airspace, as well as normal aviation regulations, planning law and the rights of local populations' safety, privacy and peaceful existence (Figure 9.1).

In the hands of amateurs or terrorists the risks of accidents between pilotless drone operations and conventional aircraft around airports is of great concern to the public, to local regulators, aircraft operators and many other involved parties. Small drones currently used for a variety of purposes such as photography, parcel delivery or entertainment, do not require any special launch facilities. Larger cargo carrying pilotless aircraft being developed, however, would need some kind of airport facilities. Although to date, no major incidents involving drones and passenger aircraft have occurred, the potential for such disasters is very much in peoples' minds. The threat of malevolent use of drones is also a serious concern and there have already been a number of airport closures, flight delays and near-collisions with commercial aircraft involving drones. The London Gatwick Airport incident in 2018 which shut down the airport for over 36 hours was caused deliberately and forced airport authorities to think hard about new security system, such as geo-fencing, to safeguard against future attempts.

The rapid growth in the use and deployment of drones in a wide variety of applications, in turn, creates appropriate international and national regulations, insurance and security measures. Similar misgivings occurred during

Figure 9.1 Delivery drone.

the early days of flight over a 100 years ago. Despite all the negative vibrations, however, the main benefits of drones are clear and attractive.

Avoiding road congestion, overcoming geographical barriers such as mountains, lakes, unnavigable rivers, rough terrain where other access does not exist, no emissions thanks to electric power. In addition, remote flight control and no crew equals low cost and greater safety plus minimal air space is required.

Apart from their use for parcel and last-mile deliveries, small drones are frequently in use inside warehouses and production facilities, alongside other robots, for delivering parts or picking goods for packing ready for delivery.

Ed De Reyes, CEO, and co-founder of Sabrewing Aircraft, Inc. pointed out that last-mile drones are more interesting for people in the city to see their food or goods arrive quickly in their backyard after ordering from a cell phone, but this may not be as interesting for people living in remote villages, also such deliveries also command a high price.

Larger Load Carrying Drone Uses

Drones are proving to be indispensable for the delivery of commercial small shipments but have proved their unique value with the accurate and secure delivery of medical and relief supplies during disaster relief operations, where normal roads or sometimes runways are badly damaged.

Cargo Drone Challenges

The main challenges faced by cargo drones include:

- Infrastructure limitations, such as the need for more investment in launching pads and charging points plus handling facilities.
- Regulations for both low and high-level flights, plus International standards and agreements for systems to maintain the quality of the cargo, such as packaging and temperature.
- Viability balance costs against commercial reality will customers pay for this service?
- People consider that drones flying in residential areas are intrusive and potentially dangerous.
- As with any new development, there will be complex technical difficulties to address.
- Manufacturers, logistics companies, distribution centres, regulators and local resident groups will need to work together to develop the necessary operating standards.

Government Regulators Involvement

The evidence of military use of drones and unmanned air than conventional delivery methods. The main integrators are already investing significantly in drones alongside electric vehicles and automation. Once again, however, the parallel situation in the early days of aviation is being repeated with the need to establish international operating facilities. This includes agreements, regulations, putting into place the necessary infrastructures, so that drones are able to operate in a safe and profitable way. The industry will thus develop rapidly. Large investments will be necessary to make commercial drones a viable option.

Operating Costs

Standard costs associated with the operation of delivery drones include:

- Ground charging station
- Batteries
- Maintenance
- Spare parts
- Computers and software systems for drone functions and control
- Operator charges
- Permanent electrical power supply
- Insurance

Next Generation Cargo Drones

The search for a new generation of environmentally friendly transport vehicles and flying machines is proceeding rapidly spurred on by the global need to cut emissions and at the same time increase transport capacities.

Electric Aircraft

There is a trend of substantial investment in developing vertical take-off aircraft for both future passenger and cargo, coupled with battery power. For example, Boeing has announced around $450 million in Wisk an advanced air mobility company (AAM) to develop all electric air taxis. According to McKinsey reported that around $7 billion had already been invested in such projects. However, the rush to create all electric vertical take-off products (EVTOL) needs to be tempered with the establishment of ground facilities, including ports and charging facilities, warehousing and handling for cargo and vertiports systems for passengers.

McKinsey categorizes vertiports as follows:

- Vertihubs," being the largest and most complex variation, as a standalone structure including multiple spaces for take-off, landing and parking, maintenance and potential retail facilities, costing an estimated $6 million – $7 million to construct and $15 million – $17 million annually to operate,

- Vertibases," which could be newbuilds or fitted onto existing rooftops, and would have about three spaces for take-off, landing and parking and maintenance. These would cost an estimated $500,000 – $800,000 in construction and $3 million – $5 million annually to operate, and
- Vertipads," being the smallest of the varieties. Like vertibases these could also be newbuilds or retrofits, with a single take-off and landing space and limited space for parking or maintenance. These are estimated to cost $200,000–$400,000 in construction and $600,000–$900,000 annually to operate.

Electric aviation equipment will be internationally regulated, both on the ground and in the air.

As Electro.Aero's CTO Josh Portlock described on the "eVTOL Insights" podcast, we have the opportunity in electric aviation to design out problems arising in existing industries, from different plugs being used in different countries, variations in the power available from local grids, the accessibility of charging units for the vehicle of different wing spans or rotor blade heights, etc. For example, learning lessons from the experience of electric cars in particular, the SAE AE-7D Aircraft Energy Storage and Charging Committee is developing standard AS6968, which "ensures that electric aircraft can be charged by one consistent internationally accepted standard, without the regional and brand-specific incompatibilities seen in the automotive industry." This means standard-compliant hardware will have to be incorporated across all eVTOL models, chargers and vertiports. Collaboration between vertiport, charger and aircraft manufacturers at the design and development stage will therefore be critical to ensure that all three are compatible and ready to go to market at the same time – which means that investment is needed across these categories, not just into aircraft development.

One of the most impressive is from the American Natilus start up company.

Natilus's larger cargo UAV designs, the 100t, pitting cargo drone technology squarely in competition with conventional aircraft.

The U.S. company is producing the world's first purpose-designed and manufactured autonomous aircraft for air freight transport and, with others, including Volatus Aerospace, Astral Aviation, Aurora and Dymond, Flexport's order brings Natilus's advanced purchase commitments to some $6bn for as many as 440 unmanned aircraft of varying sizes.

They all conform to "blended wing body" (BWB) geometry, where the aircraft's fuselage generates lift along with the wings. And despite its unusual appearance, Natilus's designs are based on established aerodynamic principles, similar to the Northrop Grumman B-2 Spirit, a stealth bomber.

The 100t, with two high-bypass turbofan engines, 110 tonnes of cargo capacity and 5,400 nautical miles of range, will likely be one of the largest examples of a BWB aircraft.

Natilus CEO Aleksey Matyushev said: "In parallel with the development of our family of autonomous aircraft, we are working closely with customers to increase the efficiency of air transport and make it more competitive and safer than ocean shipping."

Today, there are only two ways to move cargo internationally, by air and by sea. The difference between the cost and time of these two modes is dramatic. Sea freight is currently 13 times less expensive than air freight, but 50 times slower in delivery.

"Natilus intends to revolutionize the transport industry by providing the timeliness of air freight at an affordable cost reduction of 60%, making air cargo transport substantially more competitive."

Thanks to loadstar

Another example of air cargo innovation is another US-based company, MightyFly, founded by Manal Habib and Scott Parker's which is developing an unmanned battery powered vertical take-off and landing vehicle (eVTOL). The manufacturers claim that this drone will carry a payload of 100 pounds (45 kg) for 600 miles (965 km) at a speed of up to 150 mph (240 kmh) and is ideal for mid-range deliveries. The vehicle is carbo neutral and requires a small space for loading and unloading while charging its own batteries in flight. A further aircraft with a payload of 500 lb (225 km) is on the books.

Battery Power

As we are forced to abandon fossil fuels to meet our climate targets, batteries are becoming a vital factor in every aspect of lives. Not only our smartphones are powered by batteries, power tools and cars, drones and now aircraft, will be battery powered. It is estimated that by 2030 the use of batteries, large and small will increase by 15–20 times greater than today. Clearly more efficient ways of packaging and transporting them safely will need to be developed. Due to the predicted problems of obtaining some special metals, much innovation will be necessary to find practicable ways of making and supplying these batteries.

Conclusion

Despite all the technical, financial and political barriers, automation including robots, driverless vehicles in warehouses and on airports, cargo drones and crewless aircraft, success will depend on investment and government cooperation in order to develop this new era the future of the air transport industry. There will be bumps in the road as there are always in new developments especially in the aviation industry, but within a very short time we will see these innovations in daily use.

10 The Environment Challenge

Many big promises have been made by governments and big businesses to reduce the world's carbon footprint; very little action had actually occurred. The effects of the pandemic have coincided with an outbreak of extreme climatic events rarely if ever seen before. More than ever governments, businesses, environmental agencies and the public in general are insisting on action. An accusing finger is often pointed at the Aviation sector and air logistics industry in particular, for polluting our skies with emissions and noise but the realities are somewhat different. This industry is making considerable efforts to improve its environmental performance. This chapter reviews the various factors which are involved in combating emissions and noise and pollution.

Until it was hit by the COVID-19 pandemic, the aviation industry had been expanding in line with growth forecasts. Transport, especially the air cargo supply chain, is a fundamental part of modern society, always under attack from the environmental lobby over the amount of carbon-based emissions it releases into the atmosphere, adding to the "greenhouse gas" (GHG) effect and hastening global warming. Aviation's objectives are to be commercially viable and at the same time, achieve its green targets. Aviation overall is now 75% quieter than it was 40 years ago

Aircraft fuel efficiency has improved by 75% in the past 40 years, through improvements in airframe design, engine technology and rising load factors. Improved yield management techniques allow more passengers per flight and skilled loadmasters to maximize the use of cargo capacity. Before the pandemic, some 35,000 routes were in operation flying to and from over 3,500 airports. This level of activity has been greatly reduced but is gradually re-establishing itself.

With the exception of some notable cases, including Hong Kong, Dubai, Liege and Miami and several other specialist airports, cargo has traditionally been regarded as a low level, low profit activity in preference to the seemingly more glamorous passenger and retail sectors. COVID-19 brought home a sharp lesson, once the passengers had faded away, cargo was the only active business stream left in operation. Does this change the balance of both airlines and airports? This remains to be seen but returning to the theme of

DOI: 10.4324/9781003167167-10

emissions, it is not just the air pollution, there are many other activities related to cargo and aviation in general, which cause a larger carbon footprint. For example, the holding patterns of aircraft over airports are caused by missed slots and numerous different kinds of delays. Large vehicles queueing at cargo terminals waiting for their allocated slot, on airport vehicles, are misdirected and badly positioned so that aircraft are waiting on the runway for a parking slot, plus the vast amount of airport related road traffic associated with both passenger and cargo. The list is endless so that the entire aviation operation has to be examined and made more efficient in all aspects. A great deal of new technology and new attitudes have evolved and continue to evolve. It is interesting to note that aviation represents in total, 3.5% of global GDP ($3.5 trillion measured in 2018) and supports or supported some 87 million jobs worldwide. It is therefore vital that the problems of efficiency are dealt with in order to secure the future of this important human resource. According to THE INTERNATIOAL AIR CARGO ASSOCIATION (TIACA), the ocean freight industry is responsible for some 4% of global emissions, while air transport creates 2%.

The Shipping industry however carries some 96% of the world's tonnage, thus theoretically, airfreight is proportionately inefficient. There is also concern on the perceived environmental impact of air freight and the noise its activities can generate, particularly when many cargo-carrying airlines need to operate through night-time take-off and landing slots to make their business viable. Aircraft fuel efficiency has improved by 75% in the past 40 years, through improvements in airframe design, engine technology and rising load factors, where improved yield management techniques are seeing more people being moved on each flight. Upgrades in aircraft and engine design mean that air transport is now 75% quieter than it was four decades ago.

How Green Is My Cargo?

The environmental cost of aviation is a major global challenge to become green. Much work has been carried out including the introduction of cleaner fuels, more efficient aircraft, carbon offsetting and looking beyond just the aviation to its supporting infrastructure.

Aircraft produce several types of emissions that can damage the global climate and it is calculated that some 2% of global man-made carbon emissions can be directly attributed to aviation.

The main culprit is emissions of CO_2 that are produced in direct proportion to the amount of jet fuel used to fly over any distance.

Next comes water vapour created by burning jet fuels. At altitude, condensation trails form, comprising frozen ice crystals that deflect a small amount of sunlight away from the surface of the planet and reflect more infrared radiation back towards Earth. This has an overall warming effect on the atmosphere of the planet (Figure 10.1).

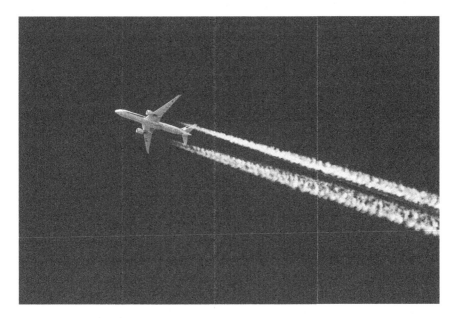

Figure 10.1 Jet trails.

The combustion of atmospheric nitrogen and oxygen in jet engines produces nitrous oxide, which catalyzes the production of ozone and the destruction of methane. The ozone layer prevents damaging ultraviolet light from reaching the Earth's surface, and methane is another GHG, so perhaps the news from that area is not all bad.

Finally, extra emissions are caused by ground handling including trucks operating on behalf of airlines carrying air freight to and from the cargo warehouses. There are also carbon emissions caused by auxiliary power units that serve the cargo facilities, like cool rooms. Some 10% of aircraft emissions of all types, except hydrocarbons and CO gas, are produced during operations on the ground and during landing and take-off, with the bulk of emissions (90%) occurring at higher altitudes. For hydrocarbons and CO, the split is closer to 30% at ground level and 70% at higher altitudes.

The noise caused by aircraft on the ground or during take-off and landing is considered a major source of environmental pollution and can be a serious nuisance for people living close to airports. However, in support of airport expansion, the creation or development of a new airport creates jobs and industry. Take the example of Paris CDG, created in the early 1970 in sparsely populated rural farmland. The new airport grew rapidly attracting industries and people seeking employment, most of whom chose to live within the airports close network of towns and villages. Today it is the ninth busiest for passengers (80 million before COVID) and eleventh for cargo (2 million tonnes) and employs many thousands directly and indirectly. Early in 2012, due to residents' pressure, the German high court upheld a temporary night-time ban previously imposed by a state court on flights between 2,300 and 0500 hours at Frankfurt-Main International Airport. Frankfurt is Germany's biggest air freight gateway and the main hub of Lufthansa Cargo, one of the world's largest cargo-carrying airlines with a fleet of MD-11 freighters operating schedules that depended for their commercial success on flying night-time schedules.

While undoubtedly there are savings to be made in terms of GHG emissions for long-distance freight movements, a voyage by sea is significantly longer. It can take almost 4 weeks for a large containership to sail from London to Singapore, compared with about 12 hours by air, and in many cases there may be a number of economic or time-sensitive advantages for the use of air freight in the first place – so keeping cargo-carrying airlines in the skies 24 hours per day is of vital economic importance for many in the industry.

Alternative Fuel Sources

Many efforts are being made to encourage the development and use of a new sustainable source of fuel to power aircraft and effectively reduce the carbon footprint. Jet aircraft use a petroleum-based fuel commonly known as "Jet A" or "Jet A-1"; the emissions problems associated with their use is discussed earlier in the chapter. Alternative fuel that is not derived from petroleum can be classified into three main categories: biofuels, synthetics and other sources like hydrogen, natural gas, ethanol, methanol and propane (LPG).

The industry body, IATA, has called for 6% of jet-fuel demand, or 8 billion litres per year, to be met by biofuels during the 2020s, adding that it expects airline demand to be 2% or less over the next few years. However, as governments expect airlines to operate in a more environmentally efficient way with the use of biofuels and convert to using a significant proportion of non-fossil fuel in their aircraft engines, they will have either to subsidize biofuel production for their airlines or introduce tough legislation requiring carriers to use a certain percentage of sustainable biofuels in their mix and force them to pay the bills. Such costs will inevitably be passed on to customers. Is this Greta's point, profit over environment?

Synthetics

Synthetic kerosene can be obtained from coal, natural gas or other hydrocarbon resources and can be produced by first turning the resource into gases, which are then recombined to form hydrocarbon liquids. However, synthetic fuel production is an energy-intensive process that produces significantly higher CO_2 emissions than the production of fuel derived from petroleum, while fuel made from vegetable products such as palm oil has caused massive land clearances, including rain forests, in order to provide commercially viable volumes.

Other Options

Several alternative options have been considered for a new source of aviation fuel, but all represent significant challenges and would require the cost-prohibitive production of new aircraft and fuel delivery systems. Hydrogen and natural gas must be used in their liquid form, which requires storage at extremely cold temperatures. Hydrogen burns cleanly, but its production is very energy intensive and it emits large quantities of water vapour with uncertain effects on cloud formation and the atmosphere. Considerable efforts and research are in progress to incorporate electrically powered engines but at present, this is still a long way from realization.

Sustainable Aviation Fuel (SAF)

SAF is one solution for cleaner fuel. It is produced from renewable feedstocks, like cooking oil and household rubbish, and is currently the most viable route to reducing CO_2 emissions in air transport. SAF can be blended with up to 50% traditional jet fuel, meaning it is safe to use in existing aircraft. In 2018 BP Air agreed a collaboration with leading fuel producer Neste to develop and supply SAF from non-palm renewable and sustainable raw materials, including used cooking oil. Although these fuels can reduce the carbon footprint of aviation fuel by up to 80% over their full life cycle they cost considerably more to produce than standard fuel. Several airlines have introduced varying amounts of SAF within a mix of conventional jet fuel but it is the high cost that is the main challenge.

However, it is hoped that in time, new technologies, especially in terms of engine design and lighter materials that reduce fuel consumption, will help to reduce cost. The use of hydrogen and a new generation of efficient batteries may be a factor in the future. Carbon offsetting has been an important method in how the aviation industry has been trying to meet CO_2 targets, which include carbon neutral growth from 2020. SAFs can be made from feedstocks, agricultural residues, algae, waste oils and even carbon

Various forms of SAF have been available in relatively small quantities so far, but it is growing in popularity. According to the Air Transport Action Group (ATAG), SAF can have up to 80% fewer GHG emissions than traditional fuels throughout their life cycle. ATAG claims that SAF also results in lower sulphur and particulate matter emissions, resulting in cleaner air. This all depends on what the SAF is made of and how much is blended with conventional fu International Airport (SFO) via pipeline.

Efficient Aircraft

Many air cargo carriers, including FedEx and UPS, Delta and Swiss World Cargo are investing in more efficient aircraft, producing lower emissions and looking at design, weight and fuel efficiency

It is reported that, for example, Delta announced a $1 billion investment in more efficient planes and carbon offsetting measures and FedEx is working to retrofit and replace aircraft to increase fuel efficiency. Optimal speed, weight and flight paths are sought by shipping companies to save money and lower CO_2 emissions. The war in Ukraine itself has obliged many carriers to use longer routes which avoid Russian airspace, costing more and increasing emissions.

Lightweight ULD

ULD manufacturers are now offering lightweight pallets and containers for the consolidated carriage of loose shipments. The reduced weight helps save fuel. In some cases, lighter ULDs could allow more packages to be shipped per container, if weight was not the limiting factor. While this wouldn't decrease fuel use for that flight, it would still result in increased efficiency as more cargo per plane could be transported.

Investments in Carbon Offsets

Many companies are setting ambitious environmental goals to be achieved in record time. Carbon offsets can help the air cargo industry bridge the gap as it researches and implements new techniques to improve the efficiency and sustainability of direct operations.

Safety

At the world cargo symposium held in October 2021 in Dublin, one of the lead subjects discussed was lithium batteries and their potential danger for both passengers and cargo. One of the frequent problems, which also applies to dangerous goods in general, for which no action is normally taken, is the false declaration of the goods by the shipper. However the main danger to aircraft from these batteries is poor packaging. Careless and inadequate packaging and preparation are a considerable danger to aircraft and it is by pure luck and a major tragedy had not occurred. It was also commented that equipment in use for cargo examination was okay looking rarely directed at detecting lithium even though the technology exists. The reluctance to use this technology by ground handling companies is based on the time taken and the potential delay to flight departures IATA's spokesman Brendan Sullivan said that governments needed to prioritize criminalizing guilty shippers. IATA has launched its CEIV lithium battery certification to ensure higher safety and security standards.

Sustainability

As airlines and logistics companies come through their most challenging 18 months, they are faced with the reality that international business is changing out of recognition but also, as the real threats of climate change become evident constantly, they will have to invest in research and technology to achieve a cleaner and greener future.

The COVID-19 pandemic forced people to stay indoors giving rise to a substantial boom in online shopping for almost everything, which has in turn increased air cargo traffic, forcing operators to plan for the best way to optimize their operations. One of the major themes through all of this has been the need for sustainability. Even though the air cargo community has been indoors, it has been a busy year as the focus has shifted towards the environment not on a short-term but instead on a long-term basis. It is to not only create goals but also to start implementing them in the next decade – from sustainable aviation fuel to reduce CO_2 emissions to using electric vehicles and encouraging others to take sustainability seriously, the industry is continuously preparing itself for a cleaner future.

In an earlier interview with STAT Trade Times, Steven Polmans, chairman of TIACA, said that sustainability for them is simply 3+2, which is people, planet and prosperity + partnerships and innovation. It is about reducing carbon footprints, attracting, retaining and developing the younger generation of air cargo employees, improving processes and efficiencies. The association also has the TIACA Sustainability Programme, which was started in 2019 and supports this vision.

The challenge faced by the industry is that Environmental protection and economic growth are almost directly conflicting objectives and therefore an extremely difficult goal to realize and balance in the future.

Weather Watch

The impact of bad and unexpected weather has been a feature of Aviation safety since the very first flights. But with the rapidly advancing impact of climate change, how significant is climate to aircraft operations now?

The vast majority of recorded incidents, accidents and disruptions caused by bad weather conditions to aircraft operations, is clearly applicable to passenger flights where high numbers of passengers have either been killed or badly injured. What is not so clear and difficult to measure, however, is the number of delays to both passenger and cargo flights as a result of weather conditions. Despite rapid advances in technology, factors such as thick fog, thunderstorms and high wind play a huge role in the accident toll. The conditions likely to endanger aircraft are broadly defined as follows:

- Fog, especially quick forming
- Ice-icing up of wings but also in the air can cause instrument failure resulting in pilot confusion and error. Layer cloud airframe icing.

- Thunderstorms: In addition to extremely heavy rain, they can contain strong wind shear, large hail and severe turbulence, each of which can damage or destroy an aircraft. And these phenomena don't just occur within the storm itself
- Lightning strikes
- Hail
- Wind shear and violent ground winds
- Sound and dust storms
- Poor atmospheric conditions for example caused by the burning of forests
- Volcanic ash (although not a climatic condition the ash is diffused into the atmosphere by winds causing frequent engine failure, especially jets.
- Clear air turbulence
- Strong to gale force winds

From the cargo operations point of view, a great deal of time and as a consequence financial loss is incurred by delays, often due to weather conditions. New technologies in climate and weather forecasting and access to real-time data can be usefully employed to avoid some of these problems but in most cases the weather will do what it wants! Airports in Alaska, for example, are geared up for permanent ice and snow whereas an airport in the middle of the United States can be hit by a sudden tornado or hurricane. Violent extremes of weather are becoming more frequent and more violent as the effects of climate change become more and more apparent. To mitigate these factors will take a great deal more than efforts from the aviation industry but everyone working in this sector is being forced to build in as many safeguards as possible for the future.

Bird Strikes

Bird strikes have caused a number of accidents and are a significant threat to flight safety, but in most cases, the collisions cause aircraft damage but prove fatal to thousands of birds. The Canada goose has been ranked as the third most hazardous wildlife species to aircraft (behind deer and vultures), with approximately 240 goose-aircraft collisions in the United States each year. 80% of all bird strikes go unreported.

Most accidents occur when a bird or flocks of birds collide with the aircraft windscreen or are sucked into the jet engine. These collisions are considered to be a contributing factor, among many others, to the worldwide decline of many avian species. Technical innovations such as pulse lights, radars, robots and remote sensing, which can deter birds, are proving to be effective. The World Birdstrike Association holds several international conferences every year to find solutions to this problem.

There is no doubt as we move towards global recovery following the COVID-19 pandemic that all nations are being forced, willingly and in some cases, unwillingly, into facing up to this climate change challenge, a real force of nature which refuses to be ignored.

The future of our lives and our planet are very largely in our hands. In the words of Sir David Attenborough "global warming and the rise of sea temperatures is a global phenomenon which we are all responsible for."

11 Career Opportunities in Air Logistics

Air Cargo Needs You

Over the last decade, the air cargo industry has welcomed new technologies and management techniques to be able to offer first class and efficient and competitive service in response to shippers and customer demands. This dynamic component of aviation is less known than its apparently more glamorous sibling – the passenger sector. Following the COVID-19 pandemic and the subsequent breakdown of traditional social activities, lock downs and other restrictions, the popular travel market has partially collapsed, while the cargo industry has experienced a dramatic demand for the urgent delivery of many kinds of goods. However, all parts of air logistics suffer from a serious shortfall in qualified new recruits. Few universities cover this sector within their teaching scope or career paths for their graduates, even though the industry desperately needs qualified engineers and computer scientists, marketing personnel and business development experts, vets and software engineers. It is a global industry offering progressive careers around the world with opportunities to travel and experience working with nationals from over 200 countries. In order to quantify some of these career opportunities, we have devoted this chapter to the subject, in the hope that young people will appreciate the outstanding opportunities that this dynamic industry can offer. Air logistics is a vital component of world trade and modern society. Most of the work within this industry takes place on the ground, in order to derive maximum capacity and yield.

Airlines

The airline sector was seriously impacted by the COVID-19 pandemic and due to changes in social habits regarding travel, may never return to the same level as before. Thanks to the considerable cargo capacity afforded by the new generation of passenger aircraft such as the Boeing 777, large quantities of belly-hold cargo can be carried on long haul flights on a regular basis. Routes are chosen on a variety of criteria – the number of passengers and tourist potential of different destinations, business travel potential on different destinations as well as possible uplift or delivery of cargo.

DOI: 10.4324/9781003167167-11

The use of freighter aircraft had become a highly specialized for the use of special cargoes where large quantities of freight were required at one time, for example, new mobile phone launch, seasonal products such as fruits or flowers while heavy equipment and machinery, cars satellite equipment, need freighter capacity as well as specially equipped aircraft for animal transport such as horses et cetera freighter aircraft such as the Boeing 747 series had, until the beginning of the pandemic, a limited function, suddenly became in demand when the passenger aircraft capacity was no longer available. Cargo has thus become a much more important part of an airlines bottom line. The job opportunities within the sector are varied and extensive. From pilots and navigation offices, loadmasters, maintenance engineers, technical managers and route planners combine with sales and marketing opportunities in a highly competitive market.

In today's competitive aviation market, cargo represents an important part of an airline's revenue and profit. The advantage of using belly-hold is that the flight operates on a regular schedule in two directions and that, any revenue from cargo that has a higher revenue than the variable cost, will contribute to the bottom line.

However, not all destinations that are served on passenger aircraft are good cargo destinations, like for example touristic destinations. In the same way, some of the destinations with high cargo demand do not have enough belly capacity to accommodate the demand. Therefore, freighters are very important in this industry, representing around 50% of all cargo carried. Other operators handle cargo only traffic very often on charters, regular or ad-hoc.

Only 1% of total freight worldwide is being transported via air but it does represent around 35% of the total value of trade due to the high value density of the products. Products are sent by air because of urgency, high value, perishability, security and high cost of inventory.

There are different types of airlines carrying cargo:

* Airlines carrying passengers with only belly-hold cargo
* Freighter operators carrying only cargo
* Mixed airlines operating both passenger and freighter aircraft
* Integrators with their own fleets of cargo freighters

Job opportunities are wide and varied and will include:

* Route planning and optimization
* Revenue and yield management
* Cargo operations overseeing handling and trucking
* Sales and marketing: Liaising with forwarders and GSSAs
* Maintenance supervising
* Flight operations
* Opportunities with airlines will often include overseas travel and postings

The aviation industry is constantly changing and evolving, creating even more career opportunities for the future. Airline careers in cargo are increasing in scope and value and as technology impacts on aircraft design, such as the use of drones, the potential for exciting careers is limitless.

Airport Management

As mentioned in the previous chapter on airports, a large proportion of these have no significant cargo interest. These are unlikely to be regional domestic airports or those specializing in low-cost travel for package deal airlines. These mostly involve smaller aircraft with little or no cargo capacity and with quick change over between stops, little time for loading or unloading cargo. In those airports where cargo is significant, however, investment in equipment and technology will be needed to ensure rapid and secure transfer of cargo. The job variety encompasses airport management and ground services, ground handling companies and ramp handling services, surface transport, specialist temperature controlled facilities and management, phytosanitary and veterinary facilities, where foodstuffs and animals are handled, secure facilities for valuable cargo, special facilities for pharmaceuticals and vaccines, cool stores and cool dollies, plus the usual management and accounting personnel.

In large cargo handling airports such as Frankfurt or Hong Kong or Miami a wide range of highly skilled personnel is required to ensure the safe and rapid passage of vital cargo there has always been criticism from the freight industry that apart from some notable exceptions, cargo is often regarded as a negative and unwanted part of airport operations. This has been brought into sharp focus during the pandemic when it was air cargo that kept airlines and airports in business. It is hoped that future airport managers will see cargo in a different and more positive light.

Airports form the link between departure and destination. There are over 8,000 registered airports around the world, ranging from the very small regional airports to the massive cargo hubs such as Paris ADP, Hong Kong, Miami or Frankfurt.

Some operate night curfews which restrict aircraft movements, while others operate 24 hours. Airports are like small towns and contain every kind of business related to the travel of both people and cargo. Many airports are the facilitator for the different actors in the air cargo supply chain. The airports derive their revenues from, amongst others, landing fees, real estate, parking and shops. Thanks to cargo many airport communities provide jobs and enable a trade to grow for the country and regions.

The career opportunities are varied and include:

- Ground management including the control of fleets of utility vehicles and equipment on the airport
- Sales and marketing to promote the airport internationally
- Automation and digitization of the cargo flows

- Security in a highly complex environment
- Ground handling
- Liaison with airlines, forwarders and handling companies
- Planning for capacity management and future development
- Customs officers, now a highly sophisticated computer-based function
- Sanitary and health inspection
- Veterinary and animal welfare operations
- Administration including marketing, press relations and communications
- Liaison with government agencies
- Control of the environment and safety management

The function of cargo processing has proved to be more important during the pandemic and the range and variety of careers in this sector have improved. As in all the other aspects of the air cargo industry, technology plays an increasing role in the progress and opens opportunities for engineers and computer experts.

Air Charters

Manufacturers and suppliers frequently need a special flight or aircraft to perform an urgent or special delivery. This may require a one-time charter of an aircraft that will meet the requirements. Charter brokers and operators are available to companies that need these special facilities and it is their task to source the correct equipment in the right location on an ad-hoc basis. Some airlines do not want to invest in their own assets and therefore lease an aircraft on a short/medium term, which might be several years, also called wet lease or aircraft, crew, maintenance and insurance (ACMI).

Some typical examples of charters are as follows:

- Seasonal deliveries such as new Beaujolais in November requiring large freighter aircraft for worldwide distribution
- Launch of a new product which demands fast bulk supplies, EG a new mobile telephone
- Transfer of large animals for rehabilitation, e.g., an endangered species such as a rhinoceros
- A consignment of heavy machinery for the construction of a power station or hospital
- The transfer of an orchestra or art exhibition and equipment
- Urgent deliveries of machinery parts or oilfield equipment

Some of the opportunities in this sector include:

- Sales to airlines and forwarders of ad-hoc capacity
- Project management that includes special air lifting
- Planning of routes
- Purchase of appropriate capacity at the right price

During the COVID pandemic and the subsequent conflict in Ukraine, the role of charters and charter brokers has increased substantially. The drastic cut back in wide bodied passenger flight and belly-hold capacity has made it imperative to employ charters. The withdrawal of the AN 124 fleet had added even greater shortages of available capacity. Added to this, high ocean freight rates and long delays have switched much more cargo onto air transport. Being a charter manager has become a very important and useful career.

Cargo Handling

Cargo spends more time on the ground than in the air. An airline can thus sometimes only differentiate itself competitively on the ground. Therefore, ground handling is of crucial importance in the air cargo supply chain. When packages and shipments arrive at the ground handling warehouse at the airport, a number of vital tasks must be performed and managed.

Today nearly all international shipments are controlled by Electronic Data Processing and in the case of a large airport, many thousands of shipments will be processed in any 24-hour period. Some larger airlines have their own handling, mainly at their hubs, but in order to remain agile and flexible they outsource the handling service to companies dedicated to the warehouse and ramp handling.

Some of the handling companies have operations in many airports all over the world. Careers and jobs in this sector carry great responsibility and the need for accuracy.

Some of your day-to-day tasks could include:

- Sales and marketing to promote their services to airlines globally
- Supervising the sorting of packages into shipments, containers and pallets, requiring excellent computer skills
- Supervising dangerous goods processes, a vital role involving meticulous and careful examination of goods and documentation
- Optimizing processes using the latest technology in order to improve efficiencies
- Dealing with Customs

The entire handling procedure is carried out under a strict management control and is a vital link between the Freight Forwarder, truckers, the airline and the recipient of the cargo. Because of tight margins and fierce competition, the management of the handling process requires very solid and flexible hands on work by the personnel. There are many really challenging possibilities in ground handling.

Freight Forwarding

Freight Forwarders are the architects of the entire transaction of transporting goods from the manufacturer or supplier to the customer. In today's fast-paced and competitive market, this could be an ideal career for young people of either sex, graduates in IT, business, management or languages.

Some of your responsibilities would include:

- Unburden shippers with their complete supply chain by offering efficient logistics solutions, ranging from air, sea, road, rail to warehouse solutions
- You would negotiate contracts with airlines and handling companies
- Liaise with the client or shipper
- Arrange packaging of goods transportation
- Find the best solution to each shipment including insurance and handling
- Manage the transaction by IT and EDI (Electronic Data Interchange).
- Provide internet technology for tracking the goods
- Deal with Customs
- Use imagination and tact to handle special cargo's such as pharmaceuticals, telecom equipment and even live animals
- Maintain communication and control of all phases of the shipment

You would work with companies and individuals in many other countries and cultures. Moreover, your customers are from different industries. You would need to be flexible and energetic and be willing to consider overseas assignments, depending on the size of the company.

General Sales and Service Agent GSSA

Some airlines prefer to appoint an independent Cargo Sales agent which allows them to concentrate on passenger business. Or in some cases the amount of (cargo) flights to a certain destination does not justify having their own sales staff. Or in less known regions the GSSA already has a commercial footprint. Sometimes an airline may have no direct flights to a country or region but can still sell cargo capacity for their main routes, this is called off-line.

The GSSA may represent several different non-competing airlines in different countries. They also offer more services than just sales. Basically, they can unburden the airline by acting as a de facto cargo department, which entails little or no investment by the airline. Digital marketplaces, where demand and supply meet, are increasing.

Some GSSAs are small-sized operations, while others are multinational. More and more airlines are handing over their cargo management to GSSAs. It is an entrepreneurial and rewarding career offering variations and great potential rewards.

You could work in different areas such as:

- Sales and marketing: liaise with airlines and forwarders to increase sales and find new customers in different international markets
- Plan and coordinate the bookings in the most efficient way

- Define the strategy, pricing and revenue optimization together with the airlines
- Digital interaction with the stake holders
- New product development to complement the sales

Logistics Service Provider

Air cargo consignments frequently travel by truck, both to feed an airport to connect with flights or deliver to customers from incoming flights. RFSs are a vital part of the air cargo supply chain. These are offered by logistics service providers which also offer other logistics facilities, like warehousing, last mile distribution, transport in other modalities and digital control towers.

An airline might decide to have a network of FTL or less than truck load (LTL) or a combination of both. In some areas around the world there are LSPs that offer an extensive road feeder network covering the whole area. Road feeder networks are mostly deployed in Europe, the United States and to a lesser extend Asia. It makes sense to use a truck instead of a flight, because of the dimensions, since short haul flights are operated by smaller planes.

Also, time and cost play a role since not all destinations are at airports. LSPs offer a wide range of truck services, including for example, secure and cool trailers. Digital platforms and control towers are growing. These companies also increasingly make use of robotization, artificial intelligence and digitization.

Some of the exiting roles you may encounter in this sector are:

- Managing and optimizing assets
- Planning and route development
- Sales and marketing: dealing with the airlines worldwide
- Process optimization through digitizing front and back office
- Market studies
- Manage the daily operations

Shipper

The shipper or customer needing to transport goods internationally may choose a mixture of transport modes but will mostly depend on the freight forwarder to manage this process.

Manufacturers and distributors employ skilled and knowledgeable transport and distribution experts to liaise with forwarders and customers or end users. The goods must arrive on time and in perfect condition with no difficulties or delays due to incorrect documentation, packaging or misdirection.

Even very heavy machinery such as jet engines, locomotives, cattle and entire orchestras may fly to destinations around the world and will include ancillary services such as refrigeration units, special road services, expert handling and quick decision-making. At the other end of the scale, highly delicate pharmaceutical products, art exhibitions and secret fashion shows, will require discrete and careful supervision. The forwarder is the link but the shipper must be hands on. Job opportunities are varied and carry responsibility and will often require travel to customer destinations.

Some of the responsibilities include:

• Liaising with forwarders to use the most efficient transportation mode
• Buying and negotiating of services
• Optimization and digitization modelling
• Planning of services in close contact with sales
• Forecasting business models

Software Companies and IT

Digitization and automation play an important role in the air cargo supply chain. There are many software companies that offer services to the industry, ranging from reservations systems to booking platforms. Information is the new gold and big data and AI and robotics are increasingly being used to streamline the processes in all parts of the supply chain.

Air cargo is adopting more and more technology solutions in all departments. Procure to pay and order to cash processes are increasingly more digitized not only to save cost but specially to improve the customer interaction and reduce errors. If you have an interest in computer or software careers, you will find them in air cargo.

Some examples of what you could do include:

• Software managers and developers
• Develop and implement yield, revenue and reservations optimization tools
• IT support for customers
• Big data analysis and develop algorithms
• IT management
• Smart solutions and (App) tools to improve performance
• Tracking and tracing technology development
• Ground handling control systems
• Digital interaction and messaging with suppliers and customers

Innovation

The air supply chain continues to change and evolve ever faster powered by the need to become faster, with lower costs, less pollution and greater efficiency. The aim is helping the shipper to send his goods to his customer at the best possible price and delivery schedule. The enterprise of a new generation of inventors, software developers, systems engineers opens up a vast and wide ranging market for new ideas in what has always been a traditional industry. Now is the time to present your ideas and inventions in any aspect of the process. On the ground, in the warehouse, and in the air, air logistics needs your ideas and inventions. The future of this industry is enormous, so why not be part of.

Training and Qualifications in Air Cargo

For those ambitious people working within the sector, there are many ways of becoming more skilful and better qualified, for enhanced promotion potential.

IATA offers around 70 varied training courses, including marketing, business development, market research, customer services, air cargo management with diplomas, revenue optimization, route profitability, temperature controlled technologies, accident prevention and safety, security and anti-theft development, ground handling, live animal transport, specialist pharmaceutical handling and management and ULD handling and management. There are many other specialist courses and the information may be obtained directly from IATA.

TIACA has also developed a programme of training and skill optimization.

For more information, visit IATA and TIACA.

Hands on Experience a Personal Reflection

Gerton Hulsman has spent over 30 years in the logistics industry. After a long and varied career, including various roles with KLM, he has wide experience of the challenges facing the on-ground service sector and its vital contribution to the smooth flow of the air logistics supply chain.

Having worked for over 40 years in the airfreight business one could say that a lot of changes have passed like a kaleidoscope.

Airplanes changed from narrow bodies to wide bodies allowing a multitude of merchandize to be transported by air. Almost every commodity was now able to be transported over vast distances around the globe, opening the doors for global trading and the benefits this entailed for economies, rich or poor.

A myriad of enterprises embarked in airfreight and saw great advantages in trading products that were not available at all in certain parts of the world. For example, think of foodstuffs, pharmaceuticals, capital goods and much more.

For young people now thinking about making a career in the airfreight industry, it is an excellent time to support developments in the field of digitization, automation and in the near future, also robotization. All this needs to be seen from a young and certainly innovative angle which will contribute to a new World of Transportation. This much-needed contribution to efficient handling involves everything being transported, not just by air but by all modes. These young entrants have an important task on their shoulders, to find ways that lead to optimal transportation including, amongst other things, the reduction of emissions which contributes to a better and safer environment.

The side effect of this international world is a beautiful environment where people from all over the world get to know each other and work together on a very important branch of the world economy.

In all these years I have enjoyed every day of working in this industry and can only wish those who chose this industry a great future.

12 Views of the Future

What Comes Next?

The world's population suffers from a continuous barrage of conflict, famine, sickness, bad weather and a hundred other negative events. Against this background the flame of optimism still burns bright.

The future of the human race during the next few decades will be heavily influenced by technology and the struggle for dominance by the mega sized tech companies such as Amazon Apple meta and Microsoft which together invested $280 billion during 2021. But with a taste of caution it can be seen that many leading companies failed by missing the next big thing. Companies such as IBM, America's most accessible company in the mid-1980s but soon a loss maker or Nokia missed out on the shift to smartphones.

In such an uncertain post–COVID-19 world nobody knows for sure what is going to happen next. What will be the most important events of the next 50 years? Will it be the environment and climate change, increasing world famine and even political and military conflict? The international logistics industry has been and continues to be a vital factor in world trade and even with the trend towards near shoring, will continue to distribute our goods and products alongside the ocean shipping industry. Air cargo has survived since the 1960s on human effort and endeavour and even with the latest technology and systems, it is the human spirit which prevails.

We have put together some personal views from people within the industry about how they feel the future will unfold. You may not agree with them and they may be right or wrong but we have set out in this book to present a true picture of the industry, its weaknesses, its strengths and its resilience.

The Digital Pathway

Air cargo's journey to digitalization has been long and winding and there is still some way to go.

IATA's electronic air waybill (e-AWB) drive has often been used as a barometer for air cargo's digital success and here progress has been slow, although gaining momentum.

DOI: 10.4324/9781003167167-12

The e-AWB, which aimed to move the industry away from paper air way-bills, was launched in 2010 and at the end of 2020 the electronic document had a market penetration level of just under 75%.

The project is more complex than it seems at first glance – a single company in the supply chain cannot drive the change to e-AWBs, it takes all the many stakeholders involved in handling a shipment to have the right digital infrastructure in place and the willingness to switch to new processes to make it happen.

It is perhaps unsurprising then that the most rapid change in air cargo's digital landscape has been driven by individual companies that can control the whole process.

For example, the last few years have seen the launch of a number of digital booking portals by both airlines and third-party companies.

These platforms allow airline customers to view schedule information, prices and book online.

The implementation of Application Program Interfaces (APIs) has also helped speed up the development of online booking. APIs allow airlines to more easily plug their systems into those of their customers or third-party booking platforms.

The development of booking portals is of particular interest; it still takes time to connect systems using APIs, so airlines tend to reserve direct connections with individual customers for larger accounts, which limits the reach of direct airline/forwarder API connections.

However, by connecting with a third-party portal, airlines can offer their capacity to multiple forwarders that have signed up to the platforms.

It is often said that the rise of digitalization in our personal lives is also helping drive the move towards a digital future in cargo. If, as an individual, I can book holidays, order food and even buy a car online, why can't I book my next cargo shipment online?

And this trend has accelerated because of COVID-19. The pandemic has undeniably increased our use of e-commerce on a personal level and several airline and booking portal executives have said it has had the same effect on air cargo as people move towards a homeworking environment.

But what of the digital projects that involve multiple stakeholders, after all this is probably where the largest efficiency gains will be made.

It should be noted that there has also been progress on this front. The last few years have seen a gradual rise in the number of cargo communities established around an airport.

These communities will often implement systems that allow the various stakeholders to share information through a centralized and independent digital platform.

These centralized systems have allowed various projects to be launched that aim to create efficiencies to benefit the whole airport community.

IATA's One Record project has similar ambitions but across the whole industry.

However, these cargo communities would probably admit that a lot more could be achieved if companies were willing to share more information, something that requires a change in mentality.

But there could be some hope here as well. COVID-19 has not only resulted in companies increasing their use of digital solutions, but it has also forced companies to review all facets of their business.

Sustainability is also pushing companies to take another look at how their businesses run.

This has the potential to push competitive collaboration, where companies team up on mutually beneficial projects.

Examples of companies outside of air cargo collaborating in this way range from ice cream firm Ben and Jerry's teaming up with sportswear brand Nike on marketing, Intel and Microsoft teaming up on a development project and pharma firms Pfizer and Merck working together on cancer treatments.

There are also examples in logistics; as well as the community platforms, ground handlers have shared infrastructure and shippers have collaborated on sharing truck capacity to name a few examples.

So, while air cargo's move to a digital future is still at an early stage, it does at least seem as if the journey is picking up speed.

The Future Air Cargo Logistics from an It Perspective, Working Together As One

Air cargo logistics traditionally is being handled by a chain of stakeholders to complete the transportation from origin to the final destination. The stakeholders involved in the logistic chain to deliver a shipment from the shipper to the final consignee are transport companies, forwarding agents, Customs brokers, handling companies, GSAs and airlines. In order to successfully comply with transport, as well as Customs, security and safety regulations all stakeholders are forced to exchange information and communications.

Due to the non-existence of an integrated electronic data and communication platform, which would enable stakeholders to access and retrieve public information from each stakeholder involved, data and communication are exchanged from shipper to agent, from agent to transporter, from transporter to handler and from handler to airline. The same applies in reverse, from airline to handler, to agent, to transporter and to finally the consignee. This involved much paperwork, endless emails and telephone calls between the logistic parties in order to be informed and keep track on shipment status information and relevant supporting actions to support a smooth transportation from origin to its final destination.

It goes without saying that this information exchange and communication process is extremely labour intensive, inefficient and often not up to date and last but not least does to support nowadays customers' expectations on the end-to-end supply chain visibility, traceability and predictability on air cargo shipments.

With the reality of online buying and selling the e-commerce and consequently customers' expectations are higher than ever before. Air cargo traditionally must be a fast way of transportation and customers anno 2022 now wants to know "everything."

One way of controlling the supply chain and connecting all data and communication channels from an efficiency and customer centric perspective is to become in control of all stakeholders involved just like integrators are operating. Recent examples of supply chain integrations are from Amazon and Maersk starting whom started its own air transport services.

For the many forwarders, handlers, transport companies and airlines who are struggling to compete in a low margin volume-based market the only way to move forward is to increase the competitiveness by further optimizing their processes. Although this has been an aim for decades with little success the current digital transformation mindset within the cargo industry has been activated as never before. With recent introduced technologies such as the IATA ONE record data model and IT platforms facilitating single window access and system to system data integration by data sharing, the next coming year will offer major opportunities to create the highly needed visibility, traceability and predictability enabling all stakeholders involved to work together as ONE.

Raoul Paul, CEO CargoHub Technologies PIC

Training For the Next Generation Shaping the Future of Air Cargo

Out of the blue, the COVID-19 pandemic shattered global commerce, social behaviour and human interchange. Transport of people and goods almost collapsed and governments rushed to acquire vital medical supplies. The devastation has revealed some serious weaknesses in our social behaviour and our ability to re-establish a "new normal" (Figure 12.1).

Figure 12.1 Stan Wraight.

There is the need to define the future now. Increasingly, leaders are admitting that air cargo should be established as a core business rather than an add on that reverts to where it was before the pandemic. For far too long, aviation operators, especially carriers and airports, have ignored the important role played by cargo, placing most investments and resources in passenger traffic development and on-airport retail, claiming that cargo generates no significant money. The screeching halt of passenger related activity has pushed airlines and airports into panic mode and has clearly demonstrated the world's dependence on air cargo deliveries, previously either taken for granted or merely unknown.

If cargo is going to be a core business in the future, a new business model, such as virtual integration, would be required to meet the challenges and opportunities that present themselves. To achieve these changes successfully, a collaborative approach is needed, requiring an additional set of skills. Some forward-thinking carriers had already started this process before the pandemic but the urgent need to mitigate the destructive effect of COVID-19 on the aviation industry has accelerated. The race is on for companies to position themselves as cargo leaders. With passenger travel slow to recover, cargo traffic may well be the primary source of income for airlines, handlers, forwarders and airports, for the foreseeable future.

Most current economic forecasts predict a slow recovery over the next 3 to 4 years. During this period, the demand for goods, especially time sensitive, will continue to expand, often at the expense of traditional retail.

How do operators exploit the opportunities which e-commerce presents? As has been demonstrated, large operators such as Amazon have been investing in their own transport fleets but will always call on the cargo airline operators to supply the necessary capacity. How will personnel requirements need to change from the handlers, airport operators, road feeder networks? Near-shoring of supply chains and geopolitical impact on demand and capacity and when employees are geographically dispersed and face-to-face personal interaction is restricted, will be some of the factors in play.

New Skills and Technologies

As individuals and businesses have become comfortable with online learning platforms and their speed of delivery, numerous opportunities will emerge. However, recognizing and creating a new product and service portfolio will require a set of skills not traditionally available in logistics-focused education and training programmes. This industry is based on service and to improve business outcomes, considerable investment in developing employees will be vital. Learning and development are usually one of the first casualties of cost reductions, but the air Logistics business needs to focus even more on training and developing of personnel to support new objectives (Figure 12.2).

A new business model in a new normal requires new mindsets and practices, but don't throw the baby out with the bath water! The technical skills

Figure 12.2 Warehouse drone.

that can meet the immediate and future needs of a company are still needed. Questions to ask are what are the skillsets that are relevant during this time and what will take the industry into the future to operate effectively and profitably in the new environment? Do current leaders have the capability to be flexible and resilient to adapt, engage the employees and lead in different situations using different tools.

Digital Transformation

Air cargo customers expect the same easy access to booking and tracking shipments as in arranging flights and hotels. To achieve this type of service for air cargo, digitization is the entry point for evolving systems. This results in streamlined and seamless process so there are fewer points of disruption in the flow of information.

The Air Cargo Industry – and indeed the supply chain as a whole – has been based on complicated paper documents and systems for far too long. Much of the necessary paper trail stems from a history of regulations that require forms and stamps, often in triplicate. New standards are slowly being approved and adopted that will reduce hard-copy requirements and allow industry players to leverage digital documentation. This will eventually generate significant time savings and increase accuracy. The IATA has said that an air cargo booking is manually retyped as many as 97 times as it passes from one system to the next. That is 97 opportunities for an error. The manual retyping is a result of many systems that have sprung up in an attempt to automate, but which unfortunately do not integrate with each other.

In addition, such digitization will allow greater visibility into operations and produce reliable data from which business decisions can be driven. Digitization will not only help air cargo carriers meet evolving customer needs for greater transparency in the transportation of their cargo, but it will also help customers streamline their own operations.

The frequently ignored but vital part of the air cargo chain, handling and RFS, is a good example of how a technology application can vastly improve and streamline the process. Take one instance of technical innovation, Trucking CDM platform from Netherlands-based CargoHub eliminates the guesswork of trucks waiting, sometimes for hours, not knowing where their shipment is or where to deliver to the handler. In the CDM platform all truck movements are visible to the handling agents and expected arrival times are continually updated. Predictability and transparency of truck movements are necessary for all parties involved at the various airports in order to facilitate road transport of air cargo to its loading and unloading destinations as efficient as possible. The more parties sharing their data on the CDM platform, the more benefits can be reached through the entire logistics chain.

Airlines also have the possibility of following the entire transport process in real time. The loading time, departure time, any eventual damage identified during loading or unloading as well as the location of trucks in combination with expected arrival times can, via an account, be fully transparent. In this way airlines can keep their customers accurately informed.

Working in close collaboration with future developments of CDM with the Holland University of applied sciences assures that the best available technology and thinking are driving the system.

According to Giovanni Douven, project manager, The Trucking CDM platform is the starting point for future research into a comprehensive Cross Chain Control Centre (4C) project for air cargo. The complexity of connections between parties involved provides extensive research and education possibilities for InHolland. The 4C project forms a "living laboratory" or eco system, as it were, to further examine and educate. After all, the connection between parties goes beyond the mere pick-up and delivery of shipments. The air cargo industry is, despite many improvements, a fairly traditional sector involving many different parties. InHolland believes that everyone in the air cargo industry should be connected in the cloud, where each player should share relevant data with other parties involved.

Similar systems are either in use or being developed throughout the industry.

Change of Habits

The air cargo industry will also need experienced cargo practitioners and those willing and motivated to learn and stay in cargo for the long haul. They will exhibit critical thinking and the capability to solve problems and innovate in a much more complicated and restricted business environment with even complex supply chains. The pandemic has also surfaced the urgency to review an organization's competency framework and learning strategy in its workforce planning. Many employees have been experiencing the joys and tribulations of working from home and juggling family life and will probably wish to continue to do so for many months to come. Some companies are already re-evaluating the need to maintain expensive office facilities. However, the need to keep up to date with industry trends and products, building new skills and growing competences demands a solution or multiple solutions

Organizations can support and guide with the aid of a structured learning process such as the competency framework and enhance virtual self-learning using technology. This provides the flexibility for the learners to choose what they would need and/or like to learn within a structure, how and when, in addition to their own informal learning. Organizations can facilitate personalized learning objectives.

For example, many of us have been in the situation where we had seen/read and "filed" something away electronically and when we need it, we cannot recall where we had "filed" it under. Think of the times when we google for an answer to the questions we have. Likewise, organizations are trying new ways to push "bite-sized" content into the "home and workspace" so that the employees can "pull" it at the time he/she needs it.

As part of the structured formal and informal learning, the organization creates the environment where the employee pulls the required content on demand but is able to access curated resources for much deeper learning at another time. A mix-and-match of different subjects would be available and aligned with their professional and personal needs along the competency pathway.

To illustrate, SASI provides in-classroom training programmes such as the Air Cargo Professional Advancement which is the first aviation-related programme accredited by the Chartered Institute of Logistics (UK). This programme is composed of a series of modules. Customers can mix-and-match individual modules that fit into their competency levels and learn at their own pace within a time guideline.

Virtual training cannot replace the personal interactions and getting the "how to" experiences that come with face-to-face training due to the limited time and a variety of reasons. However, organizations can simulate that, to a large extent, through discussions, feedback, setting tasks and creating group work through breakout sessions. In addition, forums where subject matter experts (SMEs) can answer questions that have been raised online will also add to the knowledge capture and motivate the SMEs to contribute to the community of practice [3].

By integrating interactive elements into the virtual training, you can engage the participants more effectively and establish accountability through deadlines. The participants can practise the content in a safe environment, measure their progress, reflect and apply the learnings on the job. This will also help the group to bond and generate the sense of achievement that occurs when groups have spent time interacting and working together.

Bonding is a very important outcome especially within organizations which follow a traditional structure. Individuals from different departments learn about other processes and meet individuals they might have emailed for months. Creating a team is essential in the new normal as the melding of different perspectives as well as levels of skills, knowledge and expertise is essential for survival.

Conclusion – If your organization considers cargo to be a strategic asset, then now's the time to invest or start planning to invest in training and developing the employees who will help carry your organization through these uncertain times. They are the backbone of your future success.

Reshaping the Future

Alessandro Bombelli

As global supply chains are re-shaping, so is the air freight logistics industry. A couple of years ago, before the world got hit by an unprecedented (at least for recent times) pandemic, future scenarios for the air freight industry looked very different with respect to the future scenarios the air freight industry is envisioning now. Notwithstanding, the COVID-19 pandemic generated new opportunities for the air freight industry. Due to the soaring of e-commerce and a simultaneous drop in the available capacity of belly space of passenger aircraft and ground and water transport, full-cargo airlines and integrators saw their market share rise as they were the only cargo service providers capable of offering a level of service basically unscathed, if not fostered, by the pandemic (Figure 12.3).

Figure 12.3 Professor Bombelli.

With e-commerce pushing new frontiers in terms of demand volumes and time windows between purchase and delivery, integrators seem to have a very fertile soil to exploit even more, being the only players to currently offer door-to-door services. This does not imply combination air lines and full-cargo carriers will lag behind without taking countermeasures. Efforts towards a higher digitalization, reduced paper-based documentation and enhancements to limit bottlenecks in the cargo supply chain have been made in the past years by stakeholders involved in different levels of the air cargo supply chain. Air freight will face many logistics challenges in the near future. For example, at the beginning of 2019, the e-AWB became the default contract of carriage for shipments, in an effort to switch-over from manual and paper-based processes. But, while the adoption of e-AWBs has improved performances, stakeholders need to have access and share accurate, real time information with each other for a seamless supply chain. This level of coordination has not been achieved yet and leads to our first perspective to analyse the future of air logistics, i.e., improvements in coordination and collaboration along the air cargo supply chain.

If we exclude integrators, where freight forwarding and ground handling facilities together with the aircraft fleet are owned by the same stakeholder, in air freight logistic services a package can be handled by several stakeholders along its journey from origin to destination. This makes coordination and collaboration paramount to enable a seamless delivery. While coordination and collaboration are strongly intertwined and might be used interchangeably, in this context we keep them separate. With coordination, we imply the capabilities of consecutive stakeholders in the supply chain to communicate efficiently to enable a seamless transition of air freight forward in the supply chain. With cooperation, we imply the potential collaboration between stakeholders at the same level (horizontal collaboration) or at different levels of the chain (vertical collaboration). On top of the aforementioned e-AWB paradigm, the concept of the Physical Internet (PI) has been mentioned in the last decade as a potential game-changer (ALICE, 2021) in global logistics networks, as the air freight one. In a nutshell, the PI is an open, global logistics network in which physical cargo is shipped the same way digital information travels through the digital internet. One of the key aspects of PI is collaboration and data sharing, but collaboration is challenging especially when entails stakeholders at the same level of the supply chain, that are de facto competitors. Collaboration has been identified by many stakeholders as key to improve air logistics, especially when it addresses the ground side (Aircargoweek, 2021). Still, as long as the involved stakeholders are reluctant to collaborate with their competitors, despite a tangible gin for everybody due to better resource management, collaboration initiatives in the context of air freight logistic will remain scarce.

The second perspective we analyse is, not surprisingly, environmental sustainability. The airline industry as a whole has set the ambitious goal to reduce emissions by a considerable amount (up to 50%) by 2030 (AFKLMP,

2021). While these figures seem a bit far-fetched, it is clear that actions are being taken in the context of air freight logistics as well to decrease the environmental impact. In the years to come, CO_2 emission will be reduced by means of a more efficient aircraft fleet, but this entails investments in new aircraft, which not all airlines are willing to make now, or new fuels, which are still being developed and tested. This being said, efforts are already being made in this sense. For example, according to FedEx, thanks to a more modern fleet, 255 million gallons of fuel were saved in the fiscal year 2020, which resulted in more than 2.38 million metric tonnes of CO_2 emissions being avoided (FedEx, 2021). As it concerns aircraft ground operations, joint-ventures between airlines, airports, private companies and research institutions are quickly developing a new breed of electric towing tractors for aircraft taxiing (Taxibot, 2021). As a matter of fact, taxiing operations for aircraft account for a non-negligible component of overall CO_2 emissions, since they are carried out by aircraft using their own power. Replacing these operations with fully electric towing tractors will drastically reduce CO_2 emissions due to taxiing. While this is something that the whole airline industry an benefit from, if we focus more specifically on air freight logistics, the main advancements in terms of sustainability in the short run should mostly come from the ground transport leg.

This leads us to our third perspective, i.e., last mile delivery enhancements. It should not be forgotten that the air freight industry, the only transport mode capable of offering seamless cargo connections worldwide in a limited time-frame, must offer efficient last mile delivery services so as not to jeopardize the aforementioned advantage. The last few years witnessed an unprecedented transition in the way last mile delivery is carried out. First, more and more electric vehicles are being used. This is a common trend for freight forwarders owning their own fleet, dedicated trucking companies, and integrators. On top of being more environmental sustainable, electric vehicles should be an investment that is economically sustainable in the long run, especially for densely populated areas where congestion and traffic jams imply a high fuel consumption (and costs) when performing deliveries. On a similar note, another current trend implies a return to the tradition by employing bicycles to perform deliveries. The new touch is, again, given by the fact these new bicycles are e-bikes. In this case, the advantages with respect to a classic delivery truck are two-fold. First, reduction in emissions, again. Second, reduction of delivery time (especially in high-congestion areas), due to better routing capabilities and ease of parking with respect to trucks. E-bikes are currently deployed for package delivery in many major cities such as Toronto (FedExB, 2021), Dublin (UPS, 2021), and Miami (DHL, 2021). Of course, e-bikes are mostly performing in those countries and cities with a good bicycle network and infrastructure. Countries such as the Netherlands, world leaders when it comes to the cycling culture, have been using e-bikes for a long time to perform mail delivery, for example (PostNL, 2021). In recent years, advancements in robotics opened a new venue for last mile delivery, i.e., robot deliveries. Potential use cases for such a technology range from pizza delivery to delivery of auto parts, with candidate robots capable of performing manoeuvres such as climbing the curb, travelling up the sidewalk and climbing deep terrace step (DEKA, 2021). Of course, a huge challenge hindering the applicability scale of such devices is the integration with the environment in terms of obstacles, humans and other vehicles. Finally, while last mile deliveries have been historically carried out on the ground, recent advancements in drone technology are making aerial last mile deliveries closer and closer to an actual implementation. As highlighted in a report by Roland Berger (Berger, 2021), drones can revolutionize first and last mile deliveries, which are historically the most expensive and least efficient part of a delivery. Drones can take advantage of the fact they are not bounded to the ground road infrastructure to further reduce delivery times. On the other hand, using drones to perform last mile deliveries comes with its own set of challenges. So far, there is no well-established regulatory framework defining where, when and how drones can fly, especially in dense urban environments. Related to this, urban environments in the metropolis are not easy to navigate due to the presence of many obstacles (skyscrapers, cables, etc.). It is also expected that drones will be characterized by a high turnaround time between deliveries due to the necessity to re-charge. In addition, they will be severely limited in terms of transportable payload (it is expected to be no more than a few kilograms), and safety regulations regarding their operations in highly populated areas must be defined. A scenario where packages (albeit reasonably light) start falling from the sky due to poor grasping capabilities of the drones is not ideal and extremely dangerous. Related to this point is the issue of societal acceptance of this new technological stream. Will customers be willing to accept deliveries carried out by drones or robots? In a world dominated by technology, and the air freight industry is not different, we should always remember that final decisions are taken by human beings.

To summarize, the future of air freight logistics looks driven by the pillars, common to any supply chain given the historical times we live in, of sustainability and technological advancements and automation. Given its unique multi-stakeholder and multimodal nature, it is paramount that players involved in air freight logistics improve their coordination and collaboration to achieve better resource utilization and meet the constantly increasing demand. This is challenging when collaboration should be performed with direct competitors, but emerging concepts such as synchromodality (AliceB, 2021) are showing that the gain is for everyone to be shared. Technological advancements entail as well an increased user's involvement and better traceability of cargo. Many forwarders such as Kuehne+Nagel are already working towards tangible improvements in this direction (Kuehne+Nagel, 2021). All in all, one of the lessons learned from the COVID-19 pandemic is that the air freight supply chain is vital to seamlessly connect such a globalized world. A supply chain that, historically speaking, has mostly relied on the status quo, rather than on the exploration of uncharted territories, has witnessed a deep transformation in the last few years and is currently researching and testing ground-breaking new technologies encompassing all the aspects of the supply chain. Biofuels, hydrogen-based fuels, more efficient aircraft, better routing strategies, automation applied to warehousing and last mile delivery, drones are just a handful of concepts that might be taking the air freight supply chain by storm in the decades to come. Maybe, for the future generation, having the latest smartphone or a new book delivered by a shiny drone or a talking robot just outside the front door will be the new normal of air freight logistics.

A Major Industry Trend

Significant developments are changing the structure of the global transport scene. The rapidly growing fusion of air and ocean, forwarders and carriers is creating new powerful alliances which are going to transform the supply chain into a true multimodal mechanism for the future.

In May 2022, Air France-KLM Group and the CMA CGM Group announced that they have signed a long-term strategic partnership in the air cargo market. This exclusive partnership would see both parties combine their complementary cargo networks, full freighter capacity and dedicated services in order to build an even more competitive combining the unrivalled know-how and global footprint of Air France-KLM and CMA CGM, merging cargo networks and freight capacity. The integrated fleet will consist of 10 freighters, with another 12 on order. CMA CGM currently owns four A330-200Fs, operated by Air Belgium while the line applies for its AOC. It also has eight aircraft on order, with a 777F due to arrive shortly, another a little later and four A350Fs due to deliver from 2025. AF-KLM has six freighters, with orders for four more.

The partnership declared that it presented one voice to the customer and it would "generate significant revenue synergies including, the joint design of the full freighter networks and enhanced products and services mix opportunities."

It acknowledged that the shipping line would leverage

> Air France-KLM's vast franchise, experience and capabilities in air freight, backed by a global cargo network. CMA CGM large commercial network and global logistics platform would complete this offer with innovative logistics and multimodal solutions, particularly in sea and land transport.

With money burning a hole in CMA CGM's pocket – AF-KLM made a net loss in 2021 of €3.29 billion ($3.46 billion), although cargo revenues were €3.5 billion – the line is becoming a reference shareholder of AF-KLM Group and will take up to 9% of AF-KLM's ex-post share capital during the period of the partnership. The pair said the investment "could be made as part of the contemplated capital increase of AF-KLM whose shareholders approving the appointment of a CMA CGM board member."

Rodolphe Saadé, chairman and CEO of Marseilles-based CMA CGM Group, said the partnership "allows us to significantly accelerate the development of our air division, CMA CGM Air Cargo, which was created just over a year ago, and to position our two companies among the world's leading players in air freight."

CMA CGM Air Cargo had come under scrutiny from airfreight executives who had questioned some strategic decisions that, one said, indicated a lack of experience. This tie-up boosts CMA's credentials – and ensures a steady line of business for AF-KLM.

Observers will ask, however, whether the Dutch element of the partnership, which has long struggled with strategic divergence from its French counterpart, will enjoy further French influence

The move could also put pressure on Lufthansa and MSC to complete a deal for new Italian airline ITA currently examining.

No number (or date) has been put on the investment, but it is said to be in the hundreds-of-millions-of-euros ballpark. And this doesn't look like the end of CMA's ambitions: boss Rodolphe Saadé intimated that more could be on the cards in CMA's strategy to become "a global integrator."

One Dutch air executive. "That is special. But it is also an interesting angle. Will commercial decisions be driven for the network by cargo, not passengers?"

"Cargo and passengers differ as much as airfreight differs from sea. Can you run an airline like you run a shipping line? And who will be in control, ultimately?"

Others argue that the move of an airline into a vertically integrated logistics company will change the way air cargo is sold – i.e., directly to the shipper.

> This step will bring a mindset change within the airline, as there is no secret to the fact that Ceva and the whole purpose of establishing a cargo airline by CMA CGM was to offer competitive and relevant services direct to BCOs, not forwarders,

said one air cargo executive.

"To deliver competitive products for your clients, you have to be in control of the total air logistics chain, and now AF-KLM will have to accept that philosophy as well, "no more are we only forwarder-friendly."

"Valuable, vulnerable or high-yield verticals will fly on their own controlled capacity. What that does for airlines which don't have this massive scale of client bases will be interesting to see," added the executive.

The sales aspect will certainly be interesting. Sources have revealed that there were some challenges in the Ceva/CMA CGM Air Cargo relationship, sales-wise. But CMA has a strong history of M&A

This experience, along with (as noted by AF-KLM) its own valuable experience in revenue optimization, is likely to put this particular partnership in good stead.

The January 2022 online World International conference, attended by many of the industry's experts, dealt with a selection of vital subjects, ending with "Looking Ahead – Where Next for the Air Logistics Industry?" Moderated by Joachim von Winning, Executive Director of the Air Cargo Community Frankfurt, Jessica Tyler, President Cargo & VP Operations Innovation and Delivery at American Airlines, Andrés Bianchi, CEO of LATAM Cargo, Denis Choumert, Vice President of the European Shippers Council, Dr. Ulrich Ogiermann, Chief Commercial Officer of AlisCargo Airlines, and Sebastiaan Scholte, CEO of Kales Group.

A View of the Future

After some 23 months of the COVID Pandemic, there is still much uncertainty about the recovery of passenger operations. However, the majority opined that there would be a partial return to more belly capacity as the year progressed. As Jessica Tyler of American Airlines stated "Our teams need to stay really agile and make decisions with best info we have." She predicted a "continued struggle" in the first quarter of 2022, "building up to better rest of the year."

Andrés Bianchi revealed that LATAM Cargo have prepared four separate possible budgets suggestions for 2022, "All of us are trying to figure out what will happen in 2022. It keeps changing!" he explained that passenger growth, cargo operations, the effects and developments of COVID-19, political pressures, the state of the global economic and the care of the environment, were all in play. He expressed satisfaction in the carrier's airline's decision to increase its freighter fleet. "Freighters are very handy!" he exclaimed, announcing that LATAM Cargo would be doubling its freighter fleet over the next few years. "A freighter fleet helps to match supply and demand better when overlaid with passenger fleet," he concluded.

Freighters, a Rare Commodity

Ulrich Ogiermann described the experience of launching new airline 18 months ago in the raging middle of the pandemic. "We would have loved to start much earlier, but were caught in pandemic turmoil," he stated. "We are currently forced to operate with P2F, which is not ideal, but the market warrants it for now." Acquiring the appropriate freighter aircraft has become much more complicated.

Shipper Fears

So how do shippers view the developments in air cargo throughout the pandemic and what next? Denis Choumert of the European Shippers Council outlined the period of the recent 18 months which he described as "hectic and messy." The reliable rates and an availability of data was replaced by short-term planning, rerouting and renegotiating rates daily.

Expecting that the first half of the year would be similar, but also stressed that many small freight forwarders had suffered due to their inability to access capacity on freighters which larger freight forwarders had, which led to shippers having to source capacity themselves. Also, the larger freighter forwarders were now "very rich" and even buying their own aircraft. Was this a short-term back-up or a long-term disruption in the industry, with a move to greater end-to-end trade control in both sea and air freight, he questioned? Was there now the danger of cartel style situations developing, especially with rates being vastly higher than in 2019, coupled with lower service quality, this would spell a lose-lose situation for shippers, he warned. Trust and resilience were important.

Changes in Behaviour

"The market has become a little bit more patient about disruptions because they are a continuous thing these days," Sebastiaan Scholte observed. The pandemic also brought customers and airlines closer together. Jessica Tyler declared that at American Airlines, "[We are much more] open-minded about making decisions based on partial information, making them faster, and making sure we're listening with big ears to what our customers need."

Challenging Decision-Making Models

Jessica Tyler spoke of "poking at old decision-making models." While they had not expected to be operating freighters for so long, they were optimizing assets all the time and working much closer with network planning. She illustrated that the airline had seen huge growth in its truck services – "over 600 truck flights a day!" – which it was feeding into destinations "where we have widebody services," but also talked of the challenges of forecasting. "We have changed our models of planning," she declared, emphasizing that the recruitment and preparation of staff had to get much faster. "Staffing challenges are like none we have ever seen before. Recruiting, sourcing, onboarding, training" all took far too much time with regard to all the complex background checks. This was definitely an area for urgent improvement.

More Interest in Logistics!

Yet, because "air cargo has been put a lot more on the map" (Sebastian Scholte), becoming "more sexy," there was a much greater interest amongst students in enrolling in logistics at Uni. "Hopefully this will be the positive outcome of this pandemic," he surmised.

Jessica Tyler agreed that the airline "brand pulls" and advised "we have amazing problems to solve, so we need to show our industry more" to get talent interested. Though Denis Choumert also brought up the flip side of the coin: the "dirty image of air cargo and environment" and pointed to the "FlightShame generation." Andrés Bianchi countered "FlightShaming is one side of the industry. It's our job to show the other one," talking about all the vaccine efforts that had brought a huge, positive impact on the LATAM Cargo brand. That said, the panel also agreed that while attracting talent into the aviation industry was becoming easier at academic level, it was still a major problem for "the most labour-intensive part of the air cargo chain: for the handling agent."

Be Flexible

Closing the discussion, the consensus was that data-transparency and seamlessness were the next big topics to collaborate on. Sebastiaan Scholte commented that "technology is always faster than the willingness to change. [There] should be seamless open communication." He deplored that "procurement departments focus on costs and yet essential parts of supply chain need to be seen as value instead of cost. Reward those who share errors!," he urged.

As for the industry's direction, the main prerequisites that had come up time and again during the discussion panel, were "flexibility" and "agility." There has been a palpable and positive disruptive shift brought about by the pandemic, and the air cargo industry has shown its mettle.

The Pandemic Impact

Nobody has a magic crystal ball to look into the future. No one could have predicted this pandemic, nor the capacity shortages and rate increases in the last months. The only certainty we have is that there will be a continuous uncertainty.

Unemployment levels in most developed countries are very low. The COVID crisis has functioned as a double-edged sword. People spent less on travel, which obviously led to belly capacity reduction. But the disposable income was also higher which resulted in more demand, especially on e-commerce. This "perfect storm" of reduced capacity and increased demand has caused shipping and air cargo rates to be at record levels. Add to that, shortages of drivers and warehouse personnel and capacity were even more constrained. Overall energy prices, higher transport costs, and higher wages have increased inflation levels. Strangely enough interest rates have stayed quite low, but the question is for how long.

In my opinion 2022 will be similar to 2021. There probably will be a lot of volatility and capacity will remain constraint and demand levels will be high. As soon as consumers can spend more money on travel and eating out, inflation levels will decrease. If inflation increases further, this could potentially lead to an overall slow down.

Anyone with freighter capacity basically will continue to have a licence to print money. Demand for qualified personnel will continue to be high, further putting pressure on wages. On the positive side, air cargo logistics has become a lot more attractive for younger people to join our industry, since in the last 2 years it has become obvious that air cargo is so essential for e-commerce and keeping healthcare systems going.

Long haul business travel will probably continue to be less than pre COVID levels, while shorter leisure travel will continue to improve. The question will be if travel remains restricted, how many airlines, which rely on long haul (business) travel, will be able to survive without being bailed out or getting even more debt. This could potentially lead to even further capacity reductions.

Airlines traditionally have the aircraft capacity, but in 2022 the share of freighters operated by e-commerce companies, forwarders and even shipping lines will most likely increase. As some acquisitions have shown, when profits soar in certain companies, there likely will be more consolidation as well. Much needed digitization and automation will continue to be implemented, but we should not forget the importance of skilled manpower. The shortage of labour will even further boost automation, but will also continue to cause inflation and supply chain disruptions.

As Darwin said: "It is not the strongest but the most adaptable that will survive"

Sebastiaan Scholte

Co-author

In the light of rapidly changing economic and geopolitical events, we can predict "interesting times" ahead.

PREDICTING THE FUTURE? Not even Nostradamus could solve this one, but I think that the words or Yogi Berra, the great sportsman and philosopher ring true when he said

"the future ain't what it used to be".

Mike Sales co-author

References

AFKLMP. (2021, 11 26). Sustainability. Retrieved from AFKLMP website: https://www.afklcargo.com/NL/en/common/products_and_solutions/sustainability.jsp#module_1

Aircargoweek. (2021, 11 26). Collaboration the key to a better supply chain. Retrieved from Aircargoweek website: https://www.aircargoweek.com/collaboration-key-supply-chain/

ALICE. (2021, 11 26). ALICE Roadmap to Physical Internet released! Retrieved from etp-logistics website: https://www.etp-logistics.eu/alice-physical-internet-roadmap-released/

AliceB. (2021, 12 1). Corridors, Hubs and Synchromodality. Retrieved from etp-logistics website: https://www.etp-logistics.eu/roadmaps/corridors-hubs-and-synchromodality/

Berger, R. (2021, 12 1). Cargo drones: the future of parcel delivery. Retrieved from Roland Berger website: https://www.rolandberger.com/en/Insights/Publications/Cargo-drones-The-future-of-parcel-delivery.html

DEKA. (2021, 12 1). DEKA Creating the future. Retrieved from DEKA website: http://www.dekaresearch.com/autonomous-mobility/

DHL. (2021, 12 1). DHL and reef technology launch pilot to use ecofriendly cargo bikes for deliveries in downtown Miami. Retrieved from DHL website: https://www.dhl.com/us-en/home/press/press-archive/2020/dhl-and-reef-technology-launch-pilot-to-use-ecofriendly-cargo-bikes-for-deliveries-in-downtown-miami.html

FedEx. (2021, 12 1). Our approach to innovating operations. Retrieved from FedEx website: https://www.fedex.com/en-bf/about/sustainability/our-approach.html

FedExB. (2021, 12 1). On the ground: Upgrading and optimizing vehicles. Retrieved from FedEx website: https://www.fedex.com/en-bf/about/sustainability/our-approach.html#vehicles

PostNL. (2021, 12 1). A first in Zeist: PostNL delivers all mail electrically. Retrieved from PostNL website: https://www.postnl.nl/en/about-postnl/press-news/news/2019/a-first-in-zeist-postnl-delivers-all-mail-electrically.html

Taxibot. (2021, 12 1). Sustainable taxiing: Taxibot trial. Retrieved from Schiphol website: https://www.schiphol.nl/en/innovation/blog/sustainable-taxiing-taxibot-trial/

UPS. (2021, 12 1). Smart, sustainable solutions help UPS deliver. Retrieved from UPS website: https://about.ups.com/us/en/social-impact/environment/climate/smart--sustainable-solutions-help-ups-deliver.html

Glossary

Freedom	Description	Example
First	To fly over another country without Landing	Qantas: Sydney to Singapore, overflying Indonesia
Second	To make a technical stop in another country	Air New Zealand: London to Auckland, via Los Angeles
Third	To carry traffic from the home country to another country	Emirates: Dubai to Mumbai
Fourth	To carry traffic to the home country from another country	Emirates: Mumbai to Dubai
Fifth	To carry traffic between two countries by an airline of a third country on a flight with either originates or ends in the airline's home country	Iberia: Madrid to Bogota, Colombia, and Quito, Ecuador
Sixth	To carry traffic between two countries by an airline of a third country via the airline's own country	British Airways: Houston, US, to Lagos, Nigeria, via London
Seventh	To carry traffic between two countries by an airline of a third country on a route outside its own country	FedEx: Caribbean feeder services
Eighth	To carry traffic between two or more airports in a country on a service that originates or ends in the airline's own country	Cathay Pacific: Hong Kong to Cairns and Brisbane
Ninth	To carry traffic on routes within the airline's own country	Aeroflot: Moscow to Vladivostok

Glossary of Common Terms

ACI   Airports Council International

ACMI   Aircraft, crew, maintenance, insurance (wet lease)

Air cargo   Goods carried in an aircraft

Air freight   The lading, or cargo, in an aircraft (often synonymous with air cargo)

Airside   Those parts of an airport controlled by the Customs authorities that are inaccessible to the public

All-cargo carrier   An airline that does not carry passengers

Apron   Aircraft parking area, for refuelling and the handling of cargo, baggage and mail

AWB   Air waybill, giving full details of the cargo

Block space   Air freight forwarders pre-book space with airlines

BCAA break-bulk   Sorting consolidated cargo into individual consignments. Usually ground handled task

CASS   The cargo accounts settlement system

Code share   An agreement whereby an airline sells capacity on another carrier's service (generally applicable only to passenger services)

Combination carrier   An airline that operates both passenger and cargo services

Consignee   The person or organization to whom cargo is being sent

Consolidation   When the cargo from two or more shippers is carried in a single container

CTK   Cargo-tonne-kilometre – a key airline performance indicator

Curfew   Those hours, usually at night, when flights to and from an airport are banned or restricted

Dangerous goods   Cargo that can only be carried under strictly regulated circumstances and on specific flights

Door-to-door   The movement of cargo from the consignor to consignee by a single operator (usually an express operator or integrator)

Dry lease   Lease of an aircraft, with the lessee operator providing its own crew, maintenance and insurance

e-AWB   Electronic air waybill

EDI   Electronic data interchange

FAA   Federal Aviation Administration (US)

FF   Freight forwarder

Flag carrier   The national airline of a country (often government-owned)

GHA   Ground handling agent

GSSA   General sales and services agent

HAWB   House air waybill

Hub-and-spoke   The route network where smaller aircraft feed cargo into a main hub which in turn is linked to other main hubs around the world by big long-haul aircraft

IATA   International Air Transport Association

ICAO   International Civil Aviation Organization

Integrator   An air express operator, usually with its own hub-and-spoke network

JIT   Just-in-time

KPI   Key performance indicator

MAWB   Master air waybill

MTOW   Maximum takeoff weight

Multimodal   The use of more than one transport mode – air, sea, road or rail

Noise footprint   The sound map made by an aircraft, usually when landing at or taking off from an airport in built-up areas

Offline   A destination not served by a scheduled airline

Oversize cargo   Cargo that will not fit in a standard container, or in a specific aircraft

Pallet   A ULD on which cargo is placed prior to being loaded into an aircraft

Reefer   Refrigerated vehicle or container

RFS   Road feeder service

Split charter   Where two or more consignors share space on a chartered aircraft

Tech stop   Where an aircraft lands at an airport prior to arriving at its destination airport, usually for refuelling purposes

TIACA   The International Air Cargo Association

Tonne   Metric weight measurement, equal to 1,000 kg

Traffic rights   Inter-governmental agreements stating which airlines may fly on specific routes between two countries

ULD   Unit load device

WCO   World Customs Organization

Wet lease   See ACMI and Dry lease

Index

Note: **Bold** page numbers refer to tables and *italic* page numbers refer to figures.

Printed in the United States
by Baker & Taylor Publisher Services